Two Studies in the History of Doctrine

AUGUSTINE AND THE PELAGIAN CONTROVERSY.
THE DEVELOPMENT OF THE DOCTRINE
OF INFANT SALVATION.

BY

BENJAMIN B. WARFIELD

Wipf and Stock Publishers
EUGENE, OREGON

Wipf and Stock Publishers
199 West 8th Avenue, Suite 3
Eugene, Oregon 97401

Two Studies in the History of Doctrine
Augustine and the Pelagian Controversy and the Development of the Doctirne of Infant Salvation
By Warfield, Benjamin B.
ISBN: 1-57910-530-0
Publication date 3/7/2001
Previously published by Christian Literature Crusade, 1897

PREFACE.

THE papers contained in this volume, neither of which is here printed for the first time, are reprinted to render them more accessible than they have come to be in the lapse of time. Some of their peculiarities are explained by the circumstances of their original publication. The former one was prepared as prolegomena to a translation of Augustine's Anti-Pelagian treatises, and owes it to this fact that those treatises are described and abstracted and not extracted in it, while incidental passages bearing on the subject from others of Augustine's writings are illustratively quoted. It is reprinted here practically unaltered. The latter paper, which originally appeared in a monthly magazine, has, on the contrary, been considerably enlarged and in some parts rewritten for this reissue.

Princeton, September, 1897.

CONTENTS.

PAGE

AUGUSTINE AND THE PELAGIAN CONTROVERSY...1-139

THE ORIGIN AND NATURE OF PELAGIANISM....................3-12
The first task of the Church, 3 ; inevitableness of this heresy, 4 ; the author of it, 4 ; its novelty, 4 ; its anti-Christian basis, 4 ; its roots, 5 ; its central and formative principle, 6 ; its three chief contentions, 7 ; its attitude to grace, 8 ; to sin, 9 ; its crass individualism, 10 ; five claims made for it, 12.

THE EXTERNAL HISTORY OF THE PELAGIAN CONTROVERSY.....13-22
Pelagius' work in Rome, 13 ; Pelagius and Cœlestius in Africa, 13 ; Cœlestius' condemnation at Corinth, 14 ; Pelagius' examination before John of Jerusalem, 15 ; his trial at Diospolis, 15 ; his condemnation at Carthage and Mileve, 16 ; Innocent's acquiescence, 17 ; wavering policy of Zosimus, 17 ; the interference of the State, 18 ; final action of the Africans, 18 ; stringent action of Zosimus, 19 ; Julian of Eclanum, 20 ; rise of semi-Pelagianism, 20 ; condemnation of semi-Pelagianism, 21.

AUGUSTINE'S PART IN THE CONTROVERSY....................23-126
Augustine's readiness for the controversy, 23 ; first oral stage of it, early anti-Pelagian sermons, 24 ; occasion, object, and contents of the first two books of the treatise, *On the Merits and Forgiveness of Sins*, 28 ; of the third book, 31 ; of *On the Spirit and the Letter*, 32 ; the letter to Anastasius, 36 ; the note to Pelagius, 37 ; the first letter to Paulinus of Nola, 38 ; controversial sermons of this period, 39 ; the progress of the controversy, 43 ; Sicilian Pelagianism and the letter to Hilary, 43 ; Timasius and James, 46 ; occasion, object, and contents of the treatise *On Nature and Grace*, 46 ; Paulus Orosius, 51 ; letter to Jerome on the Origin of Souls, 51 ; Cœlestius' *Definitions*, 53 ; occasion, object, and contents of *On the Perfection of Man's Righteousness*, 53 ; news of the doings in Palestine, 55 ; Pelagian view of "Forgive us our debts," 55 ; councils in Africa and letters to Innocent, 57 ; letter to Hilary of Norbonne, 58 ; letter to John of Jerusalem, 59 ; letter to Julianna, 60 ; occasion, object,

and contents of *On the Proceedings in Palestine*, 62 ;
second letter to Paulinus of Nola, 63 ; the sharpest period
of controversy, 65 ; Augustine's policy, 66 ; Zosimus' discomfiture, 68 ; occasion and object of *On the Grace of
Christ* and *On Original Sin*, 69 ; contents of *On the
Grace of Christ*, 70 ; of *On Original Sin*, 72 ; Augustine's sermons of this period, 73 ; letter to Optatus on the
soul, 80 ; correspondence with Sixtus, 83 ; letter to Mercator, 86 ; letter to Asellicus, 88 ; occasion, object, and
contents of the first book *On Marriage and Concupiscence*, 89 ; second letter to Optatus, 92 ; occasion, object, and contents of *On the Soul and its Origin*, 93 ;
advent of Julian, 95 ; his first controversial writings, 96 ;
occasion, object, and contents of the second book of *On
Marriage and Concupiscence*, 98 ; and of *Against Two
Letters of the Pelagians*, 99 ; and of *Against Julian*,
103 ; the *Enchiridion* on sin and grace, 106 ; occasion of
On Grace and Free Will, 108 ; object and contents of this
treatise, 110 ; occasion, object, and contents of *On Rebuke and Grace*, 111 ; the letter to Vitalis, 113 ; Julian's
reply to the second book of *On Marriage and Concupiscence*, 117 ; occasion of *On Heresies*, 117 ; its account of
Pelagianism, 118 ; rise of semi-Pelagianism in Gaul, 120 ;
occasion, object, and contents of *On the Perseverance
of the Saints* and *On the Gift of Perseverance*, 120 ;
contents of the *Unfinished Work*, 124 ; Augustine's
crowning anti-Pelagian work, 126.

THE THEOLOGY OF GRACE............................127–139
Roots and formative principles of Augustine's theology,
127 ; grace its central idea, 127 ; the *Necessity of Grace*,
128 ; the fall, 128 ; free-will, 129 ; the *Nature of Grace*,
130 ; prevenient grace, 132 ; gratuitous grace, 132 ; sovereignty of grace, 132 ; the *Effects of Grace*, 133 ; irresistible grace, 133 ; indefectible grace, 133 ; *Predestination*, 134 ; the *Means of Grace*, 135 ; infant damnation, 137 ; Scriptural basis of Augustine's theology, 138.

THE DEVELOPMENT OF THE DOCTRINE OF INFANT
SALVATION....................................141–239

INTRODUCTORY.......................................143–144

THE PATRISTIC DOCTRINE............................144–151
Infants' need of and capacity for salvation recognized, 144 ;
prevalence of legalistic conception, 145 ; Gregory of Nyssa's views, 146 ; externalism of conception, 147 ; baptism held necessary to salvation, 148 ; teachings of Augustine, 148 ; outcome of patristic thought, 150.

THE MEDIÆVAL MITIGATION...........................151–154
The inherited doctrine, 151 ; the scholastic doctrine of

CONTENTS. vii

poena damni, 152 ; abortive attempt to apply to infants baptism of intention, 153 ; John Wycliffe, 154.

THE DRIFT IN THE CHURCH OF ROME...................154-165
Four opinions held in post-Reformation Romanism, 154 ; the Tridentine doctrine, 155 ; popular teaching on its basis, 155 ; baptism of intention rejected for infants, 156 ; discrimination in favor of heathen infants, 158 ; protests of the heart, 161 ; "happiness in hell," 163 ; modern Pelagianizing views, 164.

THE LUTHERAN TEACHING.................................165-174
Protestant doctrine of the Church, 166 ; assertion of the necessity of baptism, 167 ; baptism of intention applied to infants, 168 ; Gerhard's teaching, 169 ; fate of heathen infants, 170 ; four opinions, 171 ; agnosticism the historical Lutheran position, 172 ; modern Lutheran opinion, 172 ; difficulties of Lutheranism, 173.

THE ANGLICAN POSITION................................174-194
Romanizing teaching of early formularies, 175 ; salvation of baptized children affirmed, 177 ; implication of baptismal regeneration, 178 ; unsuccessful efforts to revise, 181 ; implied loss of unbaptized, 183 ; at least no hope extended for unbaptized, 185 ; pure agnosticism as to unbaptized children, 186 ; opinions of English Reformers, 187 ; Cranmer, 187 ; Becon, 188 ; Hooper, 190 ; variety of seventeenth century opinions, 191 ; Hooker, 192 ; Low Church opinions, 193 ; recent High Church drift, 193.

THE REFORMED DOCTRINE................................195-220
Consistent application of Protestant doctrine of the Church, 195 ; High Church views of Jurieu, 195 ; free-grace and electing love, 196 ; Zwingli's teaching, 197 ; doctrine of the covenant fundamental, 199 ; Calvin and Bullinger, 199 ; essential Reformed postulates, 202 ; five distinguishable opinions, 202 ; 1. All dying infants saved, 203 ; 2. Fate of all infants uncertain to us, 205 ; condemned by Dort, 205 ; Gataker, 205 ; Baxter, 206 ; why neither view acceptable to earlier Calvinists, 208 ; 3. All covenanted infants saved and uncovenanted lost, 209 ; 4. All covenanted infants and some uncovenanted saved, 210 ; 5. All covenanted infants saved, agnostic as to uncovenanted, 211 ; Jonathan Dickinson, 211 ; the Reformed Confessions, 213 ; the Synod of Dort, 213 ; the Westminster Confession, 214 ; implications of " elect infants dying in infancy," 215 ; drift in late eighteenth and early nineteenth centuries, 217 ; Lyman Beecher, 218 ; modern Calvinistic opinion, 219.

ETHICAL TENDENCIES..................................220-236
The most serious peril to the orderly development of the doctrine, 220 ; early Pelagianizing conceptions, 221 ; in-

dividual Pelagianizing assaults on the Reformed doctrine, 221 ; the Remonstrant contention and its inconsequence, 222 ; Wesleyan Arminianism, 223 ; its difficulty, 223 ; Dr. James Strong's solution, 224 ; original Wesleyanism, 225 ; minor differences, 226 ; Pelagianizing Arminianism, 228 ; its consequences, 229 ; post-mortem probation, 230 ; Dr. Kedney's construction, 232 ; Dr. Emory Miller's, 234.

CONCLUSION..................................236-239
Three generic views, 236 ; their relations, 237 ; steps in the development of the doctrine, 237 ; the doctrine a test of systems, 238 ; consonant with the Reformed system alone, 238.

I.

AUGUSTINE AND THE PELAGIAN CONTROVERSY.

AUGUSTINE AND THE PELAGIAN CONTROVERSY.

THE ORIGIN AND NATURE OF PELAGIANISM.

IT was natural that the energy of the Church in intellectually realizing and defining its doctrines in relation to one another, should first be directed towards the objective side of Christian truth. The chief controversies of the first four centuries and the resulting definitions of doctrine, concerned the nature of God and the Person of Christ. It was not until these Theological and Christological questions were well upon their way to final settlement, that the Church could turn its attention to the more subjective side of truth. Meanwhile she bore in her bosom a full recognition, side by side, of the freedom of the will, the evil consequences of the fall, and the necessity of divine grace for salvation. Individual writers, or even entire sections of the Church, might exhibit a special tendency to emphasize one or another of the elements that made up this deposit of faith that was the common inheritance of all. The East, for instance, laid especial stress on free will. The West dwelt more pointedly on the ruin of the human race and the absolute need of God's grace for salvation. But the Eastern theologians did not forget the universal sinfulness and need of redemption, or the necessity, for the realization of that redemption, of God's gracious influences. Nor did those of the West deny the self-determination or accountability of men. All the elements of the composite doctrine of man were everywhere confessed. But they were variously emphasized, according to the temper of the writers or the controversial demands of the times. Such a state of affairs, however, was an invitation to heresy, and a prophecy of controversy; just as the simultaneous confession of the Unity of God and the Deity of Christ, or of the Deity and the Humanity of Christ, inevitably carried in its train a series of heresies and controversies, until the definitions of the doctrines of the Trinity and of the Person of Christ were complete. In like manner, it was inevitable that sooner or later some one should arise who would throw so one-sided a stress upon one element or the other of the Church's teaching as to salvation, as to betray himself into heresy, and drive the Church, through controversy with him, into a more precise definition of the doctrines of free will and grace in their mutual relations.

This new heresiarch came, at the opening of the fifth century, in the person of the British monk, Pelagius. The novelty of the doctrine which he taught is repeatedly asserted by Augustine,[1] and is evident to the historian. But it consisted less in the emphasis that he laid on free will, than in the fact that, in order to emphasize free will, he denied the ruin of the race and the necessity of grace. This was not only new in Christianity; it was even anti-Christian. Jerome, as well as Augustine, saw this at the time, and spoke of Pelagianism as the " heresy of Pythagoras and Zeno."[2] Modern writers of various schools have more or less fully recognized it. Thus Dean Milman thinks that "the greater part" of Pelagius' letter to Demetrias "might have been written by an ancient academic."[3]

[1] *On the Merits and Remission of Sins*, iii. 6, 11, 12; *Against Two Letters of the Pelagians*, iv. 32; *Against Julian*, i. 4; *On Heresies*, 88; and often elsewhere. JEROME found *roots* for the theory in ORIGEN and RUFINUS (*Letter* 133, 3), but this is a different matter: compare AUGUSTINE, *On Original Sin*, 25.
[2] Preface to Book iv. of his work on Jeremiah.
[3] *Latin Christianity*, i. 166, note 2.

Dr. De Pressensé identifies the Pelagian idea of liberty with that of Paganism.[1] And Bishop Hefele openly declares that the fundamental doctrine of Pelagianism, "that man is virtuous entirely of his own merit, not of the gift of grace," seems to him "to be a rehabilitation of the general heathen view of the world," and compares with it Cicero's words,[2] "For gold, lands, and all the blessings of life, we have to return thanks to the Gods; but no one ever returned thanks to the Gods for virtues."[3] The struggle with Pelagianism was thus in reality a struggle for the very foundations of Christianity. Quite as dangerously as in the previous Theological and Christological controversies, here the practical substance of Christianity was in jeopardy. The real question at issue was whether there was any need for Christianity at all; whether by his own power man might not attain eternal felicity; whether the function of Christianity was to save, or only to render an eternity of happiness more easily attainable by man.[4]

Genetically speaking, Pelagianism was the daughter of legalism; but when it itself conceived, it brought forth an essential deism. It is not without significance that its originators were "a certain sort of monks," that is, laymen of ascetic life. From that point of view the Divine law appears as a collection of separate commandments, moral perfection as a mere complex of separate virtues, and a distinct value as a meritorious demand on Divine approbation is ascribed to each good work or attainment in the exercises of piety. It was because this was essentially his point of view that Pelagius could regard man's powers as sufficient to the attainment of sanctity, and could even assert it to be possible for man to do more than is required of him. But this involves an essentially deistic conception of man's relations to his Maker. God has endowed His creature with a capacity (*possibilitas*) or ability (*posse*)

---

[1] *Trois Prem. Siècles*, ii. 375. [2] *De Natura Deorum*, iii. 36.
[3] *History of the Councils of the Church* (E. T.), ii. 446, note 3.
[4] Compare the excellent statement in THOMASIUS' *Dogmengeschichte*, i. 483.

for action; and it is for him to use it. Man is thus a machine, which, just because it is well made, needs no Divine interference for its right working; and the Creator, having once framed him and endowed him with the *posse*, henceforth leaves the *velle* and the *esse* to him.

At this point we have touched the central and formative principle of Pelagianism. It lies in the assumption of the plenary ability of man; his ability to do all that righteousness can demand—to work out not only his own salvation, but also his own perfection. This is the core of the whole theory; and all the other postulates not only depend upon it, but arise out of it. Both chronologically and logically this is the root of the system.

When we first hear of Pelagius he is already advanced in years, living in Rome in the odour of sanctity,[1] and in the enjoyment of a well-deserved reputation for zeal in exhorting others to a good life. This zeal grew especially warm against those who, when charged with their sins, endeavoured to shelter themselves behind the weakness of nature.[2] He was outraged by the excuses which were commonly made on such occasions,—" It is hard !" " It is difficult !" " We are not able !" " We are men !" " O blind madness !" he cried : " we accuse God of a twofold ignorance,—that He does not seem to know what He has made, nor what He has commanded,—as if forgetting the human weakness of which He is Himself the author, He has imposed laws on man which he cannot endure."[3] He himself tells us[4] that it was his custom, therefore, whenever he had to speak on moral improvement and the conduct of a holy life, to begin by pointing out the power and quality of human nature, and by showing what it is capable of accomplishing. For (he says) he esteemed it of little use to exhort men to do what they deem impossible : hope

---

[1] *On the Proceedings of Pelagius*, 46; *On the Merits and Remission of Sins*, iii. 1; *Epistle* 186, etc.
[2] *On Nature and Grace*, 1. [3] *Epistle to Demetrias*, 16.
[4] *Do.* 2 and 19.

must rather be our companion, and all longing and effort die when we despair of attaining. So exceedingly ardent an advocate was he of man's unaided ability to do all that God commanded, that when there was repeated in his hearing Augustine's noble and entirely scriptural prayer—"Give what Thou commandest, and command what Thou wilt"—he was unable to endure it. With such violence did he contradict it that he almost became embroiled in a quarrel.[1] The powers of man were gifts of God ; and it was, therefore (he held), a reproach against God, as if He had made man ill or evil, to believe that they were insufficient for the keeping of His law. Nay, do what we will, we cannot rid ourselves of their sufficiency : " whether we will, or whether we will not, we have the capacity of not sinning."[2] "I say," he says, " that man is able to be without sin, and that he is able to keep the commandments of God." This sufficiently direct statement of human ability is in reality the hinge of his whole system.

There were three specially important corollaries which flowed from so unmeasured an assertion of human ability, and Augustine himself recognized these as the chief elements of the Pelagian system.[3] It would be inexplicable on such an assumption, if no man had ever used his ability in keeping God's law ; and Pelagius therefore consistently asserted not only that all might be sinless if they chose, but also that many saints, even before Christ, had actually lived free from sin. Again, it would follow from man's inalienable ability to be free from sin, that each man comes into the world without entailment of sin or moral weakness from the past acts of men ; and Pelagius consistently denied the whole doctrine of original sin. And still again, it would follow from the assumption of so perfect a natural ability, that man has no need of supernatural assistance in his striving to obey righteousness ; and Pelagius consistently denied both the need

---

[1] *On the Gift of Perseverance*, 53.   [2] *On Nature and Grace*, 49.
[3] *On the Gift of Perseverance*, 4 ; *Against Two Letters of the Pelagians*, iii. 24 ; iv. 2 sq.

and the reality of divine grace in the sense of an inward help (and especially of a prevenient help) to man's weakness.

It was upon this last point that the greatest stress was laid in the controversy. Augustine was most of all disturbed that God's grace was denied and opposed. No doubt the Pelagians spoke constantly of "grace." But they meant by "grace" the primal endowment of man with free will, and the subsequent aid given him in order to its proper use by the revelation of the law and the teaching of the gospel, and, above all, by the forgiveness of past sins in Christ and by Christ's holy example.[1] Anything beyond this external help they utterly denied. And they denied that this external help itself was absolutely necessary, affirming that it only rendered it easier for man to do what otherwise he had plenary ability for doing. Chronologically, this contention seems to have preceded the assertion which must logically lie at its base—of the freedom of man from any taint, corruption, or weakness due to sin. It was in order that they might deny that man needed help, that they denied that Adam's sin had any further effect on his posterity than might arise from his bad example. "Before the action of his own proper will," said Pelagius roundly, "that only is in man which God made."[2] "As we are procreated without virtue," he said, "so also without vice."[3] In a word, "nothing that is good or evil, on account of which we are either praiseworthy or blameworthy, is born with us,—it is rather done by us; for we are born with capacity for either, but provided with neither."[4] So his follower, Julian, plainly asserts his "faith that God creates men obnoxious to no sin, but full of natural innocence, and with capacity for voluntary virtues."[5] So intrenched is free will in nature, that, ac-

---

[1] *On the Spirit and Letter*, 4; *On Nature and Grace*, 53; *On the Proceedings of Pelagius*, 20, 22, 38; *On the Grace of Christ*, 2, 3, 8, 31, 42, 45; *Against Two Letters of the Pelagians*, iv. 11; *On Grace and Free Will*, 23-26, and often.
[2] *On Original Sin*, 14.   [3] *Ibid*.   [4] *Ibid*.
[5] *The Unfinished Work*, iii. 82.

cording to Julian, it is "just as complete after sins as it was before sins;"[1] and what this means may be gathered from Pelagius' definition in the *Confession of Faith* that he sent to Innocent : " We say that man is always able both to sin and not to sin, so that we may confess that we have free will."

That sin in such circumstances was so common as to be well-nigh universal, was accounted for by the bad example of Adam and the power of habit, the latter being conceived as simply the result of imitation of the former. " Nothing makes well-doing so hard," writes Pelagius to Demetrias, " as the long custom of sins which begins from childhood and gradually brings us more and more under its power until it seems to have in some degree the force of nature (*vim naturæ*)." He is even ready to allow for the force of habit, in a broad way, on the world at large ; and so divides all history into progressive periods, marked by God's (external) grace. At first the light of nature was so strong that men by it alone could live in holiness. And it was only when men's manners became corrupt and tarnished nature began to be insufficient for holy living, that by God's grace the law was given as an addition to mere nature ; and by it " the original lustre was restored to nature after its blush had been impaired." And so again, after the habit of sinning once more prevailed among men, and " the law became unequal to the task of curing it,"[2] Christ was given, furnishing men with forgiveness of sins, exhortations to imitation of His example and the holy example itself.[3] Thus a progressive deterioration was confessed, and such a deterioration as rendered desirable at least two supernatural interpositions—in the giving of the law and the coming of Christ. Yet no corruption of nature, even by growing habit, was really allowed. It was only an ever-increasing facility in imitating vice which arose from so long a schooling in evil. And all that was

[1] *Do.* i. 91 ; compare *do.* i. 48, 60 ; ii. 20. "There is nothing of sin in man, if there is nothing of his own will." " There is no original sin in infants at all."
[2] *On Original Sin*, 30. [3] *On the Grace of Christ*, 43.

needed to rescue men from it was a new explanation of what was right (in the law), or, at the most, the encouragement of forgiveness for what was already done, and a holy example (in Christ) for imitation. Pelagius still asserted our continuous possession of "'a free will which is unimpaired for sinning and for not sinning;" and Julian, that " our free will is just as full after sins as it was before sins"—although Augustine does not fail to twit him with a charge of inconsistency.[1]

The peculiar individualism of the Pelagian view of the world comes out strongly in their failure to perceive the effect of habit on nature itself. Just as they conceived of virtue as an agglomeration of virtuous acts, so they conceived of sin exclusively as an act, or mass of disconnected acts. They appear not to have risen above the essentially heathen view which had no notion of holiness except as a series of acts of holiness, or of sin except as a like series of sinful acts.[2] Thus the will was isolated from its acts, and the acts from each other, and all organic connection or continuity of life was not only overlooked but denied.[3] After each act of the will, man stood exactly where he did before : indeed, this conception scarcely allows for the existence of a " man" —only a willing machine is left, at each click of the action of which the spring regains its original position, and is equally ready as before to perform its function. In such a conception there was no place for character : freedom of will was all. Thus it was not an unnatural mistake which they made, when they forgot the man altogether, and attributed to the faculty of free will, under the name of "*possibilitas*" or "*posse*," the ability that belongs rather to the man whose faculty it is and who is properly responsible for the use he makes of it. Here lies the essential error of their doctrine of free

---

[1] *The Unfinished Work*, i. 91 ; compare 69.
[2] Dr. MATHESON finely says (*Expositor*, i. ix. 21), "There is the same difference between the Christian and Pagan idea of prayer as there is between the Christian and Pagan idea of sin. Paganism knows nothing of sin, it knows only sins : it has no conception of the principle of evil, it comprehends only a succession of sinful acts." This is Pelagianism too.
[3] Compare SCHAFF, *Church History*, iii. 804 ; and THOMASIUS, *Dogmengeschichte*, i. 487-8.

will. They looked upon freedom in its *form* only, and not in its *matter*; and, keeping man in perpetual and hopeless equilibrium between good and evil, they allowed for no growth of character and permitted no advantage to accrue to the man himself from his successive choices of good. It need not surprise us that the type of thought which thus dissolved the organism of the man into an aggregation of disconnected voluntary acts, failed to comprehend the solidarity of the race. To the Pelagian, Adam was a man, nothing more ; and it was simply unthinkable that any act of his that left his own subsequent acts uncommitted, could entail sin and guilt upon other men. The same alembic that dissolved the individual into a succession of voluntary acts, could not fail to separate the race into a heap of unconnected units. If sin, as Julian declared, is nothing but will, and the will itself remained intact after each act, how could the individual act of an individual will condition the acts of men as yet unborn? By "imitation" of his act alone could, under such a conception, other men be affected. And this carried with it the corresponding view of man's relation to Christ. Christ could forgive us the sins we had committed ; He could teach us the true way ; He could set us a holy example ; and He could exhort us to its imitation. But He could not touch us to enable us to will the good, without destroying the absolute equilibrium of the will between good and evil. And to destroy this was to destroy the freedom of the will, which was the crowning good of our divinely created nature. Surely the Pelagians forgot that man was not made for will, but will for man.

In defending their theory, as we are told by Augustine, there were five claims that they especially made for it.[1] It allowed them to praise as was their due, the creature that God had made, the marriage that He had instituted, the law that He had given, the free will which was His greatest endowment to man, and the saints who had followed His counsels. By this they meant that they proclaimed the sinless perfection of

[1] *Against Two Letters of the Pelagians*, iii. 25, and iv. at the beginning.

human nature in every man as he was brought into the world, and opposed this to the doctrine of original sin; the purity and holiness of marriage and the sexual appetites, and opposed this to the doctrine of the transmission of sin; the ability of the law, as well as and apart from the gospel, to bring men into eternal life, and opposed this to the necessity of inner grace; the adequacy of free will to choose the good, and opposed this to the necessity of divine aid; and the perfection of the lives of the saints, and opposed this to the doctrine of universal sinfulness. Other questions, concerning the origin of souls, the necessity of baptism for infants, the original immortality of Adam, lay more upon the skirts of the controversy. As it was an obvious fact that all men died, they could not admit that Adam's death was a consequence of sin lest they should be forced to confess that his sin had injured all men; they therefore asserted that physical death belonged to the very nature of man, and that Adam would have died even had he not sinned.[1] So, as it was impossible to deny that the Church everywhere baptized infants, they could not refuse them baptism without confessing themselves innovators in doctrine; and therefore they contended that infants were not baptized for forgiveness of sin, but in order to attain a higher state of bliss than that which naturally belongs to innocence. Finally, they conceived that if it were admitted that souls are directly created by God for each birth, it could not be asserted that they come into the world soiled by sin and under condemnation; and therefore they loudly championed the creationist theory of the origin of souls.

The teachings of the Pelagians, it will be readily seen, easily welded themselves into a system, the essential and formative elements of which were entirely new in the Christian Church. It was this startlingly new reading of man's condition, powers, and dependence for salvation that broke like a thunderbolt upon the Western Church at the opening of the fifth century, and forced her to reconsider, from the foundations, her whole teaching as to man and his salvation.

[1] This belongs to the earlier Pelagianism; JULIAN was ready to admit that death came from Adam, but not that sin did.

The External History of the Pelagian Controversy.

PELAGIUS seems to have been already somewhat softened by increasing age when he came to Rome about the opening of the fifth century. He was also constitutionally averse to controversy. In his zeal for Christian morals, and in his conviction that no man would attempt to do what he was not persuaded he had natural power to perform, he diligently propagated his doctrines privately. But he was careful to arouse no opposition, and was content to make what progress he could quietly and without open discussion. His methods of work sufficiently appear in the pages of his *Commentary on the Epistles of Saint Paul*, which was written and published during these years, and which exhibits learning and a sober and correct but somewhat shallow exegetical skill. In this work, he manages to give expression to all the main elements of his system. But he always introduces them indirectly, not as the true exegesis but by way of objections to the ordinary teaching which were in need of discussion. The most important fruit of his residence in Rome was the conversion to his views of the Advocate Cœlestius, who brought the courage of youth and the argumentative training of a lawyer to the propagation of the new teaching. It was through him that it first broke out into public controversy, and received its first ecclesiastical examination and rejection. Fleeing from Alaric's second raid on Rome, the two friends landed together in Africa (A.D. 411), whence Pelagius soon afterwards departed for Palestine, leaving the bolder and more contentious[1] Cœlestius behind at Carthage. Here Cœlestius sought ordination as a presbyter. But the Milanese deacon Paulinus stood forward in accusation

---
[1] *On Original Sin*, 13.

of him as a heretic, and the matter was brought before a synod under the presidency of Bishop Aurelius.[1]

Paulinus' charge consisted of seven items,[2] which asserted that Cœlestius taught the following heresies: that Adam was made mortal, and would have died whether he sinned or did not sin; that the sin of Adam injured himself alone, not the human race; that new-born children are in that state in which Adam was before his sin; that the whole human race does not, on the one hand, die on account of the death or the fall of Adam, nor, on the other, rise again on account of the resurrection of Christ; that infants, even though not baptized, have eternal life; that the law leads to the kingdom of heaven in the same way as the gospel; and that, even before the Lord's coming, there had been men without sin. Only two fragments of the proceedings of the synod in investigating this charge have come down to us.[3] But it is easy to see that Cœlestius was contumacious and refused to reject any of the propositions charged against him, except the one which had reference to the salvation of infants that die unbaptized,—the sole one that admitted of sound defence. As touching the transmission of sin, he would only say that it was an open question in the Church, and that he had heard both opinions from Church dignitaries; so that the subject needed investigation, and should not be made the ground for a charge of heresy. The natural result was, that, on refusing to condemn the propositions charged against him, he was himself condemned and excommunicated by the synod. Soon afterwards he sailed to Ephesus, where he obtained the ordination which he sought.

Meanwhile Pelagius was living quietly in Palestine, whither in the summer of 415 a young Spanish presbyter, Paulus Orosius by name, came with letters from

---

[1] Early in 412, or, less probably, according to the BALLERINI and HEFELE, 411.

[2] See *On Original Sin*, 2, 3, 12; *On the Proceedings of Pelagius*, 23. They are also given by MARIUS MERCATOR (Migne, xlviii. 69, 70), by whom the fifth item (on the salvation of unbaptized infants) is omitted,—though apparently by an error.

[3] Preserved by AUGUSTINE, *On Original Sin*, 3, 4.

Augustine to Jerome, and was invited, near the end of July in that year, to a diocesan synod presided over by John of Jerusalem. There he was asked about Pelagius and Cœlestius, and proceeded to give an account of the condemnation of the latter at the synod of Carthage, and of Augustine's literary refutation of the former. Pelagius was sent for, and the proceedings became an examination into his teachings. The chief matter brought up was his assertion of the possibility of men living sinlessly in this world. But the favour of the bishop towards him, the intemperance of Orosius, and the difficulty of communication between the parties arising from difference of language, combined so to clog proceedings that nothing was done ; and the whole matter, as Western in its origin, was referred to the Bishop of Rome for examination and decision.[1]

Soon afterwards two Gallic bishops,—Heros of Arles and Lazarus of Aix,—who were then in Palestine, lodged a formal accusation against Pelagius with the metropolitan, Eulogius of Cæsarea. He convened a synod of fourteen bishops which met at Lydda (Diospolis), in December of the same year (415), for the trial of the case. Perhaps no greater ecclesiastical farce was ever enacted than this synod exhibited.[2] When the time arrived, the accusers were prevented from being present by illness, and Pelagius was confronted only by the written accusation. This was unskilfully drawn, and was, moreover, written in Latin which the synod did not understand. It was, therefore, not even consecutively read, and was only head by head rendered into Greek by an interpreter. Pelagius began by reading aloud several letters to himself from various men of reputation in the episcopate,—among them a friendly note from Augustine. Thoroughly acquainted with both Latin and Greek, he was enabled skillfully to thread every difficulty, and pass safely through the ordeal. Jerome called this a " miserable synod," and

[1] An account of this synod is given by Orosius himself in his *Apology for the Freedom of the Will.*
[2] A full account and criticism of the proceedings are given by Augustine in his *On the Proceedings of Pelagius.*

not unjustly. At the same time it is sufficient to vindicate the honesty and earnestness of the bishops intentions, that, even in such circumstances and despite the more undeveloped opinions of the East on the questions involved, Pelagius escaped condemnation only by a course of most ingenious disingenuousness, and only at the cost both of disowning Cœlestius and his teachings, of which he had been the real father, and of leading the synod to believe that he was anathematizing the very doctrines which he was himself proclaiming. There is really no possibility of doubting, as any one will see who reads the proceedings of the synod, that Pelagius obtained his acquittal here either by a "lying condemnation or a tricky interpretation"[1] of his own teachings; and Augustine is perfectly justified in asserting that the "heresy was not acquitted, but the man who denied the heresy,"[2] and who would himself have been anathematized had he not anathematized the heresy.

But, however obtained, the acquittal of Pelagius was an accomplished fact. Neither he nor his friends delayed to make the most widely extended use of their good fortune. Pelagius himself was jubilant. Accounts of the synodal proceedings were sent to the West, not altogether free from uncandid alterations; and Pelagius soon put forth a work, *In Defence of Free-Will*, in which he triumphed in his acquittal and "explained his explanations" at the synod. Nor were the champions of the opposite opinion idle. As soon as the news arrived in North Africa, and before the authentic records of the synod had reached that region, the condemnation of Pelagius and Cœlestius was reaffirmed in two provincial synods—one, consisting of sixty-eight bishops, met at Carthage about midsummer of 416; and the other, consisting of about sixty bishops, met soon afterwards at Mileve (Mila). Thus Palestine and North Africa were arrayed against each other, and it became of great importance to obtain the support of the Patriarchal See of Rome. Both sides

[1] *On Original Sin*, 13, at the end.
[2] AUGUSTINE'S *Sermons* (Migne, v. 1511).

made the attempt, but fortune favored the Africans. Each of the North-African synods sent a synodal letter to Innocent I., then Bishop of Rome, engaging his assent to their action. To these, five bishops, Aurelius of Carthage and Augustine among them, added a third "familiar" letter of their own, in which they urged upon Innocent to examine into Pelagius' teaching, and provided him with the material on which he might base a decision. The letters reached Innocent in time for him to take advice of his clergy and send favorable replies on Jan. 27, 417. In these he expressed his agreement with the African decisions, asserted the necessity of inward grace, rejected the Pelagian theory of infant baptism, and declared Pelagius and Cœlestius excommunicated until they should return to orthodoxy.

In about six weeks more Innocent was dead. Zosimus, his successor, was scarcely installed in his place before Cœlestius appeared at Rome in person to plead his cause; while shortly afterwards letters arrived from Pelagius, addressed to Innocent, and by an artful statement of his belief and a recommendation from Praylus, lately become bishop of Jerusalem in John's stead, attempting to enlist Rome in his favor. Zosimus, who appears to have been a Greek and therefore inclined to make little of the merits of this Western controversy, went over to Cœlestius at once, upon his profession of willingness to anathematize all doctrines which the pontifical see had condemned or should condemn; and wrote a sharp and arrogant letter to Africa, proclaiming Cœlestius "catholic," and requiring the Africans to appear within two months at Rome to prosecute their charges, or else to abandon them. On the arrival of Pelagius' papers, this letter was followed by another (September, 417), in which Zosimus, with the approbation of his clergy, declared both Pelagius and Cœlestius to be orthodox, and severely rebuked the Africans for their hasty judgment.

It is difficult to understand Zosimus' action in this matter. Neither of the Confessions presented by the accused teachers ought to have deceived him. And if he was seizing the occasion to magnify the Roman see, his mistake was dreadful. Late in 417, or early in 418, the African bishops assembled at Carthage, in number more than two hundred, and replied to Zosimus that they had decided that the sentence pronounced against Pelagius and Cœlestius should remain in force until those heretics should unequivocally acknowledge that " we are aided by the grace of God, through Christ, not only to know, but also to do what is right, in each single act, so that without grace we are unable to have, think, speak, or do anything pertaining to piety." This firmness made Zosimus waver. He answered swellingly but timidly, declaring that he had maturely examined the matter, but it had not been his intention finally to acquit Cœlestius; and now he had left all things in the condition in which they were before, but he claimed the right of final judgment to himself. Matters were hastening to a conclusion, however, that would leave him no opportunity to escape from the mortification of an entire change of front. This letter was written on the 21st of March, 418; it was received in Africa on the 29th of April; and on the very next day an imperial decree was issued from Ravenna ordering Pelagius and Cœlestius to be banished from Rome, with all who held their opinions; while on the next day, May 1, a plenary council of about two hundred bishops met at Carthage, and in nine canons condemned all the essential features of Pelagianism. Whether this simultaneous action was the result of skilful arrangement, can only be conjectured. Its effect was in any case necessarily crushing. There could be no appeal from the civil decision, and it played directly into the hands of the African definition of the faith.

The synod's nine canons part naturally into three triads.[1] The first of these deals with the relation of mankind to original sin, and anathematizes in turn those who assert that physical death is a necessity of nature, and not a result of Adam's sin; those who assert that newborn children derive nothing of original sin from Adam to be expiated by the laver of regeneration; and those

[1] Compare Canon BRIGHT's *Introduction* to his *Select Anti-Pelagian Treatises*, p. xli.

who assert a distinction between the kingdom of heaven and eternal life, for entrance into the former of which alone baptism is necessary. The second triad deals with the nature of grace, and anathematizes those who assert that grace brings only remission of past sins, not aid in avoiding future ones; those who assert that grace aids us not to sin, only by teaching us what is sinful, not by enabling us to will and do what we know to be right; and those who assert that grace only enables us to do more easily what we should without it still be able to do. The third triad deals with the universal sinfulness of the race, and anathematizes those who assert that the apostles' confession of sin (1 John i. 8) is due only to their humility; those who say that "Forgive us our trespasses" in the Lord's Prayer, is pronounced by the saints, not for themselves, but for the sinners in their company; and those who say that the saints use these words of themselves only out of humility and not truly. Here we see a careful traversing of the whole ground of the controversy, with a conscious reference to the three chief contentions of the Pelagian teachers.[1]

The appeal to the civil power, by whomsoever made, was, of course, indefensible, although it accorded with the opinions of the day and was entirely approved by Augustine. But it was the ruin of the Pelagian cause. Zosimus found himself forced either to go into banishment with his wards, or to desert their cause. He appears never to have had any personal convictions on the dogmatic points involved in the controversy, and so, all the more readily, yielded to the necessity of the moment. He cited Cœlestius to appear before a council for a new examination. But that heresiarch consulted prudence and withdrew from the city. Zosimus, possibly in the effort to appear a leader in the cause he had opposed, not only condemned and excommunicated the men whom less than six months before he had pronounced "orthodox" after a "mature consideration of the matters involved," but, in obedience to the imperial decree, issued a stringent paper which

---

[1] See above, p. 7, and the passages in AUGUSTINE cited in note [3].

condemned Pelagius and the Pelagians, and affirmed the African doctrines as to corruption of nature, true grace, and the necessity of baptism. To this he required subscription from all bishops as a test of orthodoxy. Eighteen Italian bishops refused their signatures, with Julian of Eclanum, henceforth to be the champion of the Pelagian party, at their head, and were therefore deposed, although several of them afterwards recanted and were restored. In Julian, the heresy obtained an advocate who, if aught could have been done for its re-instatement, would surely have proved successful. He was the boldest, the strongest, at once the most acute and the most weighty, of all the disputants of his party. But the ecclesiastical standing of this heresy was already determined. The policy of Zosimus' test act was imposed by imperial authority on North Africa in 419. The exiled bishops were driven from Constantinople by Atticus in 424; and they are said to have been condemned at a Cilician synod in 423, and at an Antiochian one in 424. Thus the East itself was preparing for the final act in the drama. The exiled bishops were with Nestorius at Constantinople in 429; and that patriarch unsuccessfully interceded for them with Cœlestine, then Bishop of Rome. The conjunction was ominous. And at the ecumenical synod at Ephesus in 431, we again find the "Cœlestians" side by side with Nestorius, sharers in his condemnation.

But Pelagianism did not so die as not to leave a legacy behind it. "Remainders of Pelagianism"[1] soon showed themselves especially in Southern Gaul, where a body of monastic leaders attempted to find a middle ground on which they could stand, by allowing the Augustinian doctrine of assisting grace but retaining the Pelagian conception of man's self-determination to good. We first hear of them in 428, through letters from two laymen, Prosper and Hilary, to Augustine. They are described as men who accepted original sin and the necessity of grace, but asserted that men began their turning to God, and God helped their beginning.

---

[1] Prosper's phrase.

They taught[1] that all men are sinners, and that they derive their sin from Adam ; that they can by no means save themselves, but need God's assisting grace ; and that this grace is gratuitous in the sense that men cannot really deserve it, and yet that it is not irresistible, nor given always without the occasion of its gift having been determined by men's attitude towards God ; so that, though not given on account of the merits of men, it is given according to those merits, actual or foreseen. The recognized head of this new, semi-Pelagian movement was John Cassian, a pupil of Chrysostom—to whom he attributed all that was good in his life and will—and the fountain-head of Gallic monasticism ; by his side stood Vincent of Lerins. The treatise which Augustine wrote upon the appeal of Hilary and Prosper, so far from ending the controversy, gave additional offence. The middle ground which the semi-Pelagians assumed was supported by appeals to doctrinal tradition, and not only commended itself to the ruling monastic consciousness, but was easily given the appearance of well-balanced moderation. The tide of Gallic thought set strongly in its channels and departed ever more widely from Augustinianism until it found in Faustus of Rhegium a philosophical thinker who compacted it into something like a unitary system. There was an appearance that Gallic theology had broken out a path of its own which was destined to produce a permanent breach between it and the rest of the Church, and especially with Rome, where the torch of Augustinianism was burning brightly.[2]

The Augustinian opposition was at first led by the vigorous controversialist Prosper of Aquitaine, "the Troubadour of Augustinianism," who in prose and verse alike, but to little apparent effect, assaulted the "ingrates" who would not give its full rights to the

[1] AUGUSTINE gives their teaching carefully in his *On the Predestination of the Saints*, 2.
[2] An admirable account of the development of semi-Pelagianism in Gaul is given by Dr. C. F. ARNOLD, in his *Cæsarius von Arelate und die gallische Kirche seiner Zeit*, p. 314. Cf. HARNACK'S *Dogmengeschichte*, iii. 219 sq. (ed. 1 and 2) ; HOCH's *Lehre des Johannes Cassianus von Natur und Gnade ;* and KOCH's *Der heilige Faustus*.

grace of God. Already in 431 he obtained a letter from Pope Cœlestine, addressed to the Gallican bishops and designed to close the controversy in favor of Augustinianism ; and from that time the whole influence of the Roman see was freely used to this end. It was not, however, until nearly a century later that the contest was brought to a conclusion in a victory for a weakened Augustinianism, under the leadership of the wise and good Cæsarius of Arles. As a nurseling of Lerins, Cæsarius came himself out of the centre of the semi-Pelagian circle, and owed his Augustinianism apparently to a certain Pomerius, a rhetorician by profession, whom he met at Arles. Under the influence of Cæsarius the second Council of Orange, which convened at that ancient town on the third day of July, 529, drew up a series of articles which condemned the distinctive features of semi-Pelagianism, and affirmed an anxiously guarded and somewhat attenuated Augustinianism. These articles were framed with the aid of Felix IV. and received the ratification of Boniface II. in the following year. So far as a formal condemnation could reach, distinctive semi-Pelagianism was suppressed by them in the whole Western Church. This result could not have been attained by leadership less great than that of Cæsarius. But the serious consequence attended the method of compromise by which he secured this great achievement, that a weakened Augustinianism thus became the norm of church-doctrine for the future. Crass Gallic synergism was forever excluded from Western church-teaching ; but equally a pure and complete Augustinianism was put henceforth beyond its reach. Distinctive semi-Pelagianism must hereafter rank as heresy ; the Augustinian doctrine of " prevenient grace" became an essential element of the Church's system. But consistent Augustinianism might easily also come to be looked upon as heresy, and the very terms " predestination" and " particular redemption" might fall under the ban. In a word, the decrees of Trent are the natural sequence of the canons of Orange ; and we must trace it back to these canons that Thomism has proved the supreme height of doctrine attainable in the Latin Church.

Augustine's Part in the Controversy.

BOTH by nature and by grace, Augustine was very specially fitted to be the champion of truth in this controversy. Of a naturally philosophical temperament, he saw into the springs of life with a vividness of perception to which most men are strangers. And his own experiences in his long resistance and final yielding to the drawings of grace gave him a clear apprehension of the great evangelic principle that God seeks men, not men God, such as no sophistry could cloud. Whatever change his philosophy or theology might undergo in other particulars, there was one conviction too deeply imprinted upon his heart ever to fade or alter,—the conviction of the ineffableness of God's grace. Grace,—man's absolute dependence on God as the source of all good,—this was the common and even the formative element in all stages of his doctrinal development, which was marked only by the ever growing consistency with which he built his theology around this central principle. Already in 397,—the year after he became bishop,—we find him enunciating with admirable clearness all the essential elements of his teaching, as he afterwards opposed them to Pelagius.[1] It was inevitable, therefore, that although he was rejoiced when he heard, some years later, of the zealous labours of this pious monk in Rome towards stemming the tide of luxury and sin, and although he esteemed him for his devout life and loved him for his Christian activity, he yet was deeply troubled when subsequent rumours reached him that Pelagius was "disputing against the grace of God."

He tells us over and over again, that this was a thing no devout heart could endure. And we perceive that,

---

[1] Compare his work written this year, *On Several Questions to Simplicianus*. For the development of Augustine's theology, see the admirable statement in NEANDER's *Church History*, E. T., ii. 625 sq.

from this moment, Augustine was only biding his time, and awaiting a fitting opportunity to join issue with the denier of the holy of holies of his whole, we need not say theology merely, but life. " Although I was grieved by this," he says, " and it was told me by men whom I believed, I yet desired to have something of such sort from his own lips or in some book of his, so that, if I began to refute it, he would not be able to deny it." [1] Thus he actually apologises for not entering into the controversy earlier. When Pelagius came to Africa, then, it was almost as if he had deliberately sought his fate. Circumstances secured a lull before the storm. He visited Hippo ; but Augustine was absent, though he did not fail to inform himself on his return that Pelagius while there had not been heard to say " anything at all of this kind." The controversy against the Donatists was now occupying all the energies of the African Church, and Augustine himself was a ruling spirit in the great conference now holding at Carthage with them. While there, he was so immersed in this business that, although he once or twice saw the face of Pelagius, he had no conversation with him. His ears were wounded by a casual remark which he heard, to the effect " that infants were not baptized for remission of sins but for consecration to Christ," but he allowed himself to pass the matter over, " because there was no opportunity to contradict it and those who said it were not such men as could cause him solicitude for their influence."[2]

Early Anti-Pelagian Sermons.

It appears from these facts, given us by himself, that Augustine was not only ready but was looking for the coming controversy. It can scarcely have been a surprise to him when Paulinus accused Cœlestius (412). He was not a member of the council which condemned him, but it was inevitable that he should at once take the leading part in the consequent controversy.

[1] *On the Proceedings of Pelagius*, 46.
[2] *On the Merits and Remission of Sins*, iii. 12.

Cœlestius and his friends did not silently submit to the judgment that had been passed upon their teaching. They could not openly propagate their heresy, but they were diligent in spreading their plaints privately and by subterraneous whispers among the people.[1] This was met by the Catholics in public sermons and familiar colloquies held everywhere. But this wise rule was observed,—to contend against the erroneous teachings but to keep silence as to the teachers, that so (as Augustine explains[2]) "the men might rather be brought to see and acknowledge their error through fear of ecclesiastical judgment than be punished by the actual judgment." Augustine was abundant in these oral labours. Many of his sermons directed against Pelagian error have come down to us, though it is often impossible to be sure as to their dates. For one of them (170) he took his text from Phil. iii. 6–16, "As touching the righteousness which is by the law blameless; howbeit what things were gain to me, those have I counted loss for Christ." He begins by asking how the apostle could count his blameless conversation according to the righteousness which is from the law as dung and loss, and then proceeds to explain the purpose for which the law was given, our state by nature and under law, and the kind of blamelessness that the law is able to produce, ending by showing that man can have no righteousness except from God, and no perfect righteousness except in heaven.

Three other sermons (174, 175, 176) had as their text I Tim. i. 15, 16, and developed its teaching, that the universal sin of the world and its helplessness in sin constituted the necessity of the incarnation; and especially that the necessity of Christ's grace for salvation is just as great for infants as for adults. Much is very forcibly said in these sermons which was afterwards incorporated in Augustine's treatises. "There was no reason," he insists, "for the coming of Christ the Lord except to save sinners. Take away diseases, take away wounds, and there is no reason for medi-

---

[1] *Epistle* 157, 22.
[2] *On the Proceedings of Pelagius*, 46.

cine. If the great Physician came from heaven, a great sick man was lying ill through the whole world. That sick man is the human race" (175, 1). "He who says, 'I am not a sinner,' or 'I was not,' is ungrateful to the Saviour. No one of men in that mass of mortals which flows down from Adam, no one at all of men is not sick : no one is healed without the grace of Christ. Why do you ask whether infants are sick from Adam? For they, too, are brought to the church ; and, if they cannot run thither on their own feet, they run on the feet of others that they may be healed. Mother Church accommodates others' feet to them so that they may come, others' heart so that they may believe, others' tongue so that they may confess ; and, since they are sick by another's sin, so when they are healed they are saved by another's confession in their behalf. Let, then, no one buzz strange doctrines to you. *This* the Church has always had, has always held ; this she has received from the faith of the elders ; this she will perseveringly guard until the end. Since the whole have no need of a physician, but only the sick, what need, then, has the infant of Christ, if he is not sick ? If he is well, why does he seek the physician through those who love him ? If, when infants are brought, they are said to have no sin of inheritance (*peccatum propaginis*) at all, and yet come to Christ, why is it not said in the church to those that bring them, 'Take these innocents hence ; the physician is not needed by the well, but by the sick ; Christ came not to call the just, but sinners' ? It never has been said, and it never will be said. Let each one therefore, brethren, speak for him who cannot speak for himself. It is much the custom to intrust the inheritance of orphans to the bishops ; how much more the grace of infants ! The bishop protects the orphan lest he should be oppressed by strangers, his parents being dead. Let him cry out more for the infant who, he fears, will be slain by his parents. Who comes to Christ has something in him to be healed ; and he who has not, has no reason for seeking the physician. Let parents choose one of two things : let them either confess that there is sin to be healed in their infants, or let them cease bringing them to the physician. This is nothing else than to wish to bring a well person to the physician. Why do you bring him? To be baptized. Whom? The infant. To whom do you bring him? To Christ. To Him, of course, who came into the world? Certainly, it is said. Why did He come into the world? To save sinners. Then he whom you bring has in him that which needs saving?"[1]

So again : " He who says that the age of infancy does not need Jesus' salvation, says nothing else than that the Lord Christ is not *Jesus* to faithful infants ; i.e., to infants baptized in Christ. For what is *Jesus? Jesus* means saviour. He is not Jesus to those whom He does not save, who do not need to be saved. Now, if your hearts can bear that Christ is not *Jesus* to any of the baptized, I do not know how you can be acknowledged to have sound faith. They are infants, but they are made members of Him. They are infants, but they receive His sacraments. They are infants, but they become partakers of His table, so that they may have life."[2] The preveniency of grace is explicitly asserted in these sermons. In one he says, " Zaccheus was seen, and saw ; but unless he had been seen, he would not have seen. For ' whom He predestinated, them also He called.' In order that we may see, we are seen ; that we may love, we are loved. ' My God, may His pity prevent me !'"[3] And in another, at more length : " His calling has prevented you, so that you may have a good will. Cry out, ' My God, let Thy mercy prevent me ' (Ps. lviii. 11). That you may be, that you may feel, that you may hear, that you may consent, His mercy prevents you. It prevents you in all things ; and do you too prevent His judgment in something. In what, do you say ? In what ? In confessing that you have all these things from God, whatever you have of good ; and from yourself whatever you have of evil" (176, 5). " We owe therefore to Him that we are, that we are alive, that we under-

---

[1] *Sermon* 176, 2.   [2] *Ibid.* 174.   [3] *Ibid.* 174.

stand : that we are men, that we live well, that we understand aright, we owe to Him. Nothing is ours except the sin that we have. For what have we that we did not receive?" (1 Cor. ix. 7) (176, 6).

The Treatise on " The Merits and Remission of Sins."

It was not long, however, before the controversy was driven out of the region of sermons into that of regular treatises. The occasion for Augustine's first appearance in a written document bearing on the controversy, was given by certain questions which were sent to him for answer by "the tribune and notary" Marcellinus, with whom he had cemented his intimacy at Carthage the previous year, when this notable official was presiding, by the emperor's orders, over the great conference between the Catholics and Donatists.[1] The mere fact that Marcellinus, still at Carthage where Cœlestius had been brought to trial, appealed to Augustine at Hippo for written answers to important questions connected with the Pelagian heresy, speaks volumes for the prominent position he had already assumed in the controversy. The questions that were sent concerned the connection of death with sin, the transmission of sin, the possibility of a sinless life, and especially infants' need of baptism.[2] Augustine was immersed in abundant labours when they reached him.[3] But he could not resist this appeal, and that the less

---

[1] Flavius Marcellinus was a Christian man of high character and devout mind. Honorius mentions him as a "man of conspicuous renown," in a law enacted August 30th, 414 (*Cod. Theod.* xvi., 5, line 55). He was appointed by Honorius to preside over the commission of inquiry into the disputes between the Catholics and Donatists in 411, and held the famous conference between the parties that met in Carthage on the 1st, 3d, and 8th of June, 411. He discharged this whole business with singular patience, moderation, and good judgment ; which appears to have cemented the intimate friendship between him and Augustine. Augustine's treatise on *The Spirit and Letter* is also addressed to him, and the *City of God* was undertaken on his suggestion. He was put to death in September, 413, "having, though innocent, fallen a victim to the cruel hatred of the tyrant Heraclius," as Jerome writes in his book iii. against the Pelagians.

[2] *On the Merits and Remission of Sins*, iii. 1.

[3] *Ibid.* i. 1. Compare *Epistle* 139.

since the Pelagian controversy had already grown to a place of the first importance in his eyes. The result was his treatise, *On the Merits and Remission of Sins and on the Baptism of Infants*, which consisted of two books, and was written in 412.

The first book of this work is an argument for original sin, drawn from the universal reign of death in the world (2-8), from the teaching of Rom. v. 12-21 (9-20), and chiefly from the baptism of infants (21-70).[1] It opens by exploding the Pelagian contention that death is of nature and that Adam would have died even had he not sinned, by showing that the penalty threatened to Adam included physical death (Gen. iii. 19), and that it is due to him that we all die (Rom. viii. 10, 11 ; 1 Cor. xv. 21) (2-8). Then the Pelagian assertion that we are injured in Adam's sin only by its bad example, which we imitate, not by any propagation from it, is tested by an exposition of Rom. v. 12 sq. (9-20). And then the main subject of the book is reached, and the writer sharply presses the Pelagians with the universal and primitive fact of the baptism of infants, as a proof of original sin (21-70). He tracks out all their subterfuges,—showing the absurdity of the assertion that infants are baptized for the remission of sins that they have themselves committed since birth (22), or in order to obtain a higher stage of salvation (23-28), or because of sin committed in some previous state of existence (31-33). Then turning to the positive side, he shows at length that the Scriptures teach that Christ came to save sinners, that baptism is for the remission of sins, and that all that partake of it are confessedly sinners (34 sq.) ; then he points out that John ii. 7, 8, on which the Pelagians relied, cannot be held to distinguish between ordinary salvation and a higher form, under the name of " the kingdom of God" (58 sq.) ; and he closes

[1] On the prominence of infant baptism in the controversy, and why it was so, see *Sermon* 165, 7 sq. " What do you say ? 'Just this,' he says, ' that God creates every man immortal.' Why, then, do infant children die ? For if I say, ' Why do adult men die ? ' you would say to me, ' They have sinned.' Therefore I do not argue about the adults : I cite infancy as a witness against you," and so on, eloquently developing the argument.

by showing that the very manner in which baptism was administered, with its exorcism and exsufflation, implied the infant to be a sinner (63), and by suggesting that the peculiar helplessness of infancy, so different not only from the earliest age of Adam, but also from that of many young animals, may possibly be itself penal (64–69).

The second book treats, with similar fulness, the question of the perfection of human righteousness in this life. After an exordium which speaks of the will and its limitations and of the need of God's assisting grace (1–6), the writer raises four questions. First, he asks whether it may be said to be possible for a man, by God's grace, to attain a condition of entire sinlessness in this life (7). This he answers in the affirmative. Secondly, he asks whether any one has ever done this, or may ever be expected to do it. This he answers in the negative on the testimony of Scripture (8–25). Thirdly, he asks why not, and replies briefly because men are unwilling, explaining at length what he means by this (26–33). Finally, he inquires whether any man has ever existed, exists now, or will ever exist, entirely without sin. This question differs from the second inasmuch as that inquired after the attainment in this life of a state in which sinning should cease, while this seeks a man who has never been sinful, implying the absence of original as well as of actual sin. After answering this in the negative (34), Augustine discusses anew the question of original sin. Here he first expounds from the positive side (35–38) the condition of man in paradise, the nature of his probation, and of the fall and its effects both on him and his posterity, and the kind of redemption that has been provided in the incarnation. He then proceeds to reply to certain cavils (39 sq.), such as, "Why should children of baptized people need baptism?"—"How can a sin be remitted to the father and held against the child?"—"If physical death comes from Adam, ought we not to be released from it on believing in Christ?" He concludes with an exhortation to hold fast to the exact truth, turning neither to the right nor left,—neither saying that we have no sin, nor surrendering ourselves to our sin (57 sq.).

After these books were completed, Augustine came into possession of Pelagius' *Commentary on Paul's Epistles*, which was written while he was living in Rome (before 410). He found it to contain some arguments that he had not treated,—such arguments, he tells us, as he had not imagined could be propounded by any one.[1] Unwilling to re-open his finished treatise, he began a long supplementary letter to Marcellinus, which he intended to serve as a third and concluding book to his work. He was some time in completing this letter. He had asked to have the former two books returned to him ; and it is a curious indication of his overworked state, that he forgot what he wanted with them.[2] He visited Carthage while the letter was in hand, and saw Marcellinus personally. Even after his return to Hippo, it dragged along, amid many distractions, slowly towards completion.[3] Meanwhile, a long letter was written to Honoratus, in which a section on the grace of the New Testament was incorporated. At length the promised supplement was completed. It was professedly a criticism of Pelagius' *Commentary*, and therefore naturally mentioned his name. But Augustine even goes out of his way to speak as highly of his opponent as he can.[4] It is nevertheless apparent that his esteem for the strength of Pelagius' mind was not very high, and that he had even less patience with the moral quality that led to Pelagius' odd, oblique way of expressing his opinions. There is even a half sarcasm in the way he speaks of Pelagius' care and circumspection, which was certainly justified by the event.

The letter opens by stating and criticising in a very acute and telling dialectic, the new arguments of Pelagius. These were such as the following : " If Adam's sin injured even those who do not sin, Christ's righteousness ought likewise to profit even those who do

[1] *On the Merits and Remission of Sins*, iii. 1.
[2] *Letter*, 139, 3.   [3] *Letter*, 140.   [4] See chaps. 1 and 5.

not believe" (2-4); "No man can transmit what he has not; and hence, if baptism cleanses from sin, the children of baptized parents ought to be free from sin;" "God remits one's own sins, and can scarcely, therefore, impute another's to us; and if the soul is created, it would certainly be unjust to impute Adam's alien sin to it" (5). The stress of the letter, however, is laid upon two contentions: 1. That whatever else may be ambiguous in the Scriptures, they are perfectly clear that no man can have eternal life except in Christ, who came to call sinners to repentance (7); and 2. That original sin in infants has always been, in the Church, one of the fixed facts, to be used as a basis of argument in order to reach the truth in other matters, and has never itself been called in question before (10-14). At this point, the writer returns to the second and third of the new arguments of Pelagius mentioned above, and discusses them more fully (15-20). He closes with a recapitulation of the three great points that had been raised: viz., that both death and sin are derived from Adam's sin by all his posterity; that infants need salvation, and hence baptism; and that no man ever attains in this life such a state of holiness that he cannot truly pray, "Forgive us our trespasses."

The Treatise on "The Spirit and the Letter."

Augustine was now to learn that one service often entails another. Marcellinus wrote to say that he was puzzled by what had been said in the second book of this work, as to the possibility of man's attaining to sinlessness in this life, while yet it was asserted that no man ever had attained or ever would attain, it. How, he asked, can that be said to be possible which is, and which will remain, unexampled? In reply, Augustine wrote, during this same year (412), and sent to his noble friend, another work, which he calls *On the Spirit and the Letter*, from the prominence which he gives in it to the words of 2 Cor. iii. 6.[1] He did not

---

[1] *Sermon* 163 treats the text similarly.

content himself with a simple, direct answer to Marcellinus' question. He goes at length into a profound disquisition into the roots of the doctrine. Thus he gives us, not a mere explanation of a former contention, but a new treatise on a new subject,—the absolute necessity of the grace of God for any good living.

He begins by explaining to Marcellinus that he has affirmed the possibility while denying the actuality of a sinless life, on the ground that all things are possible to God,—even the passage of a camel through the eye of a needle, which nevertheless has never occurred (1, 2). For, in speaking of man's perfection, we are speaking really of a work of God,—and one which is none the less His work because it is wrought through the instrumentality of man and in the use of his free will. The Scriptures, indeed, teach that no man lives without sin. But this is only the proclamation of a matter of fact; and although it is thus contrary to fact and Scripture to assert that men may be found that live sinlessly, yet such an assertion would not be fatal heresy. What is unbearable, is that men should assert it to be possible for man, unaided by God, to attain this perfection. This is to speak against the grace of God. It is to put in man's power what is only possible to the almighty grace of God (3, 4). No doubt, even these men do not, in so many words, exclude the aid of grace in perfecting human life. They affirm God's help; but they make it consist in His gift to man of a perfectly free will, and in His addition to this of commandments and teachings which make known to him what he is to seek and what to avoid, and so enable him to direct his free will to what is good. What, however, does such a "grace" amount to? (5). Man needs something more than to know the right way. He needs to love it, or he will not walk in it. And all mere teaching, which can do nothing more than bring us knowledge of what we ought to do, is but the letter that killeth. What we need is some inward, Spirit-given aid to the keeping of what by the law we know ought to be kept. Mere knowledge slays; while to lead a holy life is the gift of God,—not only because He has given us will, nor only because He has taught us the right way, but because by the Holy Spirit He sheds love abroad in the hearts of all those whom He has predestinated and will call and justify and glorify (Rom. viii. 29, 30).

To prove this, Augustine states to be the object of the present treatise ; and, after investigating the meaning of 2 Cor. iii. 6 and showing that " the letter" there means the law as a system of precepts, which reveals sin rather than takes it away, points out the way rather than gives strength to walk in it and therefore slays the soul by shutting it up under sin,—while " the Spirit" is God's Holy Ghost who is shed abroad in our hearts to give us strength to walk aright, —he undertakes to prove this position from the teachings of the Epistle to the Romans at large. This contention, it will be seen, cut at the very roots of Pelagianism. If all mere teaching slays the soul, as Paul asserts, then all that what they called "grace" could, when alone, do, was to destroy ; and the upshot of "helping" man by simply giving him free will and pointing out the way to him, would be the loss of the whole race. Not that the law is sin : Augustine teaches that it is holy and good and God's instrument in salvation. Not that free will is done away : it is by free will that men are led into holiness. But the purpose of the law (he teaches) is to make men so feel their lost estate as to seek the help by which alone they may be saved ; and will is only then liberated to do good when grace has made it free. " What the law of works enjoins by menace, that the law of faith secures by faith. What the law of works does is to say, ' Do what I command thee ; ' but by the law of faith we say to God, ' Give me what thou commandest.' " (22).[1]

In the midst of this argument, Augustine is led to discuss the differentiating characteristics of the Old and New Testaments. He expounds at length (33–42) the passage in Jer. xxxi. 31–34, showing that, in the

---

[1] See this prayer beautifully illustrated from Scripture in *On the Merits and Remission of Sins*, ii. 5.

prophet's view, the difference between the two covenants is that in the Old, the law is an external thing written on stones ; while in the New, it is written internally on the heart, so that men now wish to do what the law prescribes. This writing on the heart is nothing else, he explains, than the shedding abroad by the Holy Spirit of love in our hearts, so that we love God's will, and therefore freely do it. Towards the end of the treatise (50-61), he treats in an absorbingly interesting way of the mutual relations of free will, faith, and grace, contending that all co-exist without the voiding of any. It is by free will that we believe ; but it is only as grace moves us, that we are able to use our free will for believing ; and it is only after we are thus led by grace to believe, that we obtain all other goods. In prosecuting this analysis, Augustine is led to distinguish very sharply between the faculty and use of ree will (58), as well as between ability and volition (53). Faith is an act of the man himself ; but only as he is given the power from on high to will to believe, will he believe (57, 60).

By this work, Augustine completed, in his treatment of Pelagianism, the circle of that triad of doctrines which he himself looked upon as most endangered by this heresy,[1]– original sin, the imperfection of human righteousness, the necessity of grace. In his mind, the last was the kernel of the whole controversy ; and this was a subject which he could never approach without some heightened fervour. This accounts for the great attractiveness of the present work,—through the whole fabric of which runs the golden thread of the praise of God's ineffable grace. In Canon Bright's opinion, it " perhaps, next to the *Confessions*, tells us most of the thoughts of that ' rich, profound, and affectionate mind ' on the soul's relations to its God."[2]

[1] See above, p. 7.   [2] As quoted above, p. 18.

The Letters to Anastasius and Paulinus.

AFTER the publication of these treatises, the controversy certainly did not lull. But it relapsed for nearly three years, again, into less public courses. Meanwhile, Augustine was busy, among other most distracting cares (Ep. 145, 1), still defending the grace of God by letters and sermons. A fair illustration of his state of mind at this time may be obtained from his letter to Anastasius (145), which assuredly must have been written soon after the treatise *On the Spirit and the Letter*. Throughout this letter, there are adumbrations of the same train of thought that filled that treatise; and there is one passage which may almost be taken as a summary of it. Augustine is weary of the vexatious cares that oppressed his life. He is ready to long for the everlasting rest. Yet he bewails the weakness which allowed the sweetness of external things still to insinuate itself into his heart. Victory over, and emancipation from, this, he asserts, "cannot, without God's grace, be achieved by the human will, which is by no means to be called free so long as it is subject to enslaving lusts." Then he proceeds as follows: "The law, therefore, by teaching and commanding what cannot be fulfilled without grace, demonstrates to man his weakness, in order that the weakness, thus proved, may resort to the Saviour, by whose healing the will may be able to do what it found impossible in its weakness. So, then, the law brings us to faith, faith obtains the Spirit in fuller measure, the Spirit sheds love abroad in us, and love fulfils the law. For this reason the law is called a schoolmaster, under whose threatening and severity 'whosoever shall call on the name of the Lord shall be delivered.' But 'how shall they call on Him in whom they have not believed?' Wherefore, that the letter without the Spirit may not kill, the life-giving Spirit is given to those that believe and call upon Him; but the love of God is poured out into our hearts by the Holy Spirit who is given to us, so that the words of the same apostle, ' Love is the fulfilling of the law,' may be realized. Thus the law is good to him that uses it lawfully; and he uses it lawfully, who, understanding wherefore it was given, betakes himself, under the pressure of its threatening, to liberating grace. Whoever ungratefully despises this grace by which the ungodly is justified, and trusts in his own strength for fulfilling the law, being ignorant of God's righteousness and going about to establish his own righteousness, is not submitting himself to the righteousness of God ; and therefore the law is made to him not a help to pardon, but the bond of guilt ; not because the law is evil, but because ' sin,' as it is written, ' works death to such persons by that which is good.' For by the commandment he sins more grievously, who, by the commandment, knows how evil are the sins which he commits."

Although Augustine states clearly that this letter is written against those " who arrogate too much to the human will, imagining that, the law being given, the will is of its own strength sufficient to fulfil the law, though not assisted by any grace imparted by the Holy Ghost, in addition to instruction in the law,"—he refrains still from mentioning the names of the authors of this teaching, evidently out of a lingering tenderness in his treatment of them. This will help us to explain the courtesy of a note which he sent to Pelagius himself at about this time, in reply to a letter he had received from him some time before, and of which Pelagius afterward (at the Synod of Diospolis) made, to say the least of it, an ungenerous use. This note,[1] Augustine tells us, was written with "tempered praises" (wherefrom we see his lessening respect for the man), and in such a manner as to admonish Pelagius to think rightly concerning grace,—so far as could be done without raising the dregs of the controversy in a formal note. He sought to accomplish this by praying from the Lord for Pelagius, those good things by which he might be good forever, and might live

---

[1] *Epistle* 146. See *On the Proceedings of Pelagius*, 50, 51, 52.

eternally with Him who is eternal ; and by asking his prayers in return, that he, Augustine, too, might be made by the Lord such as Pelagius seemed to suppose he already was. How Augustine could really intend these prayers to be understood as an admonition to Pelagius to look to God for what he was seeking to work out for himself, is fully illustrated by the closing words of this almost contemporary letter to Anastasius. "Pray, therefore, for us," he writes, "that we may be righteous,—an attainment wholly beyond a man's reach, unless he know righteousness and be willing to practise it, but one which is immediately realized when he is perfectly willing ; but this cannot be in him unless he is healed by the grace of the Spirit, and aided to be able." The point had already been made in the controversy that so much power was attributed to the human will by the Pelagian doctrine that no one ought to pray, "Lead us not into temptation, but deliver us from evil."

If he was anxious to avoid personal controversy with Pelagius himself in the hope that he might even yet be reclaimed, Augustine was equally anxious to teach the truth on all possible occasions. Pelagius had been intimate, when at Rome, with the pious Paulinus, bishop of Nola ; and it was understood that there was some tendency at Nola to follow the new teachings. It was, perhaps, as late as 414, when Augustine made reply in a long letter,[1] to a request which Paulinus had sent him about 410[2] for an exposition of certain difficult passages of Scripture. Among these passages was Rom. xi. 28 ; and, in explaining it, Augustine did not withhold a tolerably complete account of his doctrine of predestination, involving the essence of his whole teaching as to grace. "For when he had said," he remarks, "'according to the election they are beloved for their father's sake,' he added, 'for the gifts and calling of God are without repentance.' You see that those are certainly meant who belong to the number of the predestinated. . . . 'Many indeed are called

---

[1] *Epistle* 149. See especially 18 sq.   [2] *Ibid.* 121.

but few chosen;' but those who are elect, these are 'called according to His purpose;' and it is beyond doubt that in them God's foreknowledge cannot be deceived. These He foreknew and predestinated to be conformed to the image of His Son, in order that He might be the first born among many brethren. But ' whom He predestinated, them He also called.' This calling is ' according to His purpose,' this calling is ' without repentance,'" etc., quoting Rom. v. 28–31. Then continuing, he says : "Those are not in this vocation who do not persevere unto the end in the faith that worketh by love, although they walk in it a little while. . . . But the reason why some belong to it and some do not, can easily be hidden, but cannot be unjust. For is there injustice with God? God forbid ! For this belongs to those high judgments which, so to say, terrified the wondering apostle to look upon."

Controversial Sermons.

Among the most remarkable of the controversial sermons that were preached about this time, especial mention is due to two that were delivered at Carthage in the midsummer of 413. The former of these[1] was preached on the festival of John the Baptist's birth (June 24), and naturally took the forerunner for its subject. The nativity of John suggesting the nativity of Christ, the preacher spoke of the marvel of the incarnation. He who was in the beginning, and was the Word of God, and was Himself God, and who made all things, and in whom was life, even this one " came to us. To whom? To the worthy? Nay, but to the unworthy ! For Christ died for the ungodly and the unworthy, though He was worthy. We indeed were unworthy whom He pitied ; but He was worthy who pitied us, to whom we say, ' For Thy pity's sake, Lord, deliver us !' Not for the sake of our preceding merits, but ' for Thy pity's sake, Lord, deliver us ;' and ' for Thy name's sake be propitious to our sins,' not for our merit's sake. . . . For the merit of sins is,

[1] *Sermon* 293.

of course, not reward, but punishment." The preacher then dwelt upon the necessity of the incarnation, and the necessity of a mediator between God and "the whole mass of the human race alienated from Him by Adam." Then, quoting 1 Cor. iv. 7, he asserts that it is not our varying merits but God's grace alone that makes us differ, and that we are all alike, great and small, old and young, saved by one and the same Saviour. "'What then,' some one says," he continues, "'even the infant needs a liberator?' Certainly he needs one. And the witness to it is the mother that faithfully runs to church with the child to be baptized. The witness is Mother Church herself, who receives the child for washing, and either for dismissing him [from this life] delivered, or nurturing him in piety. . . . Last of all, the tears of his own misery are witness in the child himself. . . . Recognize the misery, extend the help. Let all put on bowels of mercy. By as much as they cannot speak for themselves, by so much more pityingly let us speak for the little ones." Then follows a passage calling on the Church to take the grace of infants in their charge as orphans committed to their care, which is in substance repeated from a former sermon.[1] The speaker proceeded to quote Matt. i. 21, and apply it. If Jesus came to save from sins, and infants are brought to Him, it is to confess that they, too, are sinners. Then, shall they be withheld from baptism? "Certainly, if the child could speak for himself, he would repel the voice of opposition, and cry out, 'Give me Christ's life! In Adam I died: give me Christ's life; in whose sight I am not clean, even if I am an infant whose life has been but one day in the earth.'" "No way can be found," adds the preacher, "of coming into the life of this world except by Adam; no way can be found of escaping punishment in the next world except by Christ. Why do you shut up the one door?" Even John the Baptist himself was born in sin; and absolutely no one can be found who was born apart from sin, unless we

---

[1] *Sermon* 176, 2.

can find one who has been born apart from Adam. "' By one man sin entered into the world, and by sin, death; and so it passed through upon all men.' If these were my words, could this sentiment be expressed more expressly, more clearly, more fully?"

Three days afterwards,[1] on the invitation of the Bishop of Carthage, Augustine preached a sermon professedly directed against the Pelagians,[2] which took up the threads hinted at in the former discourse, and developed a full polemic with reference to the baptism of infants. He began, formally enough, with the determination of the question in dispute. The Pelagians concede that infants should be baptized. The only question is, For what are they baptized? We say that they would not otherwise have salvation and eternal life; but they say it is not for salvation, not for eternal life, but for the kingdom of God. "The child, they say, although not baptized, by the desert of his innocence, in that he has no sin at all, either actual or original, either from himself or contracted from Adam, necessarily has salvation and eternal life even if not baptized; but is to be baptized for this reason,—that he may enter into the kingdom of God, i.e., into the kingdom of heaven." He then showed that there is no eternal life outside the kingdom of heaven, no middle place between the right and left hand of the judge at the last day, and that, therefore, to exclude one from the kingdom of God is to consign him to the pains of eternal fire; while, on the other side, no one ascends into heaven unless he has been made a member of Christ, and this can only be by faith,—which, in an infant's case, is professed by another in his stead. He next treated, at length, some of the puzzling questions with which the Pelagians were wont to try the catholics; and then, breaking off suddenly, he took a

---

[1] The inscription says, "V Calendas Julii," i.e., June 27. But it also says, "*In natalis martyris Guddentis*," whose day appears to have been July 18. Some of the martyrologies assign the 28th of June to Gaudentius (which some copies read here), but possibly none to Guddene.
[2] *Sermon* 294.

volume in his hands. "I ask you," he said, "to bear with me a little: I will read somewhat. It is St. Cyprian whom I hold in my hand, the ancient bishop of this see. What he thought of the baptism of infants, —nay, what he has shown that the Church always thought,—learn in brief. For it is not enough for them to dispute and argue I know not what impious novelties: they even try to charge us with asserting novelties. It is on this account that I read here St. Cyprian, in order that you may perceive that the orthodox understanding and catholic sense reside in the words which I have been just now speaking to you. He was asked whether an infant ought to be baptized before he was eight days old, seeing that by the ancient law no infant was allowed to be circumcised until he was eight days old. A question arose from this as to the day of baptism,—for concerning the origin of sin there was no question; and therefore from this thing of which there was no question, that question that had arisen was settled." Whereupon he read to them the passage out of Cyprian's letter to Fidus, which declares that he, and all the council with him, unanimously thought that infants should be baptized at the earliest possible age, lest they should die in their inherited sin and so pass into eternal punishment.[1] The sermon closed with a tender warning to the teachers of these strange doctrines. He might call them heretics with truth, but he will not; let the Church seek still their salvation, and not mourn them as dead; let them be exhorted as friends, not striven with as enemies. "They disparage us," he says, "we will bear it; let them not disparage the rule [of faith], let them not disparage the truth; let them not contradict the Church, which labours every day for the remission of infants' original sin. This thing is settled. The errant disputer may be borne with in other questions that have not been thoroughly canvassed, that are not yet settled by the full authority of the Church,—their

[1] The passage is quoted at length in *On the Merits and Remission of Sins*, iii. 10. Compare *Against Two Letters of the Pelagians* iv. 23.

error should be borne with: it ought not to extend so far that they endeavour to shake even the very foundations of the Church!" He hints that although the patience hitherto exhibited towards them is "perhaps not blameworthy," yet patience may cease to be a virtue, and become culpable negligence. In the mean time, however, he begs that the catholics should continue amicable, fraternal, placid, loving, long suffering.

Letter to Hilary of Sicily.

Augustine himself gives us a view of the progress of the controversy at this time, in a letter written in 414.[1] The Pelagians had everywhere scattered the seeds of their new error. Some of them, by his ministry and that of his brother workers, had, "by God's mercy," been cured of their pest. Yet they still existed in Africa, especially about Carthage, and were everywhere propagating their opinions in subterraneous whispers, for fear of the judgment of the Church. Wherever they were not refuted they were seducing others to their following; and they were so spread abroad that he did not know where they would break out next. Nevertheless, he was still unwilling to brand them as heretics, and was more desirous of healing them as sick members of the Church than of cutting them off finally as too diseased for cure. Jerome also tells us that the poison was spreading in both the East and the West, and mentions particularly as seats where it showed itself the islands of Rhodes and Sicily. Of Rhodes we know nothing further; but from Sicily an appeal came to Augustine in 414 from one Hilary,[2] setting forth that there were certain Christians about Syracuse who taught strange doctrines, and beseeching Augustine to help him in dealing with them. The doctrines were enumerated as follows: "They say (1) that man can be without sin, (2) and can easily keep the commandments of God if he will; (3) that an unbaptized infant, if he is cut off by death, cannot justly

---

[1] *Epistle* 157, 22. [2] *Epistle* 156 among Augustine's *Letters*.

perish, since he is born without sin ; (4) that a rich man that remains in his riches cannot enter the kingdom of God, except he sell all that he has ; . . . (5) that we ought not to swear at all ;" and (6) apparently, that the Church is to be in this world without spot or blemish. Augustine suspected that these Sicilian disturbances were in some way the work of Cœlestius, and therefore in his answer[1] informs his correspondent of what had been done at the Synod of Carthage (412) against that heretic.

The long letter that was thus called forth follows the inquiries in the order they were put by Hilary. To the first of these Augustine replies substantially as he had treated the same matter in the second book of the treatise, *On the Merits and Forgiveness of Sins,*—that it is opposed to Scripture to hold that man can live sinlessly in this life, but that it is less a heresy than the wholly unbearable opinion that this state of sinlessness can be attained without God's help. "But when they say that free will suffices to man for fulfilling the precepts of the Lord, even though unaided to good works by God's grace and the gift of the Holy Spirit, it is to be altogether anathematized and detested with all execration. For those who assert this are inwardly alien from God's grace, because being ignorant of God's righteousness, like the Jews of whom the apostle speaks, and wishing to establish their own, they are not subject to God's righteousness, since there is no fulfilment of the law except love ; and of course the love of God is shed abroad in our hearts, not by ourselves, nor by the force of our own will, but by the Holy Ghost who is given to us." Dealing next with the second point, he drifts into the matter he had more fully developed in his work *On the Spirit and the Letter.* "Free will avails for God's works," he says, "if it be divinely aided, and this comes by humble seeking and doing ; but when deserted by divine aid, no matter how excellent may be its knowledge of the law, it will by no means possess solidity of righteousness, but only the

[1] *Epistle* 157, 22.

inflation of ungodly pride and deadly arrogance. This is taught us by that same Lord's Prayer; for it would be an empty thing for us to ask God ' Lead us not into temptation,' if the matter was so placed in our power that we would avail for fulfilling it without any aid from Him. For this free will is free in proportion as it is sound, but it is sound in proportion as it is subject to divine pity and grace. For it faithfully prays, saying, ' Direct my ways according to Thy word, and let no iniquity reign over me.' For how is that free over which iniquity reigns? But see who it is that is invoked by it, in order that it may not reign over it. For it says not, ' Direct my ways according to free will because no iniquity shall rule over me,' but ' Direct my ways according to *Thy word, and let no iniquity rule over me.*' It is a prayer, not a promise; it is a confession, not a profession; it is a wish for full freedom, not a boast of personal power. For it is not ' every one who confides in his own power,' but ' every one who calls on the name of God,' that ' shall be saved.' 'But how shall they call upon Him,' he says, ' in whom they have not believed?' Accordingly, then, they who rightly believe, believe in order to call on Him in whom they have believed, and to avail for doing what they receive in the precepts of the law; since what the law commands, faith prays for." " God, therefore, commands continence, and gives continence; He commands by the law, He give by grace; He commands by the letter, He gives by the spirit: for the law without grace makes the transgression to abound, and the letter without the Spirit kills. He commands for this reason,—that we who have endeavoured to do what He commands and are worn out in our weakness under the law, may know how to ask for the aid of grace; and, if we have been able to do any good work, that we may not be ungrateful to Him who aids us." The answer to the third point traverses the ground that was fully covered in the first book of the treatise *On the Merits and Forgiveness of Sins*, beginning by opposing the Pelagians to Paul in Rom. v. 12–19: " But when they say that an infant, cut off by death unbaptized, cannot perish since he is born without sin,—it is not this that the apostle says; and I think that it is better to believe the apostle than them." The fourth and fifth questions were new in this controversy; and it is not certain that they belong properly to it, though the legalistic asceticism of the Pelagian leaders may well have given rise to a demand on all Christians to sell what they had and give to the poor. This one of the points, Augustine treats at length, pointing out that many of the saints of old were rich, and that the Lord and His apostles always so speak that their counsels avail to the right use, not the destruction of wealth. Christians ought so to hold their wealth that they are not held by it and by no means prefer it to Christ. Equal good sense and mildness are shown in his treatment of the question concerning oaths; he points out that they were used by the Lord and His apostles, but advises that they be used as little as possible, lest by the custom of frequent oaths we learn to swear lightly. The question as to the Church, he passes over as having been sufficiently treated in the course of his previous remarks.

The Treatise on "Nature and Grace."

To the number of those who had been rescued from Pelagianism by his efforts, Augustine was now to have the pleasure of adding two others, in whom he seems to have taken much delight. Timasius and James were two young men of honourable birth and liberal education, who had been moved by the exhortations of Pelagius to give up the hope that they had in this world and to enter upon the service of God in an ascetic life.[1] Naturally, they had turned to him for instruction, and had received from him a book to which they had given their study. They met somewhere with some of Augustine's writings, however, and were deeply affected by what he said as to grace, and now began to see that the teaching of Pelagius opposed the grace of God by which man becomes a Christian.

[1] *Epistles* 177, 6; and 179, 2.

They gave their book, therefore, to Augustine, saying that it was Pelagius', and asking him for Pelagius' sake, and for the sake of the truth, to answer it. This was done; the resulting book, *On Nature and Grace*, was sent to the young men; and they returned a letter of thanks[1] in which they professed their conversion from their error. In this book, too, which was written in 415, Augustine refrained from mentioning Pelagius by name,[2] still feeling it better to spare the man while not sparing his errors. But he tells us, that, on reading the book of Pelagius' to which it was an answer, it became clear to him beyond any doubt that Pelagius' teaching was distinctly anti-Christian;[3] and when speaking of his own book privately to a friend, he allows himself to call it " a considerable book against *the heresy* of Pelagius, which he had been constrained to write by some brethren whom Pelagius had persuaded to adopt his fatal error, denying the grace of Christ."[4] Thus his attitude towards the persons of the new teachers was becoming ever more and more strained, despite his recognition of the excellent motives that might lie behind their "zeal not according to knowledge."

The treatise which was thus called out opens with a recognition of the zeal of Pelagius. As it burned most ardently against those who, when reproved for sin, take refuge in censuring their nature, Augustine compares it with the heathen view as expressed in Sallust's saying, " The human race falsely complains of its own nature."[5] He charges it therefore with not being according to knowledge, and proposes to oppose it by an equal zeal against all attempts to render the cross of Christ of none effect. He then gives a brief but excellent summary of the more important features of the catholic doctrine concerning nature and grace (2–7). Opening the work of Pelagius which had been placed

---
[1] *Epistle* 168. *On the Proceedings of Pelagius*, 48.
[2] *On the Proceedings of Pelagius*, 47; and *Epistle* 186, 1.
[3] Compare *On Nature and Grace*, 7; and *Epistle* 186, 1.
[4] *Epistle* 169, 13.
[5] *On Nature and Grace*, 1; Sallust's *Jugurtha*, prologue.

in his hands, he examines his doctrine of sin, its nature and effects. Pelagius, he points out, draws a distinction, sound enough in itself, between what is "possible" and what is "actual," but applies it unsoundly to sin, when he says that every man has the *possibility* of being without sin (8–9), and therefore without condemnation. Not so, says Augustine: an infant who dies unbaptized has no possibility of salvation open to him ; and the man who has lived and died in a land where it was impossible for him to hear the name of Christ has had no possibility open to him of becoming righteous by nature and free will. If this be not so, Christ is dead in vain, since all men in that case might have accomplished their salvation, even if Christ had never died (10). Pelagius, moreover, he shows, exhibits a tendency to deny the sinful character of all sins which are impossible to avoid, and so treats of sins of ignorance as to imply that he entirely excuses them (13–19). When he argues that no sin, because it is not a substance, can change nature, which is a substance, Augustine replies that this destroys the Saviour's work,—for how can He save from sins if sins do not corrupt? And, again, if an act cannot injure a substance, how can abstention from food, which is a mere act, kill the body? In the same way sin is not a substance ; but God is a substance,—yea, the height of substance and only true sustenance of the reasonable creature ; and the consequence of departure from Him is to the soul what refusal of food is to the body (22). To Pelagius' assertion that sin cannot be punished by more sin, Augustine replies that the apostle thinks differently (Rom. i. 21–31). Then putting his finger on the main point in controversy, he quotes the Scriptures as declaring the present condition of man to be that of spiritual death. " The Truth then designates as *dead* those whom this man declares to be unable to be damaged or corrupted by sin,—because, forsooth, he has discovered sin to be no substance !" (25). It was by free will that man passed into this state of death ; but a dead man needs something else to revive him,—he needs nothing less than a Vivifier. But of vivifying grace, Pelagius knows nothing ; and by knowing nothing of a Vivifier, he knows nothing of a Saviour ; but rather by making nature of itself able to be sinless, he glorifies the Creator at the expense of the Saviour (39). Next is examined Pelagius' contention that many saints are enumerated in the Scriptures as having lived sinlessly in this world. While declining to discuss the question of fact as to the Virgin Mary (42), Augustine opposes to the rest the declaration of John in 1 John i. 8 as final, but still pauses to explain why the Scriptures do not mention the sins of all, and to contend that all who ever were saved, under the Old Testament or under the New, were saved by the sacrificial death of Christ and by faith in Him (40-50). Thus we are brought, as Augustine says, to the core of the question, which concerns, not the fact of sinlessness in any man, but man's ability to be sinless. This ability Pelagius affirms of all men, and Augustine denies of all '' unless they are justified by the grace of God through our Lord Jesus Christ and Him crucified" (51). Accordingly, the whole discussion concerns grace, which Pelagius does not admit in any true sense, but places only in the nature that God has made (52).

We are next invited to attend to another distinction of Pelagius', in which he discriminates sharply between the nature that God has made, the crown of which is free will, and the use that man makes of this free will. The endowment of free will is a "capacity;" it is, because given by God in our making, a necessity of nature, and not in man's power to have or not have. It is the right use of it only, which man has in his power. This analysis Pelagius illustrates at length by appealing to the difference between the possession and use of the various bodily senses. The ability to see, for instance, he says, is a necessity of our nature : we do not make it ; we cannot help having it ; it is ours only to use it. Augustine criticises this presentation of the matter with great acuteness (although he is not averse to the analysis itself), with a view to showing the inapplicability of the illustrations used. For, he asks, is it not possible for us to blind ourselves, and so no longer have the ability to see? And would not many a man like to control the " use" of his " capacity" to hear when a screechy saw is in the neighbourhood? (55). The falsity of the contention illustrated, he argues, is evident from the fact that Pelagius has ignored the fall, and, even were that not so, has so ignored the need of God's aid for all good, in any state of being, as to deny it (56). Moreover, it is altogether a fallacy, Augustine argues, to contend that men have the " ability" to make every use we can conceive of our faculties. We *cannot* wish for unhappiness ; God *cannot* deny Himself (57) : and just so, in a corrupt nature, the mere possession of a *faculty of choice* does not imply the ability to use that faculty for not sinning. " Of a man, indeed, who has his legs strong and sound, it may be said admissibly enough, ' whether he will or not, he has the capacity of walking ; ' but if his legs be broken, however much he may wish to walk, he has not the ' capacity ' to do so. The nature of which our author speaks is corrupted" (57). What, then, can he mean by saying that, whether we will or not, we have the capacity of not sinning,—a statement so opposite to Paul's in Rom. vii. 15 ? Some space is next given to an attempted rebuttal by Pelagius of the testimony of Gal. v. 17, on the ground that the " flesh" there does not refer to the baptized (60-70). Then the passages are examined which Pelagius had quoted against Augustine out of earlier writers,—Lactantius (71), Hilary (72), Ambrose (75), John of Constantinople (76), Xystus,—a blunder of Pelagius', who quoted from a Pythagorean philosopher, mistaking him for the Roman bishop Sixtus (57), Jerome (78), and Augustine himself (80). All these writers, Augustine shows, admitted the universal sinfulness of man,—and especially he himself had confessed the necessity of grace in the immediate context of the passage quoted by Pelagius. The treatise closes (82 sq.) with a noble panegyric on that love which God sheds abroad in the heart by the Holy Ghost, and by which alone we can be made keepers of the law.

Letter to Jerome on the Origin of Souls.

The treatise *On Nature and Grace* was as yet unfinished when the over-busy[1] scriptorium at Hippo was invaded by another young man seeking instruction. This time it was a zealous young presbyter from the remotest parts of Spain,—"from the shore of the ocean,"—Paulus Orosius by name. His pious soul had been afflicted with grievous wounds by the Priscillianist and Origenist heresies that had broken out in his country, and he had come with eager haste to Augustine on hearing that he could get from him the instruction which he needed for confuting them. Augustine seems to have given him his heart at once. But feeling too little informed as to the special heresies which Orosius wished to be prepared to controvert, he persuaded him to go on to Palestine to be taught by Jerome, and gave him introductions which described him as one "who is in the bond of catholic peace a brother, in point of age a son, and in dignity a fellow-presbyter,—a man of quick understanding, ready speech and burning zeal." His departure to Palestine gave Augustine an opportunity to consult with Jerome on the one point that had been raised in the Pelagian controversy on which he had not been able to see light. The Pelagians had early argued[2] that, if souls are created new for men at their birth, it would be unjust in God to impute Adam's sin to them. And Augustine found himself unable either to prove that souls are transmitted ("traduced," as the phrase is), or to show that it would not involve God in injustice to create a soul only to make it subject to a sin committed by another. Jerome had already put himself on record as a believer in both original sin and the creation of souls at the time of birth. Augustine feared the logical consequences of this assertion, and yet was unable to refute

---
[1] For Augustine's press of work just now, see *Epistle* 169, 1 and 13.
[2] The argument occurs in Pelagius' *Commentary on Paul*, written before 410, and is already before Augustine in *On the Merits and Forgiveness of Sins*, etc., iii. 5.

it. He therefore seized this occasion to send a long treatise on the origin of the soul to his friend, with the request that he would consider the subject afresh, and answer his doubts.[1]

In this treatise he stated that he was fully persuaded that the soul had fallen into sin by no fault of God or of nature, but of its own free will; and asked when could the soul of an infant have contracted the guilt which, unless the grace of Christ should come to its rescue by baptism, would involve it in condemnation, if God (as Jerome held, and as he was willing to hold with him, if this difficulty could be cleared up) makes each soul for each individual at the time of birth? He professed himself embarrassed on such a supposition by the penal sufferings of infants, by the pains they endure in this life, and much more by the danger they are in of eternal damnation, into which they actually go unless saved by baptism. God is good, just, omnipotent: how, then, can we account for the fact that "in Adam all die," if souls are created afresh for each birth? "If new souls are made for men individually at their birth," he affirms, "I do not see, on the one hand, that they could have any sin while yet in infancy; nor do I believe, on the other hand, that God condemns any soul which He sees to have no sin." " And yet, whoever says that those children who depart out of this life without partaking of the sacrament of baptism, shall be made alive in Christ, certainly contradicts the apostolic declaration," and " he that is not made alive in Christ must necessarily remain under the condemnation of which the apostle says that by the offence of one judgment came upon all men to condemnation." "Wherefore," he adds to his correspondent, " if that opinion of yours does not contradict this firmly grounded article of faith, let it be mine also; but if it does, let it no longer be yours."[2] So

---

[1] *Epistle* 166.
[2] An almost contemporary letter to Oceanus (*Epistle* 180, written in 416) adverts to the same subject and in the same spirit, showing how much it was in Augustine's thoughts. Compare *Epistle* 180, 2 and 5.

far as obtaining light was concerned, Augustine might have spared himself the trouble of this composition. Jerome simply answered [1] that he had no leisure to reply to the questions submitted to him. But Orosius' mission to Palestine was big with consequences. Once there, he became the accuser of Pelagius before John of Jerusalem, and the occasion, at least, of the trials of Pelagius in Palestine during the summer and winter of 415, which issued so disastrously and ushered in a new phase of the conflict.

The Treatise on "The Perfection of Man's Righteousness."

Meanwhile, however, Augustine was ignorant of what was going on in the East, and had his mind directed again to Sicily. About a year had passed since he had sent thither his long letter to Hilary. Now his conjecture that Cœlestius was in some way at the bottom of the Sicilian outbreak, received confirmation from a paper which certain Catholic brethren brought out of Sicily, and which was handed to Augustine by two exiled Spanish bishops, Eutropius and Paul. This paper bore the title, *Definitions Ascribed to Cœlestius*, and presented internal evidence, in style and thought, of being correctly so ascribed.[2] It consisted of three parts. In the first of these were collected a series of brief and compressed " definitions," or " ratiocinations" as Augustine calls them, in which the author tries to place the Catholics in a logical dilemma, and to force them to admit that man can live in this world without sin. In the second part, there were adduced certain passages of Scripture in defence of Pelagian doctrine. In the third part, an attempt was made to deal with the texts that had been quoted against the Pelagian contention, not, however, by examining into their meaning, or seeking to explain them in the sense of the new theory, but simply by matching them with others which might be thought to make for it. In answer to this paper, Augustine at once (about the

[1] *Epistle* 172.
[2] See *On the Perfection of Man's Righteousness*, 1.

end of 415) wrote a treatise which bears the title of *On the Perfection of Man's Righteousness.*

The distribution of the matter in this work follows that of the paper to which it is a reply. First of all (1-16), the "ratiocinations" are taken up one by one and briefly answered. As they all concern sin and have for their object to prove that man cannot be accounted a sinner unless he is able, in his own power, wholly to avoid sin—that is, to prove that a plenary natural ability is the necessary basis of responsibility—Augustine argues *per contra* that man can entail a sinfulness on himself for which and for the deeds of which he remains responsible, though he be no longer able to avoid sin ; he thus allows that, for the race, plenary ability must stand at the root of sinfulness. Next (17-22), he discusses the passages of Scripture which Cœlestius had advanced in defence of his teachings. These include two classes of texts. There were (1) passages in which God commands men to be without sin. These Augustine meets by saying that the point is, whether these commands are to be fulfilled *without God's aid*, in the body of this death, while absent from the Lord (17-20). There were also (2) passages in which God declares that His commandments are not grievous. These Augustine meets by explaining that all God's commandments are fulfilled only by love, which finds nothing grievous ; and that this love is shed abroad in our hearts only by the Holy Ghost, without whom we have only fear, to which the commandments are not only grievous but impossible. Lastly, Augustine patiently follows Cœlestius through his odd "oppositions of texts," carefully explaining, in an orthodox sense, all that he had adduced (23-42). In closing, he takes up Cœlestius' statement that "it is quite possible for man not to sin even in word, if God so will," pointing out how he avoids saying "if God give him His aid," and then proceeds to distinguish carefully between the differing assertions of sinlessness that may be made. To say that any man ever lived, or will live, without needing forgiveness, is to contradict Rom. v. 12, and must imply that he does not need a Saviour, against

Matt. ix. 12. 13. To say that, after his sins have been forgiven, any one has ever remained without sin, contradicts 1 John i. 8 and Matt. vi. 12. Yet, if God's help be allowed, this contention is not so wicked as the other; the great heresy is to deny the necessity of God's constant grace, for which we pray when we say, "Lead us not into temptation."

Activity Subsequent to the Palestinian Acquittal.

Tidings were now (416) beginning to reach Africa of what was doing in the East. There was diligently circulated everywhere and finally came into Augustine's hands, an epistle of Pelagius' own "filled with vanity." In it he boasted that fourteen bishops had approved his assertion that "man can live without sin, and easily keep the commandments if he wishes," and had thus "shut the mouth of opposition in confusion" and "broken up the whole band of wicked conspirators against him." Soon afterwards a copy of an "apologetical paper," in which Pelagius used the authority of the Palestinian bishops against his adversaries, not altogether without disingenuousness, was sent by him to Augustine through the hands of a common acquaintance, Charus by name. It was not accompanied, however, by any letter from Pelagius; and Augustine wisely refrained from making public use of it. Towards midsummer Orosius came with more authentic information, and bearing letters from Jerome and Heros and Lazarus.

It was apparently before Orosius came that a controversial sermon was preached, only a fragment of which has come down to us.[1] So far as we can learn from the extant part, its subject seems to have been the relation of prayer to Pelagianism; and what we have opens with a striking anecdote. "When these two petitions—'Forgive us our debts as we also forgive our debtors,' and 'Lead us not into temptation'—are objected to the Pelagians, what do you think they re-

[1] Migne's Edition of Augustine's Works, vol. v. pp. 1719-1723.

ply? I was horrified, my brethren, when I heard it. I did not, indeed, hear it with my own ears; but my holy brother and fellow-bishop Urbanus, who used to be presbyter here and now is bishop of Sicca," when he was in Rome and was arguing with one who held these opinions, pressed him with the weight of the Lord's Prayer, and " what do you think he replied to him? 'We ask God,' he said, 'not to lead us into temptation lest we should suffer something that is not in our power—lest I should be thrown from my horse, lest I should break my leg, lest a robber should slay me, and the like. For these things,' he said, ' are not in my power; but for overcoming the temptations of my sins, I both have ability if I wish to use it, and am not able to receive God's help.'[1] You see, brethren," the good bishop adds, " how malignant this heresy is: you see how it horrifies all of you. Have a care that you be not taken by it." He then presses the general doctrine of prayer as proving that all good things come from God, whose aid is always necessary to us and is always attainable by prayer; and closes as follows: " Consider, then, these things, my brethren, when any one comes to you and says to you, ' What, then, are we to do if we have nothing in our power, unless God gives all things? God will not then crown us, but He will crown Himself.' You already see that this comes from that vein: it is a vein, but it has poison in it; it is stricken by the serpent; it is not sound. For what Satan is doing to-day is seeking to cast out from the Church by the poison of heretics, just as he once cast out from Paradise by the poison of the serpent. Let no one tell you that this one was acquitted by the bishops: there was an acquittal, but it was his confession, so to speak, his amendment, that was acquitted. For what he said before the bishops seemed catholic; but what he has written in his books, the bishops who pronounced the acquittal were ignorant of. And perchance he was really convinced and amended. For we ought not to despair of the man who perchance

---

[1] Compare the words of Cicero quoted above, vol. xiv., p. 467.

preferred to be united to the catholic faith and fled to its grace and aid. Perchance this was what happened. But, in any event, it was not the heresy that was acquitted, but the man who denied the heresy."[1]

The coming of Orosius must have dispelled any lingering hope that the meaning of the council's finding was that Pelagius had really recanted. Councils were immediately assembled at Carthage and Mileve, and the documents which Orosius had brought were read before them. We know nothing of their proceedings except what we can gather from the letters[2] which they sent to Innocent at Rome, seeking his aid in their condemnation of the heresy now so nearly approved in Palestine. To these two official letters, Augustine, in company with four other bishops, added a private letter,[3] in which care was taken that Innocent should be informed on all the points necessary to his decision. This important letter begins almost abruptly with a characterization of Pelagianism as inimical to the grace of God, and has grace for its subject throughout. It accounts for the action of the Palestinian synod as growing out of a misunderstanding of Pelagius' words, in which he seemed to acknowledge grace. Those catholic bishops naturally would understand this to mean that grace of which they read in the Scriptures, and which they were accustomed to preach to their people,—the grace by which we are justified from iniquity, and saved from weakness. While Pelagius really meant nothing more than that " grace" by which we are given free will at our creation. " For if these bishops had understood that he meant only that grace which we have in common with the ungodly and with all along with whom we are men, while he denied that by which we are Christians and the sons of God, they not only could not have patiently listened to him,—they

---

[1] Compare the similar words in *Epistle* 177, 3, which was written, not only after what had occurred in Palestine was known, but also after the condemnatory decisions of the African synods.
[2] *Epistles* 175 and 176 in Augustine's *Letters*.
[3] *Epistle* 177. The other bishops were Aurelius, Alypius, Evodius, and Possidius.

could not even have borne him before their eyes." The letter then proceeds to point out the difference between grace and natural gifts, and between grace and the law, and to trace out Pelagius' meaning when he speaks of grace and when he contends that man can be sinless without any really inward aid. It suggests that Pelagius be sent for and thoroughly examined by Innocent ; or that he should be examined by letter or in his writings ; and that he be not cleared until he should unequivocally confess the grace of God in the catholic sense, and anathematize the false teachings in the books attributed to him. The book of Pelagius which was answered in the treatise *On Nature and Grace* was enclosed with this letter, with the most important passages marked : and it was suggested that more was involved in the matter than the fate of one single man, Pelagius, who, perhaps, was already brought to a better mind ; the fate of multitudes already led astray, or yet to be deceived by these false views, was in danger.

At about this same time (417), the tireless bishop sent a short letter [1] to a Hilary who seems to be Hilary of Norbonne, which is interesting from the attempt made in it to convey a characterization of Pelagianism to one who was as yet ignorant of it. It thus brings out what Augustine conceived to be its essential features. " An effort has been made," we read, " to raise a certain new heresy, inimical to the grace of Christ, against the Church of Christ. It is not yet openly separated from the Church. It is the heresy of men who dare to attribute so much power to human weakness that they contend that this only belongs to God's grace,—that we are created with free will and the possibility of not sinning, and that we receive God's commandments, which are to be fulfilled by us ; while, for keeping and fulfilling these commandments, we do not need any divine aid. No doubt, the remission of sins is necessary for us ; for we have no power to right what we have done wrong in the past. But for avoiding and overcoming sins in the future, for conquering

[1] *Epistle* 178.

all temptations with virtue, the human will is sufficient by its natural capacity without any aid of God's grace. And neither do infants need the grace of the Saviour, so as to be delivered from perdition by it through His baptism, seeing that they have contracted no contagion of damnation from Adam."[1] He engages Hilary in the destruction of this heresy, which ought to be "concordantly condemned and anathematized by all who have hope in Christ," as a "pestiferous impiety," and excuses himself for not undertaking its full refutation in a brief letter.

A much more important letter was dispatched at about the same time to John of Jerusalem, who had conducted the first Palestinian examination of Pelagius and had borne a prominent part in the synod at Diospolis. With it was sent a copy of Pelagius' book which had been examined in the treatise *On Nature and Grace*, as well as a copy of that reply itself; and John was asked to send Augustine an authentic copy of the proceedings at Diospolis. Augustine took this occasion seriously to warn his brother bishop against the wiles of Pelagius, and to beg him, if he loved Pelagius, to let men see that he did not so love him as to be deceived by him. He pointed out that in the book sent with the letter, Pelagius called nothing the grace of God except nature; and that he affirmed, and even vehemently contended, that by free will alone human nature was able to suffice for itself for working righteousness and keeping all God's commandments. From this any one could see that he opposed the grace of God of which the apostles spoke in Rom. vii. 24, 25, and contradicted, as well, all the prayers and benedictions of the Church by which blessings were sought for men from God's grace. "If you love Pelagius, then," he continued, "let him, too, love you as himself,—nay, more than himself; and let him not deceive you. For when you hear him confess the grace of God and the aid of God, you think he means what you mean by it. But let him be openly asked whether he is willing that

[1] *Epistle* 179.

we should pray God that we sin not; whether he preaches the assisting grace of God without which we would do much evil; whether he believes that even children who have not yet been able to do good or evil are nevertheless, on account of one man by whom sin entered into the world, sinners in him, and in need of being delivered by the grace of Christ." If he frankly denies such things, Augustine would be pleased to hear of it.

Thus we see the great bishop sitting in his library at Hippo, placing his hands on the two ends of the world. That nothing may be lacking to the picture of his universal activity, we have another letter from him, coming from about this same time, that exhibits his care for the individuals who had placed themselves in some sort under his tutelage. Among the refugees from Rome in the terrible times when Alaric was a second time threatening the city, was a family of noble women, Proba, Juliana and Demetrias,[1]—grandmother, mother, and daughter—who, finding an asylum in Africa, gave themselves to God's service and sought the friendship and counsel of Augustine. In 413 the granddaughter "took the veil" under circumstances that thrilled the Christian world, and brought out letters of congratulation and advice from Augustine and Jerome, and also from Pelagius. This letter of Pelagius seems not to have fallen into Augustine's way until now (416). He was so disturbed by it that he wrote to Juliana a long letter warning her against its evil counsels.[2] It was so shrewdly phrased that, at first sight, Augustine was himself almost persuaded that it did somehow acknowledge the grace of God; but when he compared it with others of Pelagius' writings, he saw that, here too, he was using ambiguous terms in a non-natural sense. The object of his own letter (in which Alypius is conjoined as joint author) is to warn Juliana and her

---

[1] See *The Nicene and Post-Nicene Fathers*, New York ed., vol. i., p. 459, and the references there given. Compare Canon Robertson's vivid account of them in his *History of the Christian Church*, ii. 18, 145.
[2] *Epistle* 188.

holy daughter against all opinions that opposed the grace of God, and especially against the covert teaching of the letter of Pelagius to Demetrias.[1] "In this book," he says, "were it lawful for such an one to read it, a virgin of Christ would read that her holiness and all her spiritual riches are to spring from no other source than herself; and thus, before she attains to the perfection of blessedness, she would learn—which may God forbid!—to be ungrateful to God." He quotes the words of Pelagius in which he declares that "earthly riches came from others, but your spiritual riches no one can have conferred on you but yourself; for these, then, you are justly praised, for these you are deservedly to be preferred to others—for they can exist only from yourself and in yourself." And then, he continues: "Far be it from any virgin to listen to statements like these. Every virgin of Christ understands the innate poverty of the human heart, and therefore declines to be adorned otherwise than by the gifts of her Spouse. . . . Let her not listen to him who says, 'No one can confer them on you but yourself, and they cannot exist except from you and in you:' but to him who says, 'We have this treasure in earthen vessels, that the excellency of the power may be of God, and not of us.' And be not surprised that we speak of these things as yours, and not from you; for we speak of daily bread as 'ours,' but yet add, 'Give it to us,' lest it should be thought it was from ourselves." Again, he instructs her that grace is not mere knowledge, any more than mere nature; and that Pelagius, even when using the word "grace," means no inward or efficient aid, but mere nature or knowledge or forgiveness of past sins: and beseeches her not to forget the God of all grace from whom (Wisdom i. 20, 21) Demetrias had that very virgin continence which was so justly her boast.

With the opening of 417, came the answers from Innocent to the African letters.[2] They were marred by much boastful language concerning the dignity of his

---

[1] Compare *On the Grace of Christ*, 40. In the succeeding sections. some of its statements are examined.
[2] *Epistles* 181, 182, 183, among Augustine's *Letters*.

See, which could not but be distasteful to the Africans. But they admirably served their purpose in the satisfactory manner in which, on the one hand, they asserted the necessity of the " daily grace and help of God" for our good living, and, on the other, they determined that the Pelagians had denied this grace, and declared their leaders, Pelagius and Cœlestius, deprived of the communion of the Church until they should " recover their senses from the wiles of the Devil by whom they are held captive according to his will." Augustine may be pardoned for supposing that a condemnation pronounced by two provincial synods in Africa and heartily concurred in by the Roman bishop, who had already at Jerusalem been recognized as in some sort the fit arbiter of this Western dispute, should settle the matter. If Pelagius had been jubilant before, Augustine found this a suitable time for his rejoicing.

The Treatise on " The Proceedings in Palestine," and the Letter to Paulinus.

About the same time with Innocent's letters, the official proceedings of the synod of Diospolis at last reached Africa, and Augustine lost no time in publishing (early in 417) a full account and examination of them, thus providing us with that inestimable boon, a full contemporary history of the chief events connected with the controversy up to this time. He addresses this treatise to Aurelius, bishop of Carthage, and opens with an explanation of his delay in discussing Pelagius' defence of himself in Palestine, as due to his not having earlier received the official copy of the Proceedings of the Council at Diospolis (1–2*a*). Then he proceeds to discuss at length the doings of the synod, point by point, following the official record step by step (2*b*–45). He treats at large here eleven items in the indictment, with Pelagius' answers and the synod's decisions ; and shows that in all of them Pelagius either explained away his heresy, taking advantage of the judges' ignorance of his books, or else openly repudiated or anathematized it. Augustine points out that when it reached the twelfth item of the indictment (41*b*–43)—

which charged Pelagius with teaching that men cannot be sons of God unless they are sinless, and with condoning sins of ignorance, and with asserting that choice is not free if it depends on God's help and that pardon is given according to merit—the synod was so indignant, that, without waiting for Pelagius' answer, it condemned the statement ; and Pelagius at once repudiated and anathematized it (43). How could the synod act in such circumstances, he asks, except by acquitting the man who condemned the heresy? After quoting the final judgment of the synod (44), Augustine briefly characterizes it and its effect (45) as being indeed all that could be expected of the judges, but of no moral weight to those better acquainted than they were with Pelagius' character and writings. In a word, they approved his answers to them, as indeed they ought to have done ; but they by no means approved, but both they and he condemned, his heresies as expressed in his writings. To this statement, Augustine appends an account of the origin of Pelagianism and of his relations to it from the beginning, which has the very highest value as history (46-49) ; and then speaks of the character and doubtful practices of Pelagius (50-58), returning at the end (59-65) to a thorough canvass of the value of the acquittal which he obtained by such doubtful practices at the synod. He closes with an indignant account of the outrages which the Pelagians had perpetrated on Jerome (66).

This valuable treatise is not, however, the only account of the historical origin of Pelagianism that we have from Augustine's hands. Soon after the death of Innocent (March 12, 417), he found occasion to write a very long letter[1] to the venerable Paulinus of Nola, in which he summarized both the history of and the arguments against this "worldly philosophy." He begins by saying that he knows Paulinus has in the past loved Pelagius as a servant of God, but is ignorant in what way he now loves him. For he himself not only has loved him but loves him still, but in different ways. Once he loved him as apparently a brother in the true faith : now he loves him in the longing that God will

[1] *Epistle* 186, written conjointly with Alypius.

by His mercy free him from his noxious opinions
against God's grace. He is not merely following report in so speaking of him. No doubt report had for
a long time represented this of him, but the less heed
had been given to it because report is accustomed to lie.
But a book by Pelagius[1] at last came into his hands
which left no room for doubt, since in it it was asserted
repeatedly that God's grace consists of the gift to man
of the capacity to will and act, and thus was reduced to
what is common to pagans and Christians, to the ungodly and godly, to the faithful and infidels. He then
gives a brief account of the measures that had been
taken against Pelagius, and passes on to a treatment
of the main matters involved in the controversy,—all
of which gather around the one magic word of "the
grace of God." He argues first that we are all lost,
—in one mass and concretion of perdition,—and that
God's grace alone makes us to differ. It is therefore
folly to talk of deserving the beginnings of grace. Nor
can a faithful man say that he merits justification by
his faith, although it is given to faith; for at once he
hears the words, "What hast thou that thou didst not
receive?" and learns that even the deserving faith is
the gift of God. But if, peering into God's inscrutable judgments, we go farther, and ask why from the
mass of Adam, all of which undoubtedly has fallen by
one into condemnation, this vessel is made for honor,
that for dishonor,—we can only say that we do not
know more than the fact, and that God's reasons are hidden but His acts are just. Certain it is that Paul
teaches that all die in Adam ; and that God, by a
sovereign election, freely chooses out of that sinful
mass some to eternal life ; and that He knew from the
beginning to whom He would give this grace, and so
the number of the saints has always been fixed, to
whom He gives in due time the Holy Ghost. Others,
no doubt, are called ; but no others are elect, or "called
according to His purpose." On no other body of doc-

---

[1] The book given him by Timasius and James, to which *On Nature and Grace* is a reply.

trines can it be possibly explained that some infants die unbaptized and are lost. Is God unjust to punish innocent children with eternal pains? And are they not innocent if they are not partakers of Adam's sin? And can they be saved from that, save by the undeserved, and that is the gratuitous, grace of God? The account of the proceedings at the Palestinian synod is then taken up, and Pelagius' position in his latest writings is quoted and examined. "But why say more?" he adds. . . . "Ought they not, since they call themselves Christians, to be more careful than the Jews that they do not stumble at the stone of offence, while they subtly defend nature and free will just like philosophers of this world who vehemently strive to be thought, or to think themselves, to attain for themselves a happy life by the force of their own will? Let them take care, then, that they do not make the cross of Christ of none effect by the wisdom of word (1 Cor. i. 17), and thus stumble at the rock of offence. For human nature, even if it had remained in that integrity in which it was created, could by no means have served its own Creator without His aid. Since then, without God's grace it could not keep the safety it had received, how can it without God's grace repair what it has lost?" With this profound view of the Divine immanence, and of the necessity of His moving grace in all the acts of all His creatures, as over against the heathen-deistic view of Pelagius, Augustine touched in reality the deepest point in the whole controversy, and illustrated the essential harmony of all truth.[1]

The sharpest period of the whole conflict was now drawing on.[2] Innocent's death brought Zosimus to the chair of the Roman See, and the efforts which he

[1] Compare also Innocent's letter (*Epistle* 181) to the Carthaginian Council, chap. 4, which also Neander, *History of the Christian Church*, E. T., ii. 646, quotes in this connection, as showing that Innocent "perceived that this dispute was connected with a different way of regarding the relation of God's providence to creation." As if Augustine did not see this too!

[2] The book addressed to Dardanus, in which the Pelagians are confuted, but not named, belongs about at this time. Compare *Retractations*, ii. 49.

made to re-instate Pelagius and Cœlestius now began (September, 417). How little the Africans were likely to yield to his remarkable demands, may be seen from a sermon[1] which Augustine preached on the 23d of September, while Zosimus' letter (written on the 21st of September) was on its way to Africa. The preacher took his text from John vi. 54–66. "We hear here," he said, "the true master, the divine Redeemer, the human Saviour, commending to us our ransom, His blood. He calls His body food, and His blood drink; and, in commending such food and drink, He says, 'Except you eat My flesh, and drink My blood, ye shall have no life in you.' What, then, is this eating and drinking, but to live? Eat life, drink life; you shall have life, and life is whole. This will come,— that is, the body and blood of Christ will be life to every one,—if what is taken visibly in the sacrament is in real truth spiritually eaten and spiritually drunk. But that He might teach us that even to believe in Him is of gift, not of merit, He said, 'No one comes to Me, except the Father who sent Me draw him.' *Draw* him, not *lead* him. This violence is done to the *heart*, not the flesh. Why do you marvel? Believe, and you come; love, and you are drawn. Think not that this is harsh and injurious violence; it is soft, it is sweet; it is sweetness itself that draws you. Is not the sheep drawn when the succulent herbage is shown to him? And I think that there is no compulsion of the body, but an assembling of the desires. So, too, do you come to Christ; wish not to plan a long journey,—when you believe, then you come. For to Him who is everywhere, one comes by loving, not by taking a voyage. No doubt, if you come not, it is your work; but if you come, it is God's work. And even after you have come and are walking in the right way, become not proud, lest you perish from it: 'happy are those that confide in Him,' not in *themselves*, but in *Him*. We are saved by grace, not of ourselves: it is the gift of God. Why do I continually

---

[1] *Sermon* 131, preached at Carthage.

say this to you? It is because there are men who are ungrateful to grace and attribute much to unaided and wounded nature. It is true that man received great powers of free will at his creation; but he lost them by sinning. He has fallen into death; he has been made weak; he has been left half dead in the way, by robbers; the good Samaritan has lifted him up upon his ass and borne him to the inn. Why should we boast? But I am told that it is enough that sins are remitted in baptism. But does the removal of sin take away weakness too? What! will you not see that after pouring the oil and the wine into the wounds of the man left half dead by the robbers, he must still go to the inn where his weakness may be healed? Nay, so long as we are in this life we bear a fragile body; it is only after we are redeemed from corruption that we shall find no sin and receive the crown of righteousness. Grace, that was hidden in the Old Testament, is now manifest to the whole world. Even though the Jew may be ignorant of it, why should Christians be enemies of grace? why presumptuous of themselves? why ungrateful to grace? For, why did Christ come? Was not nature already here,—that very nature by the praise of which you are beguiled? Was not the law here? But the apostle says, 'If righteousness is of the law, then is Christ dead in vain.' What the apostle says of the law, that we say to these men about nature: if righteousness is by nature, then Christ is dead in vain. What then was said of the Jews, this we see repeated in these men. They have a zeal for God: I bear them witness that they have a zeal for God: but not according to knowledge. For, being ignorant of God's righteousness, and wishing to establish their own, they are not subject to the righteousness of God. My brethren, share my compassion. Where you find such men, wish no concealment; let there be no perverse pity in you: where you find them, wish no concealment at all. Contradict and refute, resist, or persuade them to us. For already two councils have, in this cause, sent letters to the Apostolic See, whence also rescripts have come back. The cause is ended: would that the error might some day end! Therefore we admonish so that they may take notice, we teach so that they may be instructed, we pray so that their way may be changed."

Here is certainly tenderness to the persons of the teachers of error, readiness to forgive, and readiness to go all proper lengths in recovering them to the truth. But here is also absolute firmness as to the truth itself, and a manifesto as to policy. Certainly, on the lines of the policy here indicated, the Africans fought out the coming campaign. They met in council at the end of this year, or early in the next (418), and formally replied to Zosimus that the cause had been tried, and was finished; and that the sentence that had been already pronounced against Pelagius and Cœlestius should remain in force until they should unequivocally acknowledge that "we are aided by the grace of God through Christ, not only to know, but to do, what is right, and that in each single act; so that without grace we are unable to have, think, speak, or do anything belonging to piety." As we may see Augustine's hand in this, so, doubtless, we may recognize it in that remarkable piece of engineering which crushed Zosimus' plans within the next few months. There is, indeed, no direct proof that it was due to Augustine, or to the Africans under his leading, or to the Africans at all, that the State interfered in the matter. It is even in doubt whether the action of the Empire was put forth as a rescript, or as a self-moved decree. But surely it is difficult to believe that such a *coup de théâtre* could have been prepared for Zosimus by chance. As it is well known both that Augustine believed in the righteousness of civil penalty for heresy, invoking it on other occasions and defending and using it on this, and that he had influential friends at court with whom he was in correspondence, it seems, on internal grounds, altogether probable that he was the *deus ex machinâ* who let loose the thunders of ecclesiastical and civil enactment simultaneously on the poor Pope's devoted head.

AUGUSTINE'S PART IN THE CONTROVERSY.

The Treatises "On the Grace of Christ" and "On Original Sin."

The "great African Council" met at Carthage on the 1st of May, 418. After its decrees were issued, Augustine remained at Carthage and watched the effect of the combination of which he was probably one of the moving causes. He had now an opportunity to betake himself once more to his pen. While still at Carthage, at short notice and in the midst of much distraction, he wrote a large work in two books, which have come down to us under the separate titles of *On the Grace of Christ* and *On Original Sin*, at the instance of another of those ascetic families which formed so marked a feature in those troubled times. Pinianus and Melania, the daughter of Albina, were husband and wife, who, leaving Rome amid the wars with Alaric, had lived together continently in Africa for some time, but now in Palestine had separated, he to become head of a monastery, and she an inmate of a convent. While in Africa, they had lived at Sagaste under the tutelage of Alypius, and in the enjoyment of the friendship and instruction of Augustine. After retiring to Bethlehem, like the other holy ascetics whom he had known in Africa, they kept up their relations with him. Like the others, also, they became acquainted with Pelagius in Palestine, and were well-nigh deceived by him. They wrote to Augustine that they had begged Pelagius to condemn in writing all that had been alleged against him, and that he had replied, in the presence of them all, that " he anathematized the man who either thinks or says that the grace of God whereby Christ Jesus came into the world to save sinners is not necessary, not only for every hour and for every moment, but also for every act of our lives," and had asserted that "those who endeavor to disannul it are worthy of everlasting punishment."[1] Moreover, they wrote, Pelagius had read to them, out of his book that he had sent to Rome,[2] his assertion " that infants

[1] *On the Grace of Christ*, 2.
[2] The so-called *Confession of Faith* sent to Innocent after the Synod of Diospolis, which, however, arrived after Innocent's death.

ought to be baptized with the same formula of sacramental words as adults."[1] They expressed their delight at hearing from Pelagius these words, which seemed exactly what they should wish to hear: and yet they felt impelled to consult Augustine about them, before they fully committed themselves regarding them.[2] It was in answer to this appeal, that the present work was written. Its two books take up the two points in Pelagius' asseveration. The theme of the first is, "the assistance of Divine grace towards our justification, by which God co-operates in all things for good to those who love Him and whom He first loved, giving to them that He may receive from them." While the subject of the second is, "the sin which by one man has entered the world along with death, and so has passed upon all men."[3]

The first book, *On the Grace of Christ*, begins by quoting and examining Pelagius' anathema of all those who deny that grace is necessary for every action (2 sq.). Augustine confesses that this would deceive all who were not fortified by knowledge of Pelagius' writings. But he asserts that in the light of these writings it is clear that Pelagius means that grace is always necessary, only because we need continually to remember the forgiveness of our sins, the example of Christ, the teaching of the law, and the like. Then he enters (4 sq.) upon an examination of Pelagius' scheme of human faculties, and quotes at length the account of them as given in his book, *In Defence of Free Will*. Pelagius distinguishes between the *possibilitas* (*posse*), *voluntas* (*velle*) and *actio* (*esse*), and declares that the first only is from God and receives aid from God, while the others are entirely ours and in our own power. Augustine opposes to this the passage in Phil. ii. 12, 13 (6), and then criticises (7 sq.) Pelagius' ambiguous acknowledgment that God is to be praised for man's good works "because the capacity for any action on man's part is from God," which reduces all

[1] *On Original Sin*, 1.   [2] *Ibid.* 5.
[3] *On the Grace of Christ*, 55.

AUGUSTINE'S PART IN THE CONTROVERSY.

grace to the primeval endowment of nature with "capacity" (*possibilitas, posse*) and the help afforded it by the law and teaching. Augustine points out the difference between law and grace, and the purpose of the former as a pedagogue to the latter (9 sq.), and then refutes Pelagius' further definition of grace as consisting in the promise of future glory and the revelation of wisdom, by an appeal to Paul's thorn in the flesh and his experience under its discipline (11 sq.). Pelagius' illustrations of his theory of natural faculty from our senses are then sharply tested (16). The criticism on the whole doctrine is then pressed (17 sq.), that it makes God equally sharer in our blame for evil acts as in our praise for good ones, since if God does help and His help is only His gift to us of ability to act in either part, then He has equally helped to the evil deeds as to the good. The assertion that this "capacity of either part" is the fecund root of both good and evil is then criticised (19 sq.), and opposed to Matt. vii. 18, with the result of establishing that we must seek two roots in our dispositions for so diverse results,—covetousness for evil, and love for good,—not a single root in nature for both. Man's "capacity," it is argued, is the root of nothing; but it is capable of both good and evil according to the moving cause, which, in the case of evil, is man-originated, while, in the case of good, it is from God (21). Next, Pelagius' assertion that grace is given according to our merits (23 sq.) is taken up and examined. It is shown, that, despite his anathema, Pelagius holds to this doctrine, and in so extreme a form as explicitly to declare that man comes and cleaves to God by his freedom of will alone, and without God's aid. He shows that the Scriptures teach just the opposite (24-26); and then points out how Pelagius has confounded the functions of knowledge and love (27 sq.), and how he forgets that we cannot have merits until we love God, while John certainly asserts that *God loved us first* (1 John iv. 10). The representation that what grace does is to render obedience *easier* (28-30), and the twin view that prayer is only relatively necessary, are next criticised (32). That Pelagius never acknowledges real grace is then demonstrated by a detailed examination of all that he had written on the subject (31-45). The book closes (46-80) with a full refutation of Pelagius' appeal to Ambrose, as if he supported him ; and an exhibition of Ambrose's contrary testimony as to grace and its necessity.

The object of the second book—*On Original Sin*—is to show, that, in spite of Pelagius' admissions as to the baptism of infants, he yet denies that they inherit original sin and contends that they are born free from corruption. The book opens by pointing out that there is no question as to Cœlestius' teaching in this matter (2-8). At Carthage he refused to condemn those who say that Adam's sin injured no one but himself and that infants are born in the same state that Adam was in before the fall ; and he openly asserted at Rome that there is no sin *ex traduce*. As for Pelagius, he is simply more cautious and mendacious than Cœlestius. He deceived the Council at Diospolis, but failed to deceive the Romans (5-13), and, as a matter of fact (14-18), teaches exactly what Cœlestius does. In support of this assertion, Pelagius' *Defence of Free Will* is quoted, wherein he asserts that we are born neither good nor bad " but with a capacity for either," and " as without virtue, so without vice ; and that previous to the action of our own proper will, that alone is in man which God has formed" (14). Augustine also quotes Pelagius' explanation of his anathema against those who say Adam's sin injured only himself, as meaning that he has injured man by setting a bad " example ;" and his even more sinuous explanation of his anathema against those who assert that infants are born in the same condition that Adam was in before he fell, as meaning that they are *infants* and he was a *man !* (16-18). With this introduction to them, Augustine next treats of Pelagius' subterfuges (19-25), and then animadverts on the importance of the issue (26-37), pointing out that Pelagianism is not a mere error but a deadly heresy, and strikes at the very centre of Christianity. A counter argument of the Pelagians is then taken up (38-45), " Does not the doctrine of original sin make marriage an evil thing?" No, says Augustine, marriage is ordained by God and is good ; but it is a diseased good, and hence what is born of it is a good nature made by God, but this good nature in a diseased condition,—the result of the Devil's work. Hence, if it be asked why God's gift produces any thing for the Devil to take possession of, it is to be answered that God gives his gifts liberally (Matt. v. 45), and makes men ; but the Devil makes these men sinners (46). Finally, as Ambrose had been appealed to in the former book, so at the end of this it is shown that he openly proclaimed the doctrine of original sin, and here too, before Pelagius, condemned Pelagius (47 sq.).

Sermons at Carthage.

What Augustine meant by writing to Pinianus and his family that he was more oppressed by work at Carthage than anywhere else, may perhaps be illustrated from his diligence in preaching while in that capital. He seems to have been almost constantly in the pulpit during this period " of the sharpest conflict with them,"[1] preaching against the Pelagians. There is one series of his sermons, of the exact dates of which we can be pretty sure, which may be adverted to here. This includes Sermons 151 and 152, preached early in October, 418 ; Sermon 155 on October 14, 156 on October 17, and 26 on October 18. They thus follow one another almost with the regularity of the days. The first was based on Rom. vii. 15-25. Augustine declares this text to contain dangerous words if it is not properly understood ; for men are prone to sin, and when they hear the apostle so speaking they do evil and think they are like him. They are meant to teach us, however, that the life of the just in this body is a war, not yet a triumph : the triumph will come only when death is swallowed up in victory. It would, no doubt, be better not to have an enemy than even to conquer. It

[1] *On the Gift of Perseverance*, 55.

would be better not to have evil desires. But we have them. Nevertheless, let us not follow after them. If they rebel against us, let us rebel against them ; if they fight, let us fight ; if they besiege, let us besiege : let us look only to this, that they do not conquer. With some evil desires we are born : others we make by bad habit. It is on account of those with which we are born that infants are baptized—that they may be freed from the guilt of inheritance, not from any evil of custom, which, of course, they have not. And it is on account of these, too, that our war must be endless : the concupiscence with which we are born cannot be done away as long as we live ; it may be diminished, but not done away. Neither can the law free us, for it only reveals the sin to our fuller apprehension. Where, then, is hope, save in the superabundance of grace?

The next sermon (152) takes up the words in Rom. viii. 1–4, and points out that the inward aid of the Spirit brings all the help we need. "We, like farmers in the field, work from without : but, if there were no one who worked from within, the seed would not take root in the ground, nor would the sprout arise in the field, nor would the shoot grow strong and become a tree, nor would branches and fruit and leaves be produced. Therefore the apostle distinguishes between the work of the workmen and the work of the Creator (1 Cor. iii. 6, 7). If God give not the increase, empty is this sound within your ears ; but if He gives, it avails somewhat that we plant and water, and our labor is not in vain." He then applies this to the individual striving against his lusts ; warns against Manichean error ; and distinguishes between the three laws,—the law of sin, the law of faith, and the law of deeds,—defending the last, the law of Moses, against the Manicheans. Then he comes to the words of the text, and explains its chief phrases, closing thus : "What else do we read here than that Christ is a sacrifice for sin? . . . Behold by what 'sin' he condemned sin : by the sacrifice which he made for sins, he condemned sin. This is the law of the Spirit of life which has freed you from the law of sin and death. For that other law, the law of the letter, the law that commands, is indeed good ; ' the commandment is holy and just and good : ' but ' it was weak through the flesh,' and what it commanded it could not bring about in us. Therefore there is one law, as I began by saying, that reveals sin to you, and another that takes it away : the law of the letter reveals sin, the law of grace takes it away."

Sermon 155 covers the same ground, and more, taking the broader text, Rom. viii. 1-11, and fully developing its teaching, especially as discriminating between the law of sin and the law of Moses and the law of faith ; the law of Moses being the holy law of God written with His finger on the tables of stone, while the law of the Spirit of life is nothing other than the same law written in the heart, as the prophet (Jer. xxx. 1, 33) clearly declares. So written, it does not terrify from without, but soothes from within. Great care is also taken, lest by such phrases as, " walk in the Spirit, not in the flesh," " who shall deliver me from the body of this death?" a hatred of the body should be begotten. " Thus you shall be freed from the body of this death, not by having no body, but by having another one and dying no more. If, indeed, he had not added, ' of this death,' perchance an error might have been suggested to the human mind, and it might have been said, ' You see that God does not wish us to have a body.' But He says, ' the body of this death.' Take away death, and the body is good. Let our last enemy, death, be taken away, and my dear flesh will be mine for eternity. For no one can ever ' hate his own flesh.' Although the ' spirit lusts against the flesh and the flesh against the spirit,' although there is now a strife in this house, yet the husband is seeking by his strife not the ruin of, but concord with, his wife. Far be it, far be it, my brethren, that the spirit should hate the flesh in lusting against it ! It hates the vices of the flesh ; it hates the wisdom of the flesh ; it hates the contention of death. This corruption shall put on incorruption,— this mortal shall put on immortality ; it is sown a natural body—it shall rise a spiritual body ; and you shall see full and perfect concord,—you shall see the creature praise the Creator." One of the special interests of such passages is to show, that, even at this early date, Augustine was careful to guard his hearers from Manichean error while proclaiming original sin. One of the sermons which, probably, was preached about this time (153), is even entitled, "Against the Manicheans openly, but tacitly against the Pelagians," and bears witness to the early development of the method that he was somewhat later to use effectively against Julian's charges of Manicheanism against the Catholics.[1]

Three days afterwards, Augustine preached on the next few verses, Rom. viii. 12-17, but can scarcely be said to have risen to the height of its great argument. The greater part of the sermon is occupied with a discussion of the law, why it was given, how it is legitimately used, and its usefulness as a pedagogue to bring us to Christ. It then passes on to speak of the need of a mediator ; and then, of what it is to live according to the flesh, which includes living according to merely human nature, and the need of mortifying the flesh in this world. All this, of course, gave full opportunity for opposing the leading Pelagian errors ; and the sermon is brought to a close by a direct polemic against their assertion that the function of grace is only to make it more easy to do what is right. "With the sail more easily, with the oar with more difficulty : nevertheless even with the oar we can go. On a beast more easily, on foot with more difficulty : nevertheless progress can be made on foot. It is not true ! For the true Master who flatters no one, who deceives no one,— the truthful Teacher and very Saviour to whom this very grievous schoolmaster has led us,—when he was speaking about good works, *i.e.*, about the fruits of the twigs and branches, did not say, ' Without me, indeed, you can do something, but you will do it more easily with me ; ' He did not say, ' You can produce your

---

[1] Compare below. Neander, in the second volume (E. T.) of his *History of the Christian Church*, discusses the matter in a very fair spirit.

fruit without me, but more richly with me.' He did not say this! Read what He said : it is the holy gospel,—bow the proud necks! Augustine does not say this : the Lord says it. What says the Lord? 'Without me you can do *nothing !* '"

On the very next day he was again in the pulpit, and taking for his text chiefly the ninety-fifth Psalm.[1] He began by quoting the sixth verse, and laying stress on the words "Our Maker." 'No Christian,' he said, ' doubted that God had made him, and that in such a sense that God created not only the first man, from whom all have descended, but that God to-day creates every man,—as He said to one of His saints, "Before that I formed thee in the womb, I knew thee." At first He created man apart from man ; now He creates man from man : nevertheless, whether man apart from man, or man from man, "it is He that made us, and not we ourselves." Nor has He made us and then deserted us ; He has not cared to make us, and not cared to keep us. Will He who made us without being asked, desert us when He is besought? But is it not just as foolish to say, as some say or are ready to say, that God made them men, but they make themselves righteous? Why, then, do we pray to God to make us righteous? The first man was created in a nature that was without fault or flaw. He was made righteous : he did not make himself righteous ; what he did for himself was to fall and break his righteousness. This God did not do : He permitted it, as if He had said, " Let him desert Me ; let him find himself ; and let his misery prove that he has no ability without Me." In this way God wished to show man what free will was worth without God. O evil free will without God! Behold, man was made good ; and by free will man was made evil! When will the evil man make himself good by free will? When good, he was not able to keep himself good ; and now that he is evil, is he to make himself good? Nay, behold, He that made us has also made us " His

---

[1] *Sermon* 26.

people" (Ps. xcv. 7). This is a distinguishing gift. Nature is common to all, but grace is not. It is not to be confounded with nature ; but if it were, it would still be gratuitous. For certainly no man, before he existed, deserved to come into existence. And yet God has made him, and that not like the beasts or a stock or a stone, but in His own image. Who has given this benefit? He gave it who was in existence : he received it who was not. And only He could do this, who calls the things that are not as though they were : of whom the apostle says that " He chose us before the foundation of the world." We have been made in this world, and yet the world was not when we were chosen. Ineffable ! wonderful ! They are chosen who are not : neither does He err in choosing nor choose in vain. He chooses, and has elect whom He is to create to be chosen : He has them in Himself, not indeed in His nature, but in His prescience. Let us not, then, glory in ourselves, or dispute against grace. If we are men, He made us. If we are believers, He made us this too. He who sent the Lamb to be slain has, out of wolves, made us sheep. This is grace. And it is an even greater grace than that grace of nature by which we were all made men.' " I am continually endeavoring to discuss such things as these," said the preacher, "against a new heresy which is attempting to rise ; because I wish you to be fixed in the good, untouched by the evil. . . . For, disputing against grace in favor of free will, they became an offence to pious and catholic ears. They began to create horror ; they began to be avoided as a fixed pest ; it began to be said of them, that they argued against grace. And they found such a device as this : . . . ' Because I defend man's free will and say that free will is sufficient in order that I may be righteous,' says one, ' I do not say that it is without the grace of God.' The ears of the pious are pricked up, and he who hears this already begins to rejoice : ' Thanks be to God ! He does not defend free will without the grace of God ! There is free will, but it avails nothing without the grace of God.' If, then, they do not defend free will without the grace of God, what evil do they say? Expound to us, O teacher, what grace you mean? 'When I say,' he says, 'the free will of man, you observe that I say *"of man"?*' What then? 'Who created man?' God. 'Who gave him free will?' God. 'If, then, God created man, and God gave man free will, whatever man is able to do by free will, to whose grace does he owe it, except to His who made him with free will?' And this is what they think they say so acutely! You see, nevertheless, my brethren, how they preach that general grace by which we were created and by which we are men; and, of course, we are men in common with the ungodly, and are Christians apart from them. It is this grace by which we are Christians, that we wish them to preach, this that we wish them to acknowledge, this that we wish,—of which the apostle says, ' I do not make void the grace of God, for if righteousness is by the law, Christ is dead in vain.' " Then the true function of the law was explained as a revealer of our sinfulness and a pedagogue to lead us to Christ: the Manichean depreciation of the Old-Testament law was attacked, but its insufficiency for salvation was pointed out; and so his hearers were brought back to the necessity of grace, which is illustrated from the story of the raising of the dead child in 2 Kings iv. 18–37: the dead child being Adam; the ineffective staff (by which we ought to walk), the law; but the living prophet, Christ with his grace, which we must preach. " The prophetic staff was not enough for the dead boy: would dead nature itself have been enough? Even this by which we are made, although we nowhere read of it under this name, we nevertheless, because it is given gratuitously, confess to be grace. But we show to you a greater grace than this, by which we are Christians. . . . This is the grace by Jesus Christ our Lord: it was He that made us,—both before we were at all it was He that made us, and now, after we are made, it is He that has made us all righteous,—and not we ourselves." There was but one mass of perdition from Adam, to which nothing was due but punishment ; and from that mass vessels have been made unto honor. " Rejoice because you have escaped ; you have escaped the death that was due,— you have received the life that was not due. ' But,' you ask, ' why did He make me unto honor, and another unto dishonor?' Will you who will not hear the apostle saying, ' O man, who art thou that repliest against God?' hear Augustine? . . . Do you wish to dispute with me ? Nay, wonder with me, and cry out with me, ' Oh the depth of the riches!' Let us both be afraid,—let us both cry out, ' Oh the depth of the riches!' Let us both agree in fear, lest we perish in error."

The Letter to Optatus.

Augustine was not less busy with his pen, during these months, than with his voice. Quite a series of letters belong to the last half of 418, in which he argues to his distant correspondents on the same themes which he was so iterantly trying to make clear to his Carthaginian auditors. One of the most interesting of these was written to a fellow-bishop, Optatus, on the origin of the soul.[1] Optatus, like Jerome, had expressed himself as favoring the theory of a special creation of each at birth ; and Augustine, in this letter as in the paper sent to Jerome, lays great stress on so holding our theories on so obscure a matter as to conform to the indubitable fact of the transmission of sin. This fact, such passages as 1 Cor. xv. 21 sq., Rom. v. 12 sq., make certain ; and in stating this, Augustine takes the opportunity to outline the chief contents of the catholic faith over against the Pelagian denial of original sin and grace : that all are born under the contagion of death and in the bond of guilt ; that there is no deliverance except in the one Mediator, Christ Jesus ; that before His coming men received him as promised, now as already come, but with the same faith ; that the law was not intended to save, but to shut up under sin and

[1] *Epistle* 190.

so to force us back upon the one Saviour ; and that the distribution of grace is sovereign.

Augustine pries into God's sovereign counsels somewhat more freely here than is usual with him. " But why those also are created who, the Creator foreknew, would belong to damnation, not to grace, the blessed apostle mentions with as much succinct brevity as great authority. For he says that God, ' wishing to show His wrath and demonstrate His power,' etc. (Rom. ix. 22). Justly, however, would He seem unjust in forming vessels of wrath for perdition, if the whole mass from Adam were not condemned. That, therefore, they are made on birth vessels of anger, belongs to the punishment due to them ; but that they are made by re-birth vessels of mercy, belongs to the grace that is not due to them. God, therefore, shows His wrath,—not, of course, perturbation of mind, such as is called wrath among men, but a just and fixed vengeance. . . . He shows also His power, by which He makes a good use of evil men, and endows them with many natural and temporal goods, and bends their evil to admonition and instruction of the good by comparison with it, so that these may learn from them to give thanks to God that they have been made to differ from them, not by their own deserts which were of like kind in the same mass, but by His pity. . . . But by creating so many to be born who, He foreknew, would not belong to His grace, so that they are more by an incomparable multitude than those whom He deigned to predestinate as children of the promise into the glory of His kingdom,—He wished to show by this very multitude of the rejected how entirely of no moment it is to the just God what is the multitude of those most justly condemned. And that hence also those who are redeemed from this condemnation may understand, that what they see rendered to so great a part of the mass was the desert of the whole of it,—not only of those who add many others to original sin, by the choice of an evil will, but as well of so many children who are snatched from this life without the grace of the Mediator, bound by no bond except that of original sin alone."

With respect to the question more immediately concerning which the letter was written, Augustine explains that he is willing to accept the opinion that souls are created for men as they are born, if only it can be made plain that it is consistent with the original sin that the Scriptures so clearly teach. In the paper sent to Jerome, the difficulties of creationism are sufficiently urged; this letter is interesting on account of its statement of some of the difficulties of traducianism also,—thus evidencing Augustine's clear view of the peculiar complexity of the problem, and justifying his attitude of balance and uncertainty between the two theories. 'The human understanding,' he says, 'can scarcely comprehend how a soul arises from a parent's soul in the offspring; or is transmitted to the offspring as a candle is lighted from a candle and thence another fire comes into existence without loss to the former one. Is there an incorporeal seed for the soul, which passes, by some hidden and invisible channel of its own, from the father to the mother, when it is conceived in the woman? Or, even more incredible, does it lie enfolded and hidden within the corporeal seed?' He is lost in wonder over the question whether, when conception does not take place, the immortal seed of an immortal soul perishes; or, whether the immortality attaches itself to it only when it lives. He even expresses doubt whether traducianism will explain what it is called in to explain, much better than creationism; in any case, who denies that God is the maker of every soul? Isaiah lvii. 16 says, "I have made every breath;" and the only question that can arise is as to method,—whether He "makes every breath from the one first breath, just as He makes every body of man from the one first body; or whether He makes new bodies indeed from the one body, but new souls out of nothing." Certainly nothing but Scripture can determine such a question; but where do the Scriptures speak unambiguously upon it? The passages to which the creationists point only affirm the admitted fact that God makes the soul; and the traducianists forget that the word "soul" in the Scriptures is ambiguous, and can

mean "man," and even a "dead man." What more
can be done, then, than to assert what is certain, viz.,
that sin is propagated, and leave what is uncertain in
the doubt in which God has chosen to place it?

This letter was written not long after the issue of
Zosimus' *Tractoria*, which demanded the signature of all
to African orthodoxy; and Augustine sends Optatus
"copies of the recent letters which have been sent
forth from the Roman See, whether specially to the
African bishops or generally to all bishops," on the
Pelagian controversy, "lest perchance they had not
yet reached" his correspondent, who, it is very evident, he was anxious should thoroughly realize "that
the authors, or certainly the most energetic and noted
teachers," of these new heresies, "had been condemned in the whole Christian world by the vigilance
of episcopal councils aided by the Saviour who keeps
His Church, as well as by two venerable overseers of
the Apostolical See, Pope Innocent and Pope Zosimus,
unless they should show repentance by being convinced and reformed." To this zeal we owe it that the
letter contains an extract from Zosimus' *Tractoria*, one
of the two brief fragments of that document that have
reached our day.

The Correspondence with Sixtus.

There was another ecclesiastic in Rome, besides
Zosimus, who was strongly suspected of favoring the
Pelagians. This was the presbyter Sixtus, who afterwards became Pope Sixtus III. But when Zosimus
issued his condemnation of Pelagianism, Sixtus sent
also a short letter to Africa addressed to Aurelius of
Carthage. This, though brief, spoke with considerable vigor against the heresy which he was commonly
believed to have before defended,[1] and which claimed
him as its own.[2] Some months afterwards, he sent another similar, but longer, letter to Augustine and
Alypius, more fully expounding his rejection of "the

[1] See *Epistle* 194, 1.   [2] *Ibid.* 191, 1.

fatal dogma" of Pelagius, and his acceptance of "that grace of God freely given by Him to small and great, to which Pelagius' dogma was diametrically opposed." Augustine was overjoyed with these developments. He quickly replied in a short letter[1] in which he expresses the delight he had in learning from Sixtus' own hand that he was not a defender of Pelagius, but a preacher of grace. And close upon the heels of this he sent another much longer letter,[2] in which he discusses the subtler arguments of the Pelagians with an anxious care that seems to bear witness to his desire to confirm and support his correspondent in his new opinions. Both letters testify to Augustine's approval of the persecuting measures which had been instituted by the Roman see in obedience to the emperor; and urge on Sixtus his duty not only to bring the open heretics to deserved punishment, but to track out those who spread their poison secretly, and even to remember those whom he had formerly heard announcing the error before it had been condemned and who were now silent through fear, and to bring them either to open recantation of their former beliefs, or to punishment.

It is pleasanter to recall the dialectic of these letters. The greater part of the second is given to a discussion of the gratuitousness of grace, which, just because grace, is given to no preceding merits. Many subtle objections to this doctrine were brought forward by the Pelagians. They said that "free will is taken away if we assert that man does not have even a good will without the aid of God:" that we make "God an accepter of persons, if we believe that without any preceding merits He has mercy on whom He will, and whom He will He calls, and whom He will He makes religious:" that "it is unjust, in one and the same case, to deliver one and punish another:" that, if such a doctrine be preached, "men who do not wish to live rightly and faithfully, will excuse themselves by saying that they have done nothing evil

[1] *Epistle* 191.   [2] *Ibid.* 194.

by living ill, since they have not received the grace by which they might live well :" that it is a puzzle " how sin can pass over to the children of the faithful, when it has been remitted to the parents in baptism :" that " children respond truly by the mouth of their sponsors that they believe in remission of sins, but not because sins are remitted to *them*, but because they believe that sins are remitted in the church or in baptism to those in whom they are found, not to those in whom they do not exist ;" and consequently they said that " they were unwilling that infants should be so baptized unto remission of sins as if this remission took place in them," for (they contended) " they have no sin ; but they are to be baptized, although without sin, with the same rite of baptism through which remission of sins takes place in any that are sinners." This last objection is especially interesting,[1] because it furnishes us with the reply which the Pelagians made to the argument that Augustine so strongly pressed against them from the very act and ritual of baptism, as implying remission of sins.[2] His rejoinder to it here is to point to the other parts of the same ritual, and to ask why, then, infants are exorcised and exsufflated in baptism. " For, it cannot be doubted that this is done fictitiously, if the Devil does not rule over them ; but if he rules over them, and they are therefore not falsely exorcised and exsufflated, why does that Prince of sinners rule over them except because of sin ?"

On the fundamental matter of the gratuitousness of grace, this letter is very explicit. " If we seek for the deserving of hardening, we shall find it. . . . But if we seek for the deserving of pity, we shall not find it ; for there is none, lest grace be made a vanity if it is not given gratis but rendered to merits. But, should we say that faith preceded and in it there is desert of grace, what desert did man have before faith that he should receive faith ? For, what did he have that he did not receive ? and if he received it, why does he

---

[1] It appears to have been first reported to Augustine by Marius Mercator, in a letter received at Carthage. See *Epistle* 193, 3.
[2] As, for example, in *On the Merits and Remission of Sins*, etc., i.

glory as if he received it not? For as man would not have wisdom, understanding, prudence, fortitude, knowledge, piety, fear of God, unless he had received (according to the prophet) the spirit of wisdom and understanding, of prudence and fortitude, of knowledge and piety and the fear of God; as he would not have justice, love, continence, except the spirit were received of whom the apostle says, 'For you did not receive the spirit of fear, but of virtue, and love, and continence:' so he would not have faith unless he received the spirit of faith of whom the same apostle says, 'Having then the same spirit of faith, according to what is written, "I believed and therefore spoke," we too believe and therefore speak.' But that He is not received by desert, but by His mercy who has mercy on whom He will, is manifestly shown where he says of himself, 'I have obtained mercy to be faithful.'" "If we should say that the merit of prayer precedes, that the gift of grace may follow, . . . even prayer itself is found among the gifts of grace" (Rom. viii. 26). "It remains, then, that faith itself, whence all righteousness takes beginning, . . . it remains, I say, that even faith itself is not to be attributed to the human will which they extol, nor to any preceding merits, since from it begin whatever good things are merits: but it is to be confessed to be the gratuitous gift of God, since we consider it true grace, that is, without merits, inasmuch as we read in the same epistle, ' God divides out the measure of faith to each' (Rom. xii. 3). Now, good works are done by man, but faith is wrought in man, and without it these are not done by any man. For all that is not of faith is sin" (Rom. xiv. 23.)

Letters to Mercator and Asellicus.

By the same messenger who carried this important letter to Sixtus, Augustine sent also a letter to Mercator,[1] an African layman who was then apparently at Rome, but who was afterwards (in 429) to render ser-

[1] *Epistle* 193.

vice by instructing the Emperor Theodosius as to the nature and history of Pelagianism, and so preventing the appeal of the Pelagians to him from being granted. Now he appears as an inquirer. Augustine, while at Carthage, had received a letter from him in which he had consulted him on certain questions that the Pelagians had raised, but in such a manner as to indicate his opposition to them. Press of business had compelled the postponement of the reply until this later date. One of the questions which Mercator had put concerned the Pelagian account of infants sharing in the one baptism unto remission of sins, which we have seen Augustine answering when writing to Sixtus. In this letter he replies: " Let them, then, hear the Lord (John iii. 36). Infants, therefore, who are made believers by others, by whom they are brought to baptism, are, of course, unbelievers by others, if they are in the hands of such as do not believe that they should be brought, inasmuch as they believe they are nothing profited; and accordingly, if they believe by believers and have eternal life, they are unbelievers by unbelievers and shall not see life, but the wrath of God abideth on them. For it is not said, ' it *comes* on them,' but ' it *abideth* on them,' because it was on them from the beginning, and will not be taken from them except by the grace of God through Jesus Christ, our Lord. . . . Therefore, when children are baptized, the confession is made that they are believers, and it is not to be doubted that those who are not believers are condemned: let them, then, dare to say now, if they can, that they contract no evil from their origin to be condemned by the just God, and have no contagion of sin." The other matter on which Mercator sought light concerned the statement that universal death proved universal sin:[1] he reported that the Pelagians replied that not even death was universal—that Enoch, for instance, and Elijah, had not died. Augustine adds those who are to be found living at the second advent, who are not to die but to be " changed;"

[1] Compare *On Dulcitius' Eight Questions*, 3.

and replies that Rom. v. 12 is perfectly explicit that there is no death in the world except that which comes from sin, and that God is a Saviour, and we cannot at all "deny that He is able to do that, now, in any that he wishes, without death, which we undoubtingly believe is to be done in so many after death." He adds that the difficult question is not why Enoch and Elijah did not die, if death is the punishment of sin ; but why, such being the case, the justified ever die ; and he refers his correspondent to his book *On the Baptism of Infants*[1] for a resolution of this greater difficulty.

It was probably at the very end of 418 that Augustine wrote a letter of some length[2] to Asellicus, in reply to one which he had written, on "avoiding the deception of Judaism," to the primate of the Bizacene province, and which that ecclesiastic had sent to Augustine for answering. He discusses in this the law of the Old Testament. He opens by pointing out that the apostle forbids Christians to Judaize (Gal. ii. 14-16), and explains that it is not merely the ceremonial law that we may not depend upon, "but also what is said in the law, ' Thou shalt not covet ' (which no one, of course, doubts is to be said to Christians too), does not justify man, except by faith in Jesus Christ and the grace of God through Jesus Christ our Lord." He then expounds the use of the law : " This, then, is the usefulness of the law : that it shows man to himself, so that he may know his weakness, and see how, by the prohibition, carnal concupiscence is rather increased than healed. . . . The use of the law is, thus, to convince man of his weakness, and force him to implore the medicine of grace that is in Christ." " Since these things are so," he adds, " those who rejoice that they are Israelites after the flesh and glory in the law apart from the grace of Christ, these are those concerning whom the apostle said that ' being ignorant of God's righteousness, and wishing to establish their own, they are not subject to God's righteousness ; '

---

[1] That is, *On the Merits and Remission of Sins*, etc., ii. 30 sq.
[2] *Epistle* 196.

since he calls ' God's righteousness ' that which is from God to man ; and ' their own,' what they think that the commandments suffice for them to do without the help and gift of Him who gave the law. But they are like those who, while they profess to be Christians, so oppose the grace of Christ that they suppose that they fulfil the divine commands by human powers, and, ' wishing to establish their own,' are ' not subject to the righteousness of God,' and so, not indeed in name, but yet in error, Judaize. This sort of men found heads for themselves in Pelagius and Cœlestius, the most acute asserters of this impiety, who by God's recent judgment, through his diligent and faithful servants, have been deprived even of catholic communion, and, on account of an impenitent heart, persist still in their condemnation."

The First Book of the Treatise " On Marriage and Concupiscence."

At the beginning of 419, a considerable work was published by Augustine on one of the more remote corollaries which the Pelagians drew from his teachings. It had come to his ears, that they asserted that his doctrine condemned marriage. "If only sinful offspring come from marriage," they asked, "is not marriage itself made a sinful thing?" The book which Augustine composed in answer to this query, he sent, along with an explanatory letter, to the Comes Valerius, a trusted servant of the Emperor Honorius and one of the most steady opponents at court of the Pelagian heresy. Augustine explains[1] why he desired to address the book to him : first, because Valerius was a striking example of those continent husbands of which that age furnishes us with many instances, and, therefore, the discussion would have especial interest for him ; secondly, because of his eminence as an opponent of Pelagianism ; and, thirdly, because Augustine had learned that he had read a Pelagian document in which Augustine was charged with condemning mar-

[1] *On Marriage and Concupiscence,* i. 2.

riage by defending original sin.[1] The book in question is the first book of the treatise *On Marriage and Concupiscence*. It is, naturally, tinged, or rather stained, with the prevalent ascetic notions of the day. Its doctrine is that marriage is good, and that God is the maker of the offspring that comes from it, although now there can be no begetting and hence no birth without sin. Sin made concupiscence, and now concupiscence perpetuates sinners. The specific object of the work, as it states it itself, is "to distinguish between the evil of carnal concupiscence, from which man who is born therefrom contracts original sin, and the good of marriage" (I. 1). After the brief introduction, in which he explains why he writes, and why he addresses his book to Valerius (1-2), Augustine points out that conjugal chastity, like its higher sister-grace of continence, is God's gift. Thus copulation, but only for the propagation of children, has divine allowance (3-5). Lust, or "shameful concupiscence," however, he teaches, is not of the essence, but only an accident, of marriage. It did not exist in Eden, although true marriage existed there; but arose from, and therefore only after, sin (6-7). Its addition to marriage does not destroy the good of marriage: it only conditions the character of the offspring (8). Hence it is that the apostle allows marriage, but forbids the "disease of desire" (1 Thess. iv. 3-5); and hence the Old Testament saints were even permitted more than one wife, because, by multiplying wives, it was not lust, but offspring, that was increased (9-10). Nevertheless, fecundity is not to be thought the only good of marriage: true marriage can exist without offspring, and even without cohabitation (11-13); and cohabitation is now, under the New Testament, no longer a duty as it was under the Old Testament (14-15), but the apostle praises continence above it. We must, then, distinguish between the goods of marriage, and seek the best (16-19). But thus it follows that it is not due to any inherent and necessary evil in mar-

---

[1] Compare the Benedictine Preface to *The Unfinished Work*.

riage, but only to the presence, now, of concupiscence in all cohabitation, that children are born under sin, even the children of the regenerate, just as from the seed of olives only oleasters grow (20-24). And yet again, concupiscence is not itself sin in the regenerate; it is remitted as guilt in baptism : but it is the daughter of sin, and it is the mother of sin, and in the unregenerate it is itself sin, as to yield to it is even to the regenerate (25-39). Finally, as so often, the testimony of Ambrose is appealed to, and it is shown that he too teaches that all born from cohabitation are born guilty (40).

In this book, Augustine certainly seems to teach that the bond of connection by which Adam's sin is conveyed to his offspring is not mere descent, or heredity, or mere inclusion in him in a realistic sense as partakers of the same numerical nature, but concupiscence. Without concupiscence in the act of generation, the offspring would not be a partaker of Adam's sin. This he had taught also previously, as, e.g., in the treatise *On Original Sin*, from which a few words may be profitably quoted as succinctly summing up the teaching of this book on the subject : "It is, then, manifest, that that must not be laid to the account of marriage, in the absence of which even marriage would still have existed. . . . Such, however, is the present condition of mortal men, that the connubial intercourse and lust are at the same time in action. . . . Hence it follows that infants, although incapable of sinning, are yet not born without the contagion of sin, . . . not, indeed, because of what is lawful, but on account of that which is unseemly : for, from what is lawful, nature is born ; from what is unseemly, sin" (42).

The Treatise "On the Soul and its Origin."

Towards the end of the same year (419), Augustine was led to take up again the vexed question of the origin of the soul. This he did not only in a new letter to Optatus,[1] but also, moved by the zeal of the same monk, Renatus, who had formerly brought Optatus' inquiries to his notice, in an elaborate treatise entitled *On the Soul and its Origin*, by way of reply to a rash adventure of a young man named Vincentius Victor, who blamed him for his uncertainty on such a subject and attempted to determine all the puzzles of the question, though, as Augustine insists, on assumptions that were partly Pelagian and partly worse.

Optatus had written in the hope that Augustine had heard by this time from Jerome, in reply to the treatise he had sent him on this subject. Augustine, in answering his letter, expresses his sorrow that he has not yet been thought by Jerome worthy of an answer, although five years had passed away since he wrote, but his continued hope that such an answer will in due time come. For himself, he confesses that he has not yet been able to see how the soul can contract sin from Adam and yet not itself be contracted from Adam ; and he regrets that Optatus, although holding that God creates each soul for its birth, has not sent him the proofs on which he depends for that opinion, nor met its obvious difficulties. He rebukes Optatus for confounding the question of whether God makes the soul, with the entirely different one of how he makes it, whether *ex propagine* or *sine propagine*. No one doubts that God makes the soul, as no one doubts that He makes the body. But when we consider how He makes it, sobriety and vigilance become necessary lest we should unguardedly fall into the Pelagian heresy. Augustine defends his attitude of uncertainty, and enumerates the points as to which he has no doubt : viz., that the soul is spirit, not body ; that it is rational or intellectual ; that it is not of the nature of God, but is so far a mortal creature that it is capable of deterioration and of alienation from the life of God, and so far immortal that after this life it lives on in bliss or punishment forever ; that it was not incarnated because of, or according to, preceding deserts ac-

---

[1] *Epistle* 202, *bis*. Compare *Epistle* 190.

quired in a previous existence, yet that it is under the curse of sin which it derives from Adam, and therefore in all cases alike needs redemption in Christ.

The whole subject of the nature and origin of the soul, however, is most fully discussed in the four books which are gathered together under the common title of *On the Soul and its Origin.* Vincentius Victor was a young layman who had recently been converted from the Rogatian heresy. On being shown by his friend Peter, a presbyter, a small work of Augustine's on the origin of the soul, he expressed surprise that so great a man could profess ignorance on a matter so intimate to his very being ; and, receiving encouragement, he wrote a book for Peter, in which he attacked and tried to solve all the difficulties of the subject. Peter received the work with transports of delighted admiration. But Renatus, happening that way, looked upon it with distrust, and, finding that Augustine was spoken of in it with scant courtesy, felt it his duty to send him a copy of it. This he did in the summer of 419. It was probably not until late in the following autumn that Augustine found time to take up the matter. He wrote then to Renatus, to Peter, and two books to Victor himself ; and it is these four books together which constitute the treatise that has come down to us.

The first book is a letter to Renatus, and is introduced by an expression of thanks to him for sending Victor's book, and of kindly feeling towards and appreciation for the high qualities of Victor himself (1-3). Then Victor's errors are pointed out,—as to the nature of the soul (4-9), including certain far-reaching corollaries that flow from these (10-15), and also as to the origin of the soul (16-30). The letter closes with some remarks on the danger of arguing from the silence of Scripture (31), on the self-contradictions of Victor (34), and on the errors that must be avoided in any theory of the origin of the soul that hopes to be acceptable. These errors are that souls become sinful by an alien original sin, that unbaptized infants need no salvation, that souls sinned in a previous state, and that they are condemned for sins which they have not committed, but would have committed had they lived longer.

The second book is a letter to Peter, warning him of the responsibility that rests on him, as Victor's trusted friend and a clergyman, to correct Victor's errors, and reproving him for the uninstructed delight he had taken in Victor's crudities. It opens by asking Peter what was the occasion of the great joy which Victor's book brought him? Could it be that he learned from it, for the first time, the old and primary truths it contained (2-3)? Or was it due to the new errors that it proclaimed,—seven of which he enumerates (4-16)? Then, after animadverting on the dilemma in which Victor stood, of either being forced to withdraw his violent assertion of creationism, or else of making God unjust in His dealings with new souls (17), he speaks of Victor's unjustifiable dogmatism in the matter (18-21), and closes with severely solemn words to Peter on his responsibility in the premises (22-23).

In the third and fourth books, which are addressed to Victor, the polemic, of course, reaches its height. The third book is entirely taken up with pointing out to Victor, as a father to a son, the errors into which he had fallen, and which, in accordance with his professions of readiness for amendment, he ought to correct. Eleven are enumerated : 1. That the soul was made by God out of Himself (3-7) ; 2. That God will continuously create souls forever (8) ; 3. That the soul has desert of good before birth (9) ; 4. (contradictingly), That the soul has desert of evil before birth (10) ; 5. That the soul deserved to be sinful before any sin (11) ; 6. That unbaptized infants are saved (12) ; 7. That what God predestinates may not occur (13) ; 8. That Wisd. iv. 1 is spoken of infants (14) ; 9. That some of the mansions with the Father are outside of God's kingdom (15-17) ; 10. That the sacrifice of Christ's blood may be offered for the unbaptized (18) ; 11. That the unbaptized may attain at the resurrection even to the kingdom of heaven (19). The book closes by reminding Victor of his professions of readiness to correct his errors, and warning him against the obstinacy that makes the heretic (20-23). The fourth book deals with the more personal elements of the controversy, and discusses the points in which Victor had expressed dissent from Augustine. It opens with a statement of the two grounds of complaint that Victor had urged against Augustine ; viz., that he refused to express a confident opinion as to the origin of the soul, and that he affirmed that the soul was not corporeal, but spirit (1-2). These two complaints are then taken up at length (2-16 and 17-37). To the first, Augustine replies that man's knowledge is at best limited, and often most limited about the things nearest to him. We do not know the constitution of our bodies ; and, above most others, this subject of the origin of the soul is one on which no one but God is a competent witness. Who remembers his birth? Who remembers what was before birth? But this is just one of the subjects on which God has not spoken unambiguously in the Scriptures. Would it not be better, then, for Victor to imitate Augustine's cautious ignorance, than that Augustine should imitate Victor's rash assertion of errors? That the soul is not corporeal, Augustine argues (18-35) from the Scriptures and from the phenomena of dreams ; and then shows, in opposition to Victor's trichotomy, that the Scriptures teach the identity of " soul" and " spirit" (36-37). The book closes with a renewed enumeration of Victor's eleven errors (38), and a final admonition to his rashness (39).

It is pleasant to know that Augustine found, in this case also, that righteousness is the fruit of the faithful wounds of a friend. Victor accepted the rebuke, and professed his better instruction at the hands of his modest but resistless antagonist.

The Second Book of " Marriage and Concupiscence."

The controversy now entered upon a new stage. Among the evicted bishops of Italy who refused to sign Zosimus' *Epistola Tractoria*, Julian of Eclanum[1]

[1] This able and learned man was much the most formidable of the Pelagian writers. He was a son of a dear friend of Augustine and

was easily the first, and at this point he appears as the champion of Pelagianism. It was a sad fate that arrayed this beloved son of an old friend against Augustine, just when there seemed to be reason to hope that the controversy was at an end and the victory won, and the plaudits of the world were greeting him as the saviour of the Church.[1] But the now fast-aging bishop was to find, that in this "very confident young man" he had yet to meet the most persistent and the most dangerous advocate of the new doctrines that had arisen. At an earlier period Julian had sent two letters to Zosimus, in which he attempted to approach Augustinian forms of speech as much as possible, his object being to gain standing ground in the Church for the Italian Pelagians. Now he appears as a Pelagian controversialist. In opposition to the book *On Marriage and Concupiscence*, which Augustine had sent Valerius, Julian published an extended work in four thick books addressed to Turbantius.[2] Extracts from the first of these books were sent by some one to Valerius, and were placed by him in the hands of Alypius, who was then in Italy, for transmission to Augustine. Meanwhile, a letter had been sent to Rome by Julian,[3] de-

was himself much loved by him. He became a "lector" in 404, and was ordained bishop by Innocent I. about 417. Under Zosimus' vacillating policy he took strong ground on the Pelagian side, and, refusing to sign Zosimus' *Tractoria*, was exiled with his seventeen fellow-recusants, and passed his long life in vain endeavours to obtain recognition for the Pelagian party. His writings included two letters to Zosimus, a *Confession of Faith*, the two letters answered in *Against Two Letters of the Pelagians* (though he seems to have repudiated the former of these), and two large books against Augustine, the first of which was his four books against the first book of *On Marriage and Concupiscence*, in reply to extracts from which the second book of that treatise was written, whilst Augustine's *Against Julian*, in six books, traverses the whole work. To this second book Julian replied in a rejoinder addressed to Florus, and consisting of eight books. Augustine's *Unfinished Work* is a reply to this. Julian's character was as noble as his energy was great and his pen acute. He stands out among his fellow-Pelagians as the sufferer for conscience' sake. A full account of his works may be read in the Benedictine Preface to Augustine's *Unfinished Work*, with which may be compared the article on him in Smith and Wace's *Dictionary of Christian Biography*.

[1] Compare *Epistle* 195.   [2] A fellow-recusant.
[3] Julian afterwards repudiated this letter, perhaps because of some falsifications it had suffered : it seems to have been certainly his.

signed to strengthen the cause of Pelagianism there. A similar one also, written in the names of the eighteen Pelagianizing Italian bishops, was addressed to Rufus, bishop of Thessalonica and representative of the Roman see in that portion of the Eastern Empire which was regarded as ecclesiastically a part of the West, the purpose of which was to obtain the powerful support of this important magnate, and perhaps, also, a refuge from persecution within his jurisdiction. These two letters came into the hands of the new Pope, Boniface, who gave them also to Alypius for transmission to Augustine. Thus provided, Alypius returned to Africa.

The tactics of all these writings of Julian were essentially the same. He attempted not so much to defend Pelagiansim as to attack Augustinianism, and thus literally to carry the war into Africa. He insisted that the corruption of nature which Augustine taught was nothing else than Manicheism; that the sovereignty of grace, as taught by him, was only the attribution of "acceptance of persons" and partiality to God; and that his doctrine of predestination was mere fatalism. He accused the anti-Pelagians of denying the goodness of the nature that God had created, of the marriage that He had ordained, of the law that He had given, of the free will that He had implanted in man, as well as the perfection of His saints.[1] He insisted that this teaching also did dishonour to baptism itself which it professed so to honour, inasmuch as it asserted the continuance of concupiscence after baptism and thus taught that baptism does not take away sins, but only shaves them off as one shaves his beard, and leaves the roots whence the sins may grow anew and need cutting down again. He complained bitterly of the way in which Pelagianism had been condemned,—that bishops had been compelled to sign a definition of dogma, not in council assembled, but sitting at home; and he demanded a rehearing of the whole case before a lawful council, lest the doctrine of the Manicheans should be forced upon the acceptance of the world.

[1] Compare *Against Two Letters of the Pelagians*, iii. 24; and see above, p. 11.

Augustine felt a strong desire to see the whole work of Julian against his book *On Marriage and Concupiscence* before he undertook a reply to the excerpts sent him by Valerius. But he did not feel justified in delaying obedience to that officer's request ; therefore he wrote at once two treatises. One of these was an answer to these excerpts, for the benefit of Valerius ; it constitutes the second book of his *On Marriage and Concupiscence*. The other was a far more elaborate examination of the letters sent by Boniface, and bears the title, *Against Two Letters of the Pelagians*.

The purpose of the second book of *On Marriage and Concupiscence*, Augustine himself states, in its introductory sentences, to be " to reply to the taunts of his adversaries with all the truthfulness and scriptural authority he could command." He begins (2) by identifying the source of the extracts forwarded to him by Valerius with Julian's work against his first book, and then remarks upon the garbled form in which he is quoted in them (3-6), and passes on to state and refute Julian's charge that the Catholics had turned Manicheans (7-9). At this point, the refutation of Julian begins in good earnest, and the method that Augustine proposes to use is stated ; viz., to adduce the adverse statements, and refute them one by one (10). Beginning at the beginning, he quotes first the title of the paper sent him, which declares that it is directed against " those who condemn matrimony and ascribe its fruit to the Devil" (11). This certainly, says Augustine, does not describe him or the Catholics. The next twenty chapters (10-30), accordingly, following Julian's order, labour to prove that marriage is good and ordained by God ; but that its good includes *fecundity* indeed, but not *concupiscence*, which arose from sin and contracts sin. It is next argued, that the doctrine of original sin does not imply an evil origin for man (31-51). In the course of this argument, the following propositions are especially defended : that God makes offspring for good and bad alike, just as He sends the rain and sunshine on just and unjust (31-34) ; that God makes everything to be found in marriage except its *flaw*, concupiscence

(35-40); that marriage is not the cause of original sin, but only the channel through which it is transmitted (41-47); and that to assert that evil cannot arise from what is good leaves us in the clutches of that very Manicheism which is so unjustly charged against the Catholics—for, if evil be not eternal, what else was there from which it could arise but something good (48-51)? In concluding, Augustine recapitulates, and argues, especially, that shameful concupiscence is of sin and the author of sin, and was not in paradise (52-54); that children are made by God, and only marred by the Devil (55); that Julian, in admitting that Christ died for infants, admits that they need salvation (56); that what the Devil makes in children is not a substance, but an injury to a substance (57-58); and that to suppose that concupiscence existed in any form in paradise introduces incongruities in our conception of life in that abode of primeval bliss (59-60).

The Treatise " Against Two Letters of the Pelagians."

The long and important treatise, *Against Two Letters of the Pelagians*, consists of four books. The first of these replies to the letter sent to Rome, and the other three to that sent to Thessalonica. After a short introduction, in which he thanks Boniface for his kindness and gives reasons why heretical writings should be answered (1-3), Augustine begins at once to rebut the calumnies which the letter before him brings against the Catholics (4-28). These are seven in number. 1. That the Catholics destroy free will. To this Augustine replies that none are " forced into sin by the necessity of their flesh" but all sin by free will, though no man can have a righteous will save by God's grace. It is really the Pelagians, he argues, who destroy free will by exaggerating it (4-8). 2. That Augustine declares that such marriage as now exists is not of God (9). 3. That sexual desire and intercourse are made a device of the Devil, which is sheer Manicheism (10-11). 4. That the Old-Testament saints are said to have died in sin (12). 5. That Paul and the other apostles are asserted to have been polluted by lust all their days. Augustine's answer to this includes a running commentary on Rom. vii. 7 sq., in which (correcting his older exegesis) he shows that Paul is giving here a transcript of his own experience as a typical Christian (13–24). 6. That Christ is said not to have been free from sin (25). 7. That baptism does not give complete remission of sins, but leaves roots from which they may again grow. To this Augustine replies that baptism does remit all sins, but leaves concupiscence, which, although not sin, is the source of sin (26–28). Next, the positive part of Julian's letter is taken up, and his profession of faith against the Catholics examined (29–41). The seven affirmations that Julian makes here are designed as the obverse of the seven charges against the Catholics. He believed: 1. That free will is in all by nature, and could not perish by Adam's sin (29); 2. That marriage, as now existent, was ordained by God (30); 3. That sexual impulse and virility are from God (31–35); 4. That men are God's work, and no one is forced to do good or evil unwillingly, but are assisted by grace to good and incited by the Devil to evil (36–38); 5. That the saints of the Old Testament were perfected in righteousness here, and so passed into eternal life (39); 6. That the grace of Christ (ambiguously meant) is necessary for all, and all children— even those of baptized parents—are to be baptized (40); 7. And that baptism gives full cleansing from all sins— to which Augustine pointedly asks, "What does it do for infants, then?" (41). The book concludes with an answer to Julian's conclusion, in which he demands a general council and charges the Catholics with Manicheism.

The second, third, and fourth books deal with the letter to Rufus in a somewhat similar way. The second and third books are occupied with the calumnies brought against the Catholics, and the fourth with the claims made by the Pelagians. The second book begins by repelling the charge of Manicheism brought against the Catholics (1–4). The pointed remark is added, that the Pelagians cannot hope to escape condemnation merely because they are willing to condemn another heresy. It then defends (with less success) the Roman clergy against the charge of prevarication in their dealing with the Pelagians (5-8), and in the course of this all that can be said in defence of Zosimus's wavering policy is said well and strongly. Next the charges against Catholic teaching are taken up and answered (9-16), especially the two important accusations that they maintain fate under the name of grace (9-12), and that they make God an "accepter of persons" (13-16). Augustine's replies to these charges are in every way admirable. The charge of "fate" rests solely on the Catholic denial that grace is given according to preceding merits; but the Pelagians do not escape the same charge when they acknowledge that the "fates" of baptized and unbaptized infants do differ. It is, in truth, not a question of "fate," but of *gratuitous bounty;* and "it is not the Catholics that assert fate under the name of grace, but the Pelagians that choose to call divine grace by the name of 'fate'" (12). As to "acceptance of persons," we must define what we mean by that. God certainly does not accept one's "person" above another's; He does not give to one rather than to another because He sees something to please Him in one rather than another : quite the opposite. He gives of His bounty to one while giving all their due to all, as in the parable (Matt. xx. 9 sq.). To ask why He does this, is to ask in vain : the apostle answers by not answering (Rom. ix.); and before the dumb infants, who are yet made to differ, all objection to God is dumb. From this point, the book becomes an examination of the Pelagian doctrine of prevenient merit (17-23), and the conclusion is reached that God gives all by grace, from the beginning to the end of every process of doing good : 1. He commands the good ; 2. He gives the desire to do it ; and, 3. He gives the power to do it ; and all, of His gratuitous mercy.

The third book continues the discussion of the calumnies of the Pelagians against the Catholics, and enumerates and answers six of them : viz., that the Catholics teach, 1, that the Old-Testament law was given, not to justify the obedient, but to serve as cause of greater sin (2–3); 2, that baptism does not give entire remission of sins, but the baptized are partly God's and partly the Devil's (4–5); 3, that the Holy Ghost did not assist virtue in the Old Testament (6–13); 4, that the Bible saints were not holy, but only less wicked than others (14–15); 5, that Christ was a sinner by necessity of His flesh (doubtless Julian's inference from the doctrine of race sin) (16); 6, that men will begin to fulfil God's commandments only after the resurrection (17–23). Augustine shows that at the basis of all these calumnies lies either misapprehension or misrepresentation. In concluding the book, he enumerates the three chief points in the Pelagian heresy, with the five claims growing out of them of which they most boasted; and then elucidates the mutual relations of the three parties, Catholics, Pelagians, and Manicheans, with reference to these points, showing that the Catholics stand asunder from both the others and condemn both (24–27).

This conclusion is really a preparation for the fourth book, which takes up these five Pelagian claims, and, after showing the Catholic position on them all in brief (1–3), discusses them in turn (4–19): viz., the praise of the creature (4–8), the praise of marriage (9), the praise of the law (10–11), the praise of free will (12–16), and the praise of the saints (17–18). At the end, Augustine calls on the Pelagians to cease to oppose the Manicheans only to fall into heresy as bad as theirs (19); and then in reply to their accusation that the Catholics were proclaiming novel doctrine, he adduces the testimony of Cyprian and Ambrose, both of whom had received Pelagius' praise, on each of the three main points of Pelagianism (20–32),[1] and closes with the declaration that the "impious and foolish doctrine," as they called it, of the Catholics, is immemorial truth (33), and with a denial of the right of the Pelagians to ask for a general council to condemn them (34). All

[1] To wit: Cyprian's testimony on original sin (20–24), on gratuitous grace (25–26), on the imperfection of human righteousness (27–28); and Ambrose's testimony on original sin (29), on gratuitous grace (30), and on the imperfection of human righteousness (31).

heresies do not need an ecumenical synod for their condemnation ; usually it is best to stamp them out locally, and not to allow what may be confined to a corner to disturb the whole world.

The Treatise "Against Julian."

These books were written late in 420, or early in 421, and Alypius appears to have conveyed them to Italy during the latter year. Before its close, Augustine, having obtained and read the whole of Julian's attack on the first book of his work *On Marriage and Concupiscence*, wrote out a complete answer to it.[1] He was the more anxious to complete this task, on perceiving that the extracts sent by Valerius were not only all from the first book of Julian's treatise, but were somewhat altered in the extracting. The resulting work, *Against Julian*, one of the longest that Augustine wrote in the whole course of the Pelagian controversy, shows its author at his best. According to Cardinal Noris's judgment, he appears in it "almost divine," and Augustine himself clearly set great store by it.

In the first book of this noble treatise, after professing his continued love for Julian, "whom he was unable not to love, whatever he [Julian] should say against him" (35), he undertakes to show that in affixing the opprobrious name of Manicheans on those who assert original sin, Julian is incriminating many of the most famous fathers, both of the Latin and Greek Churches. In proof of this, he makes appropriate quotations from Irenæus, Cyprian, Recticius, Olympius, Hilary, Ambrose, Gregory Nazianzenus, Basil, John of Constantinople.[2] Then he argues, that, so far from the Catholics falling into Manichean heresy, Julian himself plays into the hands of the Manicheans in their strife against the Catholics, by many unguarded statements, such as, *e.g.*, when he says that an evil thing cannot arise from what is good, that the work of the Devil cannot be suffered to be diffused by means of a work of

---
[1] Compare *Epistle* 207, written probably in the latter half of 421.
[2] That is, Chrysostom.

God, that a root of evil cannot be inserted within a gift of God, and the like.

The second book advances to greater detail, and, in order to test them by the voice of antiquity, adduces the five great arguments which the Pelagians urged against the Catholics. These arguments are stated as follows (2). "For you say, 'That we, by asserting original sin, affirm that the Devil is the maker of infants, condemn marriage, deny that all sins are remitted in baptism, accuse God of the guilt of sin, and produce despair of perfection.' You contend that all these follow as consequences, if we believe that infants are born bound by the sin of the first man and are therefore under the Devil unless they are born again in Christ. For, 'It is the Devil that creates,' you say, ' if they are created from that wound which the Devil inflicted on the human nature that was made at first.' ' And marriage is condemned,' you say, ' if it is to be believed to have something about it whence it produces those worthy of condemnation.' ' And all sins are not remitted in baptism,' you say, ' if there remains any evil in baptized couples whence evil offspring are produced.' ' And how is God,' you ask, ' not unjust, if He, while remitting their own sins to baptized persons, yet condemns their offspring, inasmuch as, although it is created by Him, it yet ignorantly and involuntarily contracts the sins of others from those very parents to whom they are remitted?' 'Nor can men believe,' you add, ' that virtue--to which corruption is to be understood to be contrary—can be perfected, if they cannot believe that it can destroy the inbred vices, although, no doubt, these can scarcely be considered vices, since he does not sin who is unable to be other than he was created.'" These arguments are then tested, one by one, by the authority of the earlier teachers who were appealed to in the first book, and shown to be condemned by them.

The remaining four books follow Julian's four books, argument by argument, refuting him in detail. In the third book it is urged that although God is good and made man good and instituted marriage, which is, therefore, good, nevertheless concupiscence is evil and in it the flesh lusts against the spirit. Although chaste spouses use this evil well, continent believers do better in not using it at all. It is pointed out, how far all this is from the madness of the Manicheans, who dream of matter as essentially evil and co-eternal with God ; and it is shown that evil concupiscence sprang from Adam's disobedience, and, being transmitted to us, can be removed only by Christ. It is shown, also, that Julian himself confesses lust to be evil, inasmuch as he speaks of remedies against it, wishes it to be bridled and speaks of the continent waging a glorious warfare. The fourth book follows the second book of Julian's work and makes two chief contentions : that unbelievers have no true virtues, and that even the heathen recognize concupiscence as evil. It also argues that grace is not given according to merit, and yet is not to be confounded with fate ; and explains the text that asserts that ' God wishes all men to be saved,' in the sense that ' all men ' means ' all that are to be saved,' since none are saved except by His will.[1] The fifth book, in like manner, follows Julian's third book, and treats of such subjects as these : that it is due to sin that any infants are lost ; that shame arose in our first parents through sin ; that sin can well be the punishment of preceding sin ; that concupiscence is always evil, even in those who do not assent to it ; that true marriage may exist without intercourse ; that the " flesh " of Christ differs from the " sinful flesh " of other men ; and the like. In the sixth book, Julian's fourth book is followed, and original sin is proved from the baptism of infants, the teaching of the apostles, and the rites of exorcism and exsufflation incorporated in the form of baptism. Then, by the help of the illustration drawn from the olive and the oleaster, it is explained how Christian parents can produce unregenerate offspring ; and the originally voluntary character of sin is asserted, even though it now comes by inheritance.

[1] Compare *On Rebuke and Grace*, 44 ; *Enchiridion*, 103 ; *City of God*, xxii. 1, 2.

The "Enchiridion."

After the completion of this important work, there succeeded a lull in the controversy of some years' duration; and the calm refutation of Pelagianism and exposition of Christian grace which Augustine gave in his *Enchiridion*,[1] might well have seemed to him his closing word on this all-absorbing subject. This handbook *On Faith, Hope, and Charity* was written at the instance of one Laurentius, who is not otherwise known, and certainly later than the opening of A.D. 421. In it Augustine treats briefly but pretty carefully, as he himself says, "the manner in which God is to be worshipped, which knowledge divine Scripture defines to be the true wisdom of man."[2] One of the questions which Laurentius had asked was not only "what ought to be man's chief end in life," but also "what he ought, in view of the various heresies, chiefly to avoid" (4). Accordingly, in the first part of the treatise—that consecrated to the treatment of faith, in which he unfolds the proper objects of faith, that is, what we are to believe—Augustine briefly refutes the tenets of the leading heresies, inclusive of Pelagianism. This is not done formally; he notes rather the impossibility of giving a real defence of Christianity against these assaults in a practical handbook (6): but that is said which he deemed important in order to keep the heart rightly Christian in the midst of the evil thoughts of men.

On creating man, he explains, God placed him in that protected nook of life which we call Eden (25). When man lost God's favour by sin, all his descendants, being the offspring of carnal lust, were tainted with an original sin (26), and thus the whole mass of the human race came under condemnation and lay steeped and wallowing in misery (27). Whence it is a matter of course that they cannot be restored by the merit of any good works of their own (30); for by an evil use of free will man has destroyed both himself and it, and

---

[1] See vol. iii. of *The Post-Nicene Library*, pp. 237 sq.
[2] *Retractations*, lib. ii. c. 63.

a dead man cannot restore himself to life (30). Man cannot, therefore, arrogate to himself even the merit of his own faith, "and we shall be made truly free only when God fashions us—that is, forms and creates us anew, not as men—for He has done that already—but as good men" (31). The whole work belongs to God, "who both makes the will of men righteous and thus prepares it for assistance, and assists it when prepared" (32). As the whole human race lies under just condemnation, there is need of a Mediator (33), who, being made sin for us, reconciles us to God (41); and this is symbolized in the great sacrament of baptism (42), which is given to adults and infants alike (43 and 52). "The whole human race was originally and, as we may say, radically condemned" on account of the one sin of Adam, and this sin "cannot be pardoned or blotted out except through the one Mediator between God and man, the man Christ Jesus, who alone has had power to be so born as not to need a second birth" (48). Who are to be interested in this salvation it is the prerogative of God to determine, who "changes the evil will of men whichever, whenever, and wheresoever He chooses" (98), not, therefore, according to any works of their own foreseen by Him, but according to His own good pleasure. "The whole human race was condemned in its rebellious head by a divine judgment so just that, if not a single member of the race had been redeemed, no one could justly have questioned the justice of God; and it was right that those who are redeemed should be redeemed in such a way as to show, by the greater number who are unredeemed and left in their just condemnation, what the whole race deserved, and whither the deserved judgment of God would lead even the redeemed, did not His undeserved mercy interpose, so that every mouth might be stopped of those who wish to glory in their own merits, and that he that glorieth might glory in the Lord" (99). Thus Augustine taught on the great subjects of sin and grace when his mind was measurably withdrawn from controversy and intent on the creation of right frames in the hearts of men.

The Treatise "On Grace and Free Will."

Augustine had not yet, however, given the world all he had in treasure for it. And we can rejoice in the chance that five or six years afterward drew from him a renewed discussion of some of the more important aspects of the doctrine of grace. The circumstances which brought this about are sufficiently interesting in themselves, and open to us an unwonted view into the monastic life of the times. There was an important monastery at Adrumetum, the metropolitan city of the province of Byzacium.[1] From this a monk named Florus went out on a journey of charity to his native country of Uzalis about 426. On the journey he met with Augustine's letter to Sixtus,[2] in which the doctrines of gratuitous and prevenient grace were expounded. He was much delighted with it, and, procuring a copy, sent it back to his monastery for the edification of his brethren, while he himself went on to Carthage. At the monastery, the letter created great disturbance. Without the knowledge of the abbot, Valentinus, it was read aloud to the monks, many of whom were unskilled in theological questions. Some five or more of them were greatly offended, and declared that free will was destroyed by it. A secret strife arose among the brethren, some taking extreme grounds on both sides. Of all this, Valentinus remained ignorant until the return of Florus, who was attacked as the author of all the trouble, and who felt it his duty to inform the abbot of the state of affairs. Valentinus applied first to the bishop, Evodius, for such instruction as would make Augustine's letter clear to the most simple. Evodius replied, praising their zeal and deprecating their contentiousness, and explaining that Adam had full free will, but that it is now wounded and weak, and Christ's mission was as a physician to cure and recuperate it. "Let them read," is his prescription, "the words of God's elders. . . . And when they do not understand, let them not quickly reprehend, but

---

[1] Now a portion of Tunis.   [2] *Epistle* 194.

pray to understand." This did not, however, cure the malcontents; and the holy presbyter Sabrinus was appealed to, and sent a book with clear interpretations. But neither was this satisfactory; and Valentinus, at last, reluctantly consented that Augustine himself should be consulted—fearing, he says, lest by making inquiries he should seem to waver about the truth.

Two members of the community were consequently permitted to journey to Hippo, though they took with them no introduction and no commendation from their abbot. Augustine, nevertheless, received them without hesitation, as they bore themselves with too great simplicity to allow him to suspect them of deception. Now we get a glimpse of life in the great bishop's monastic home. The monks told their story, and were listened to with courtesy and instructed with patience. As they were anxious to return home before Easter, they received a letter for Valentinus [1] in which Augustine briefly explains the nature of the misapprehension that had arisen, and points out that both grace and free will must be defended, and neither so exaggerated as to deny the other. The letter to Sixtus, he explains, was written against the Pelagians, who assert that grace is given according to merit, and briefly expounds the true doctrine of grace as necessarily gratuitous and therefore prevenient. When the monks were on the point of starting home they were joined by a third companion from Adrumetum, and were led to prolong their visit. This gave Augustine the opportunity he craved for their fuller instruction. He read with them and explained to them not only his letter to Sixtus, from which the strife had risen, but also much of the chief literature of the Pelagian controversy,[2] copies of which also were made for them to take home with them. And when they were ready to go, he sent by them another and longer letter to Valentinus, and placed in their hands a treatise composed for their especial use, which, moreover, he took the trouble to explain to them. This longer letter is essentially an ex-

[1] *Epistle* 214.   [2] *Epistle* 215, 2 sq.

hortation "to turn aside neither to the right hand nor to the left,"—neither to the left hand of the Pelagian error of upholding free will in such a manner as to deny grace, nor to the right hand of the equal error of so upholding grace as if we might yield ourselves to evil with impunity. Both grace and free will are to be proclaimed; and it is true both that grace is not given to merits, and that we are to be judged at the last day according to our works. While the treatise which Augustine composed for a fuller exposition of these doctrines is the important work *On Grace and Free Will.*

After a brief introduction, explaining the occasion of his writing, and exhorting the monks to humility and teachableness before God's revelations (1), Augustine begins this treatise by asserting and proving the two propositions that the Scriptures clearly teach that man has free will (2–5), and, as clearly, the necessity of grace for his doing any good (6–9). He next examines the passages which the Pelagians assert to teach that we must first turn to God, before He visits us with His grace (10–11). And then he undertakes to show that grace is not given to merit (12 sq.), appealing especially to Paul's teaching and example, and replying to the assertion that forgiveness is the only grace that is not given according to our merits (15–18), and to the query, "How can eternal life be both of grace and of reward?" (19–21). The nature of grace, what it is, is next explained (22 sq.). It is not the law, which gives only knowledge of sin (22–24); nor nature, which would render Christ's death needless (25); nor mere forgiveness of sins, as the Lord's Prayer (which should be read with Cyprian's comments on it) is enough to show (26). Nor will it do to say that it is given to the merit of a good will, thus distinguishing the good work which is of grace from the good will which precedes grace (27–30); for the Scriptures oppose this, and our prayers for others prove that we expect God to be the *first mover*, as indeed both Scripture and experience prove that He is. It is next shown that both free will and grace are concerned in the heart's conversion (31–32), and that love is the spring of all good in man

(33-40), which, however, we have only because God first loved us (38), and which is certainly greater than knowledge, although the Pelagians admit only the latter to be from God (40). God's sovereign government of men's wills is then proved from Scripture (41-43), and the wholly gratuitous character of grace is illustrated (44), while the only possible theodicy is found in the certainty that the Lord of all the earth will do right. For, though no one knows why He takes one and leaves another, we all know that He hardens judicially and saves graciously,-- that He hardens none who do not deserve hardening, but none that He saves deserve to be saved (45). The treatise closes with an exhortation to its prayerful and repeated study (46).

The Treatise " On Rebuke and Grace."

The one request that Augustine made, on sending the treatise *On Grace and Free-Will* to Valentinus, was that the monk Florus, through whom the controversy had arisen, should be sent to him. He wished to converse with him and learn whether he had been misunderstood, or had himself misunderstood Augustine. In due time Florus arrived at Hippo, bringing a letter[1] from Valentinus which thanked Augustine for his "sweet" and "healing" instruction, and introduced Florus as one whose true faith could be confided in. It is very clear, both from Valentinus' letter and from the hints that Augustine gives, that his loving dealing with the monks had borne admirable fruit: "none were cast down for the worse, some were built up for the better."[2] But it was reported to him that some one at the monastery had objected, to the doctrine he had taught them, that "no man, then, ought to be rebuked for not keeping God's commandments ; but only God should be besought that he might keep them."[3] In other words, it was said that if all good was, in the last resort, from God's grace, man ought not to be

---
[1] *Epistle* 216.   [2] *On Rebuke and Grace*, 1.
[3] *Retractations*, ii. 67. Compare *On Rebuke and Grace*, 5 sq.

blamed for not doing what he could not do, but God ought to be besought to do for man what He alone could do : we ought, in short, to apply to the source of power. This occasioned the composition of yet another treatise, that entitled *On Rebuke and Grace*,[1] the object of which was to explain the relations of grace to human conduct, and especially to make it plain that the sovereignty of God's grace does not supersede our duty to ourselves or to our fellow-men.

The treatise begins by thanking Valentinus for his letter and for sending Florus (whom Augustine finds well instructed in the truth), praising God for the good effect of the previous book, and recommending its continued study. This is followed by a brief exposition of the catholic faith concerning grace, free-will and the law (1-2). The general proposition that is defended is that the gratuitous sovereignty of God's grace does not supersede human means for obtaining and continuing it (3 sq.). This is shown by the apostle's example, who used all human means for the prosecution of his work and yet confessed that it was " God that gave the increase" (3). Objections are then answered (4 sq.),—especially the great one that " it is not my fault if I do not do what I have not received grace for doing" (6). To this Augustine replies (7-10) that we deserve rebuke for our very unwillingness to be rebuked, that on the same reasoning the prescription of the law and the preaching of the gospel would be useless, that the apostle's example opposes such a position, and that our consciousness witnesses that we deserve rebuke for not persevering in the right way. From this point an important discussion arises, in this interest, of the gift of perseverance (11-19) and of God's election (20-24). It is taught that no one is saved who does not persevere, and that all who are predestinated or " called according to God's purpose" (Augustine's phrase for what we should name " effectually called")

---

[1] On the importance of this treatise for Augustine's doctrine of predestination, see WIGGERS' *Augustinianism and Pelagianism*, E. T. p. 236, where a sketch of the history of this doctrine in Augustine's writings may be found.

will persevere, and yet that we co-operate by our will in all good deeds and deserve rebuke if we do not. Whether Adam received the gift of perseverance, and, in general, what the difference is between the grace given to him (which was that grace by which he was able to stand) and that now given to God's children (which is that grace by which we are made actually to stand), are next discussed (26-38), with the result of showing the superior greatness of the gifts of grace now to those given before the fall. The necessity of God's mercy at all times and our constant dependence on it, are next vigorously asserted (39-42) : even in the day of judgment, it is declared, if we are not judged " with mercy" we cannot be saved (41). The treatise is brought to an end by a concluding application of the whole discussion to the special matter in hand, *rebuke* (43-49). Seeing that rebuke is one of God's means of working out his gracious purposes, it cannot be inconsistent with the sovereignty of that grace ; for, of course, God predestinates the means with the end (43). Nor can we know, in our ignorance, whether our rebuke is, in any particular case, to be the means of amendment or the ground of greater condemnation. How dare we, then, withhold it? Let it be, however, graduated to the fault, and let us always remember its purpose (46-48). Above all, let us not venture to hold it back, lest we withhold from our brother the means of his recovery, and, as well, disobey the command of God (49).

The Letter to Vitalis.

It was not long afterwards (about 427) that Augustine was called upon to attempt to reclaim an erring Carthaginian friend, Vitalis by name, who had been brought to trial on the charge of teaching that the beginning of faith was not the gift of God but the act of man's own free will (*ex propria voluntatis*). This was essentially the semi-Pelagian position which was subsequently to make so large a figure in history ; and Augustine treats it now as necessarily implying the basal idea of Pelagianism.

In the important letter which he sent to Vitalis,[1] Augustine first argues that his position is inconsistent with the prayers of the church. He, Augustine, prays that Vitalis may come to the true faith; but does not this prayer ascribe the origination of right faith to God? The Church so prays for all men. The priest at the altar exhorts the people to pray God for unbelievers, that He may convert them to the faith; for catechumens, that He may breathe into them a desire for regeneration; for the faithful, that by His aid they may persevere in what they have begun. Will Vitalis refuse to obey these exhortations, because, forsooth, faith is of free will and not of God's gift? Nay, will a Carthaginian scholar array himself against Cyprian's exposition of the Lord's prayer? For certainly Cyprian teaches that we are to ask of God what Vitalis says is to be had of ourselves. We may go farther. It is not Cyprian but Paul who says, "Let us pray to God that we do no evil" (2 Cor. xiii. 7); it is the Psalmist who says, "The steps of man are directed by God" (Ps. xxxvi. 23). "If we wish to defend free will," Augustine urges, "let us not strive against that by which it is made free. For he who strives against grace, by which the will is made free for refusing evil and doing good, wishes his will to remain captive. Tell us, I beg you, how the apostle can say, 'We give thanks to the Father who made us fit to have our lot with the saints in light, who delivered us from the power of darkness and translated us into the kingdom of the Son of His love' (Col. i. 12, 13), if not He, but itself, frees our choice? It is, then, a false rendering of thanks to God, as if He does what He does not do; and he has erred who has said that 'He makes us fit, etc.' 'The grace of God,' therefore, does not consist in the nature of free will, and in law and teaching, as the Pelagian perversity dreams; but it is given for each single act by His will, concerning whom it is written,"—quoting Ps. lxvii. 10.

About the middle of the letter, Augustine lays down

[1] *Epistle* 217.

twelve propositions against the Pelagians, which are important as communicating to us what, at the end of the controversy, he considered the chief points in dispute. " Since, therefore," he writes, " we are catholic Christians : 1. We know that new-born children have not yet done anything in their own lives, good or evil, neither have they come into the miseries of this life according to the deserts of some previous life, which none of them can have had in their own persons ; and yet, because they are born carnally after Adam, they contract the contagion of ancient death by the first birth, and are not freed from the punishment of eternal death (which is contracted by a just condemnation, passing over from one to all), except they are by grace born again in Christ. 2. We know that the grace of God is given neither to children nor to adults according to our deserts. 3. We know that it is given to adults for each several act. 4. We know that it is not given to all men ; and to those to whom it is given, it is not only not given according to the merits of works, but it is not even given to them according to the merits of their will ; and this is especially apparent in children. 5. We know that to those to whom it is given, it is given by the gratuitous mercy of God. 6. We know that to those to whom it is not given, it is not given by the just judgment of God. 7. We know that we shall all stand before the tribunal of Christ, and each shall receive according to what he has done through the body,—not according to what he would have done, had he lived longer,—whether good or evil. 8. We know that even children are to receive according to what they have done through the body, whether good or evil. But according to what ' they have done ' not by their own act, but by the act of those by whose responses for them they are said both to renounce the Devil and to believe in God, wherefore they are counted among the number of the faithful and have part in the statement of the Lord when He says, ' Whosoever shall believe and be baptized, shall be saved.' Therefore also, to those who do not receive this sacrament, belongs what follows, ' But whosoever shall not have believed, shall be damned.' (Mark xvi. 16). Whence these too, as I have said, if they die in that early age, are judged, of course, according to what they have done through the body, i.e., in the time in which they were in the body, when they believe or do not believe by the heart and mouth of their sponsors, when they are baptized or not baptized, when they eat or do not eat the flesh of Christ, when they drink or do not drink His blood,—according to those things, then, which they have done through the body, not according to those which, had they lived longer, they would have done. 9. We know that blessed are the dead that die in the Lord; and that what they would have done had they lived longer is not imputed to them. 10. We know that those that believe, with their own heart, in the Lord, do so by their own free will and choice. 11. We know that we who already believe act with right faith towards those who do not wish to believe, when we pray to God that they may wish it. 12. We know that for those who have believed out of this number, we both ought and are rightly and truly accustomed to return thanks to God, as for his benefits."

Certainly such a body of propositions commends their author to us as Christian both in head and heart: they are admirable in every respect; and even in the matter of the salvation of infants, where he had not yet seen the light of truth, he expresses himself in a way as engaging in its hearty faith in God's goodness as it is honorable in its loyalty to what he believed to be truth and justice. Here his doctrine of the Church ran athwart and clouded his view of the reach of grace; but we seem to see between the lines the promise of the brighter dawn of truth that was yet to come. The rest of the epistle is occupied with an exposition of these propositions, which ranks with the richest passages of the anti-Pelagian writings, and which breathes everywhere a yearning for his correspondent which, we cannot help hoping, proved salutary to his faith.

The Treatise "On Heresies."

It is not without significance, that the error of Vitalis took a semi-Pelagian form. Pure Pelagianism was by this time no longer a living issue. Augustine was himself, no doubt, not yet done with it. The second book of his treatise *On Marriage and Concupiscence*, which seems to have been taken to Italy by Alypius in 421, received at once the attention of Julian and was elaborately answered by him during that same year, in eight books addressed to one of his fellow-recusants named Florus. But Julian was now in Cilicia, and his book was slow in working its way westward. It was found at Rome by Alypius, apparently in 427 or 428, and he at once set about transcribing it for his friend's use. An opportunity arising to send it to Africa before it was finished, he forwarded to Augustine the five books that were ready, with an urgent request that they should receive his immediate attention, and a promise to send the other three as soon as possible. Augustine gives an account of the progress of his reply to them in a letter written to Quodvultdeus, apparently in 428.[1] This deacon was urging Augustine to give the Church a succinct account of all heresies; and Augustine excuses himself from immediately undertaking that task by the press of work on his hands. He was writing his *Retractations*, and had already finished two books of them, in which he had dealt with two hundred and thirty-two of his works. His letters and homilies remained to be examined, and he had given the necessary reading to many of the letters. He was engaged also, he tells his correspondent, on a reply to the eight books of Julian's new work. Working night and day, he had already completed his response to the first three of Julian's books and had begun on the fourth while still expecting the arrival of the last three, which Alypius had promised to send. If he had completed the answer to the five books of Julian which he already had in hand

[1] *Epistle* 224.

before the other three reached him, he might begin the work which Quodvultdeus so earnestly desired him to undertake. In due time, whatever may have been the trials and labors that needed first to be met, the desired treatise *On Heresies* was written (about 428), and the eighty-eighth chapter of it gives us a welcome compressed account of the Pelagian heresy, which may be accepted as the obverse of the account of catholic truth given in the letter to Vitalis.

" To the grace of God, by which we have been predestinated unto the adoption of sons by Jesus Christ unto himself (Eph. i. 5), and by which we are delivered from the power of darkness so as to believe in Him and be translated into His kingdom (Col. i. 13) (wherefore He says, 'No man comes to Me, except it be given him of My Father' [John vi. 66]), and by which love is shed abroad in our hearts (Rom. v. 5), so that faith may work by love," the Pelagians, he tells us, " are to such an extent inimical that they believe that man is able, without it, to keep all the Divine commandments—whereas, if this were true, it would clearly be an empty thing for the Lord to say, ' Without Me ye can do nothing ' (John xv. 5)." " When Pelagius," he adds, " was at length accused by the brethren, because he attributed nothing to the assistance of God's grace towards the keeping of His commandments, he yielded to their rebuke so far as, not indeed to place this grace above free will, but at least to use faithless cunning in subordinating it, saying that it was given to men for this purpose, viz., that they might be able more easily to fulfil by grace what they were commanded to do by free will. By saying, ' that they might be able more easily,' he, of course, wished it to be believed that, although with more difficulty, nevertheless men were able without Divine grace to perform the Divine commands. But they say that the grace of God, without which we can do nothing good, does not exist except in free will, which without any preceding merits our nature received from Him ; and that He adds His aid only that by His law and teaching we may learn what we ought to do, but not that by the gift of His Spirit we may do what we have learned ought to be done. Accordingly, they allow that knowledge, by which ignorance is banished, is divinely given to us, but deny that love, by which we may live a pious life, is given; so that, forsooth, while knowledge, which without love puffeth up, is the gift of God, love itself, which edifieth so that knowledge may not puff up, is not the gift of God (1 Cor. viii. 11). They also destroy the prayers which the Church offers, whether for those that are unbelieving and resist God's teaching, that they may be converted to God; or for the faithful, that faith may be increased in them and they may persevere in it. For they contend that men do not receive these things from Him but we have them from ourselves, saying that the grace of God by which we are freed from impiety is given according to our merits. Pelagius was, no doubt, compelled to condemn this by his fear of being condemned by the episcopal judgment in Palestine; but he is found to teach it still in his later writings. They also go so far as to say that the life of the righteous in this world is without sin, and the Church of Christ is perfected by them in this mortality to the point of being entirely without spot or wrinkle (Eph. v. 27); as if it were not the Church of Christ, that, in the whole world, cries to God, ' Forgive us our debts.' They also deny that children, who are carnally born after Adam, contract the contagion of ancient death from their first birth. For they assert that they are so born without any bond of original sin, that there is absolutely nothing that ought to be remitted to them in the second birth; yet they are to be baptized, but only that, adopted in regeneration, they may be admitted to the kingdom of God, and thus be translated from good into better,—not that they may be washed by that renovation from any evil of the old bond. For although they be not baptized, they promise to them, outside the kingdom of God indeed, but nevertheless, a certain eternal and blessed life of their own. They also say that Adam himself, even had he not sinned, would have died in the body, and that this death would not have come as a penalty to a fault, but as a condition of nature. Certain other things also are objected to them, but these are the chief, and moreover either all, or nearly all, the others may be understood to depend on these."

The Treatise "On the Predestination of the Saints."

The composition of the work *On Heresies* was not, however, the only interruption which postponed the completion of the second elaborate work against Julian. It was in the providence of God that the later energies of this great leader in the battle for grace should be expended in dealing with the subtler forms of error, as exhibited in semi-Pelagianism. We have seen his attention being already called to modifications of Pelagianism of this sort. And now information as to the rise of this new form of the heresy at Marseilles and elsewhere in Southern Gaul was conveyed to him along with entreaties that, as "faith's great patron," he would give his aid towards meeting it, by two laymen with whom he had already had correspondence,—Prosper and Hilary.[1]

They pointed out[2] the difference between the new party and thoroughgoing Pelagianism; but, at the same time, the essentially Pelagianizing character of its formative elements. Its representatives were ready, as a rule, to admit that all men were lost in Adam, and that no one could recover himself by his own free will but all needed God's grace for salvation. But they objected to the doctrines of prevenient and of irresistible grace; and they asserted that man could initiate the process of salvation by turning first to God, and that all men could resist God's grace and no grace could be given which they could not reject; and especially they denied that the gifts of grace came irrespective of merits, actual or foreseen. They affirmed that what Augustine taught as to the calling of God's elect ac-

[1] Compare *Epistles* 225, 1, and 156. It is, of course, not certain that this is the same Hilary that wrote to Augustine from Sicily, but it seems probable.
[2] *Letters* 225, and 226.

cording to His own purpose was tantamount to fatalism, was contrary to the teaching of the fathers and the true Church doctrine, and, even if true, should not be preached, because of its tendency to drive men into indifference or despair. Hence, Prosper especially desired Augustine to point out the dangerous nature of these views, and to show that prevenient and co-operating grace is not inconsistent with free will, that God's predestination is not founded on foresight of receptivity in its objects, and that the doctrines of grace may be preached without danger to souls.

Augustine's answer to these appeals was a work in two books, *On the Predestination of the Saints*, the second book of which is usually known under the separate title of *The Gift of Perseverance*.

The former book begins with a careful discrimination of the position of his new opponents. They have made a right beginning in that they believe in original sin and acknowledge that none are saved from it save by Christ, and that God's grace leads men's wills, and without grace no one can suffice for good deeds. These things will furnish a good starting-point for their progress to an acceptance of predestination also (1-2). The first question that needs discussion in such circumstances is, whether God gives the very beginnings of faith (3 sq.). They admit that what Augustine had previously urged suffices to prove that faith is the gift of God so far as that the increase of faith is given by Him; but they deny that it will prove that the beginning of faith may not be understood to be man's, to which, then, God adds all other gifts (compare 43). Augustine insists that this contention is no other than a repetition of the Pelagian assertion of grace according to merit (3), that it is opposed to Scripture (4-5), and that it begets arrogant boasting in ourselves (6). He replies to the charge that he had himself once held this view, by confessing it, and explaining that he was converted from it by 1 Cor. iv. 7, as applied by Cyprian (7-8); and he then expounds that verse as containing in its narrow compass a sufficient answer to the present theories (9-11). He answers, further, the objection that the apostle distinguishes faith from works, and works alone are meant in such passages, by pointing to John vi. 28, and similar statements in Paul (12–16). Then he answers the objection that he himself had previously taught that God acted on foresight of faith, by showing that he was misunderstood (17–18). He next shows that no objection lies against predestination that does not lie with equal force against grace (19–22),—since predestination is nothing but God's foreknowledge of and preparation for grace, and all questions of sovereignty and the like belong to grace. Did God not know to whom He was going to give faith (19)? Or did He promise the results of faith, works, without promising the faith without which, as going before, the works were impossible? Would not this place God's fulfilment of His promise out of His power, and make it depend on man (20)? Why are men more willing to trust in their weakness than in God's strength? Do they count God's promises more uncertain than their own performance (22)? He next proves the sovereignty of grace, and of predestination which is but the preparation for grace, by the striking examples of infants, and, above all, of the human nature of Christ (23–31), and then speaks of the twofold calling, one external and one " according to purpose,"—the latter of which is efficacious and sovereign (32–37). In closing, the semi-Pelagian position is carefully defined and refuted as opposed, alike with the grosser Pelagianism, to the Scriptures of both Testaments (38–42).

The Treatise " On the Gift of Perseverance."

The purpose of the second book, which has come down to us under the separate title of *On the Gift of Perseverance*, is to show that that perseverance which endures to the end is as much of God as the beginning of faith, and that no man who has been " called according to God's purpose" and has received this gift, can fall from grace and be lost.

The first half of the treatise is devoted to this theme (1–33). It begins by distinguishing between temporary perseverance which endures for a time, and that perseverance which continues to the end (1), and by affirming that the latter is certainly a gift of God's grace, and is, therefore, asked from God : which would otherwise be but a mocking petition (2-3). This, the Lord's Prayer itself might teach us, as under Cyprian's exposition it does teach us,—each petition being capable of being read as a prayer for perseverance (4-9). Of course, moreover, it cannot be lost; otherwise it would not be " to the end." If man forsakes God, of course it is he that does it; and he is doubtless under continual temptation to do so. But if man abides with God, it is God who secures that, and God is equally able to *keep* one when drawn to Him, as He is to *draw* him to Him (10-15). He argues anew at this point, that grace is not according to merit but always in mercy ; and explains and illustrates the unsearchable ways of God in His sovereign but merciful dealing with men (16-25). He closes this part of the treatise with a defence of himself against adverse quotations from his early work on *Free Will*, which he has already corrected in his *Retractations*.

The second half of the book discusses the objections that were being urged against the preaching of predestination (34-62), as if it opposed and enervated the preaching of the Gospel. He replies that Paul and the apostles, and Cyprian and the fathers, preached both together ; that the same objections will lie against the preaching of God's foreknowledge and grace itself, and, indeed, against preaching any of the virtues, as, e.g., obedience, while declaring them God's gifts. He meets the objections in detail, and shows that such preaching is food to the soul and must not be withheld from men ; but he explains that it must be given gently, wisely, and prayerfully. The whole treatise ends with an appeal to the prayers of the Church as testifying that all good is from God (63-65), and to the great example of unmerited grace and sovereign predestination in the choice of one human nature without preceding merit, to be united in one person with the Eternal Word,—an illustration of his theme of the gratuitous grace of God which he is never tired of adducing (66–67).

The "Unfinished Work" against Julian.

These books were written in 428–429, and after their completion the unfinished work against Julian was resumed. Alypius had sent the remaining three books, and Augustine slowly toiled on to the end of his reply to the sixth book. But he was to be interrupted once more, and this time by the most serious of all interruptions. On the 28th of August, 430, while the Vandals were thundering at the gates of Hippo, he turned his face away from the strifes of earth—whether theological or secular—and full of faith and of good works entered into rest with the Lord whom he loved. The last work against Julian was already one of the most considerable in size of all his books, but it was never finished and retains until to-day the significant title of *The Unfinished Work*. Augustine had hesitated to undertake this treatise, because he found Julian's arguments too vapid either to deserve refutation or to afford occasion for really edifying discourse. Certainly the result falls below Augustine's usual level; and this can scarcely be due, as is so often said, to failing powers and great age, since nothing that he wrote surpasses in mellow beauty and chastened strength the two books *On the Predestination of the Saints*, which were written after four books of this work were completed.

The plan of the work is to state Julian's arguments in his own words, and to follow these with remarks. It thus takes on something of the form of a dialogue. It follows Julian's work, book by book. The first book states and answers certain calumnies which Julian had brought against Augustine and the catholic faith on the ground of their confession of original sin. Julian had argued that, since God is just, He cannot impute another's sins to innocent infants; since sin is nothing but evil will, there can be no sin in infants who are not yet in the use of their will; and, since the freedom of will that is given to man consists in the capacity of both sinning and not sinning, free will is denied to those who attribute sin to nature. Augustine replies to these arguments, and answers certain objections that are made to his work *On Marriage and Concupiscence*, and then corrects Julian's false explanations of certain Scriptures from John viii., Rom. vi., vii., and 2 Timothy. The second book is a discussion of Rom. v. 12, which Julian had tried, like the other Pelagians, to explain of the "imitation" of Adam's bad example. The third book examines the abuse by Julian of certain Old-Testament passages—in Deut. xxiv., 2 Kings xiv., Ezek. xviii.—in his effort to show that God does not impute the father's sins to the children; as well as his similar abuse of Heb. xi. The charge of Manicheism, which was so repetitiously brought by Julian against the catholics, is then examined and refuted. The fourth book treats of Julian's strictures on Augustine's treatise *On Marriage and Concupiscence* ii. 4-11, and proves from 1 John ii. 16 that concupiscence is evil, and not the work of God but of the Devil. Augustine argues that the shame that accompanies it is due to its sinfulness, and that there was none of it in Christ; also, that infants are born obnoxious to the first sin, and that the corruption of their origin is proved by Wisd. x. 10, 11. The fifth book defends *On Marriage and Concupiscence* ii. 12 sq., and argues that a sound nature could not feel shame on account of its members, and that regeneration is needed for what is generated by means of shameful concupiscence. Then Julian's abuse of 1 Cor. xv., Rom. v., Matt. vii. 17 and 33, with reference to *On Marriage and Concupiscence* ii. 14, 20, 26, is discussed; and then the origin of evil and God's treatment of evil in the world are examined. The sixth book traverses Julian's strictures on *On Marriage and Concupiscence* ii. 34 sq., and argues that human nature was changed for the worse by the sin of Adam, and thus was made not only sinful but the source of sinners; and that the forces of free will by which man could at first do rightly if he wished and refrain from sin if he chose, were lost by Adam's sin. An attack is made upon Julian's definition of free will as "the capacity for sinning or not sinning" (*possibilitas peccandi et non peccandi*); and it is shown that the evils of this life are the punishment of sin,—including, first of all, physical death. At the end, 1 Cor. xv. 22 is treated.

Although the great preacher of grace was taken away by death before the completion of this book, yet his work was not left incomplete. In the course of the next year (431) the Œcumenical Council of Ephesus condemned Pelagianism for the whole Christian world; and an elaborate treatise against the pure Pelagianism of Julian was in 430 already an anachronism. Semi-Pelagianism was yet to run its course, and to work its way to a permanent position in the heart of a corrupt church; but pure Pelagianism was to abate with the first generation of its advocates. As a leaven it will, of course, persist as long as an evil heart of unbelief persists among men: but under the leadership of Augustine the Church for all time found its bearings with reference to it, and henceforth it must needs assume subtler forms to menace the dominion of the doctrines of grace. As we look back now through the almost millennium and a half of years that have intervened since Augustine lived and wrote, it is to his *Predestination of the Saints,*—a completed, and well-completed, treatise, dealing with one of these subtle forms of the great error for the confutation of which he had expended so much of time and strength,—and not to *The Unfinished Work,* which was still engaged with its gross form, that we look as the crown and completion of his labors in behalf of the grace of God.

The Theology of Grace.

THE theology which Augustine opposed to the errors of Pelagianism is, briefly, the theology of grace. The roots of this theology were deeply planted in his own experience and the teaching of Scripture, especially in the teaching of that apostle whom he delights to call "the great preacher of grace," and to follow hard after whom was his great desire. The grace of God in Jesus Christ, conveyed to us by the Holy Spirit and evidenced by the love which He sheds abroad in our hearts, is the centre about which his whole system revolves.[1] As over against the Pelagian exaltation of nature, he was never weary of glorifying grace. And this high conception the more naturally became the centre of his soteriology because of its harmony with the primal principle of his whole thinking, which was theocentric and grew out of his idea of God as the immanent and vitalizing spirit in whom all things live, and move, and have their being.[2] That God is the ab-

---

[1] For the relation of AUGUSTINE's doctrine of the Church to his doctrine of grace, and the primacy of the latter in his thought, see the first two essays in REUTER's *Augustinische Studien :* "In his later years it was not the idea of the Church as the institute of grace, but that of predestinational grace that was the dominating one"; "the doctrine of predestinational grace is the fundamental datum of his religious consciousness ; it must be unconditionally maintained, and all else must yield to it" (p. 102). The ecclesiastical element was the traditional element in his teaching; but as THOMASIUS points out (*Dogmengeschichte*, i. 495) both experience and Scripture stood with him above tradition. Accordingly HARNACK tells us truly (*Dogmengeschichte* iii. 87, 89): "No Western theologian before him had so lived in the Scriptures or had drawn so much from the Scriptures as he;" and "as no Church father before him, he brought the practical element into the foreground."

[2] It is inexplicable how Professor ALLEN, in his *Continuity of Christian Thought*, can speak of the Augustinian theology as resting "upon the transcendence of Deity as its controlling principle" (p. 3), which is explained as "a tacit assumption of deism" (p. 171). A. DORNER (*Augustinus : sein theologisches System*, etc.) also finds deistic implications in certain elements of Augustine's thought. Any tendency to error in Augustine's conception of God lay, however,

solute good, and nothing is good but God and what comes from Him, so that only as God makes them good may men do good, was the foundation-stone of all his theology. His doctrine of grace appears as but a specific application of this broad doctrine.

The *necessity of grace* Augustine argued from the condition of the race as sharers in Adam's sin. God created man upright and endowed him with human faculties, including free will;[1] and gave to him freely that grace by which he was able to retain his uprightness.[2] Being thus put on probation,[3] with divine aid to enable him to stand if he chose, Adam perversely used his free choice for sinning and involved his whole race in his fall. It was on account of this sin that he died spiritually and physically; and this double death passes over from him to us.[4] That all his descendants by ordinary generation are partakers in Adam's guilt and condemnation, Augustine is sure from the teachings of Scripture. This is the fact of original sin from which no one generated from Adam is free, and from which no one is freed save as regenerated in Christ.[5] But how we are made partakers of it, he is less certain. Sometimes he speaks as if it came by some mysterious unity of the race, so that we were all personally present in the individual Adam and thus the whole race was the one man that sinned;[6] sometimes he speaks more in the sense of modern realists, as if Adam's sin corrupted the nature, and the nature now corrupts those to whom it is communicated;[7] sometimes he speaks as if it were due to simple heredity.[8] More characteris-

in precisely the opposite direction. Compare AUBREY MOORE, *Lux Mundi*, p. 83, and LEVI L. PAINE, *The New World*, December, 1895 (iv. 670-673).
[1] *On Rebuke and Grace*, 27, 28.
[2] *Ibid.*, 29, 31, sq.
[3] *Ibid.*, 28.
[4] *On the City of God*, xiii. 2, 12, 14; *On the Trinity*, iv. 13.
[5] *On the Merits and Remission of Sins*, i. 15, and often.
[6] *Against Two Letters of the Pelagians*, iv. 7; *On the Merits and Forgiveness of Sins*, iii. 14, 15.
[7] *On Marriage and Concupiscence*, ii. 57; *On the City of God*, xiv. 1.
[8] *Against Two Letters of the Pelagians*, iv. 7.

tically he speaks as if it depended on the presence of shameful concupiscence in the act of procreation, so that the propagation of guilt depends on the propagation of offspring by means of concupiscence.¹ However transmitted, it is yet a fact that sin is propagated, and all mankind became sinners in Adam. The result is that we have lost the divine image, though not in such a sense that no lineaments of it remain to us.² And, the sinning soul making the flesh corruptible, our whole nature is corrupted, and we are unable to do anything of ourselves truly good.³

This corruption includes, of course, an injury to our will. Augustine, writing for the popular eye, treats this subject in popular language. But it is clear that in his thinking he distinguished between will as a faculty and will in a broader sense. As a mere faculty, will is and always remains an indifferent thing.⁴ After the fall, as before, it continues poised in indifferency, and ready, like a weathercock, to be turned whithersoever the breeze that blows from the heart ("will," in the broader sense) may direct.⁵ It is not the faculty of willing, but the man who makes use of that faculty, that has suffered change from the fall. In paradise man stood in full ability. He had the *posse non peccare*, but not yet the *non posse peccare ;*⁶ that is, he was endowed with a capacity for either part, and possessed the grace of God by which he was able to stand if he would, but also the power of free will by which he might fall if he would. By his fall he has suffered a change, is become corrupt, and has fallen under the power of Satan. His will (in the broader sense) is now injured, wounded, diseased, enslaved—although the faculty of will (in the narrow sense) remains indifferent. Augustine's criticism of Pelagius' discrimina-

---
¹ *On Original Sin,* 42 ; *On Marriage and Concupiscence,* ii. 15.
² *Retractations,* ii. 24.
³ *Against Julian,* iv. 3, 25, 26. Compare THOMASIUS' *Dogmengeschichte,* i. 501 and 507.
⁴ *On the Spirit and Letter,* 58.
⁵ *On the Merits and Forgiveness of Sins,* ii. 30.
⁶ *On Rebuke and Grace,* 11.

tion[1] of "capacity" (*possibilitas, posse*), "will" (*voluntas, velle*) and "act" (*actio, esse*), does not turn on the discrimination itself, but on the incongruity of placing the *power, ability* in the mere capacity or possibility, rather than in the living agent who "wills" and "acts." He himself adopts an essentially similar distribution, with only this correction.[2] He thus keeps the faculty of will indifferent, but places the power of using it in the active agent, man. According, then, to the character of the *man*, will the use of the free will be. If the man be holy he will make a holy use of it, and if he be corrupt he will make a sinful use of it: if he be essentially holy, he (like God Himself) cannot make a sinful use of his will; and if he be enslaved to sin, he cannot make a good use of it. The last is the present condition of men by nature. They have free will;[3] the faculty by which they act remains in indifferency, and they are allowed to use it just as they choose. But such as they cannot desire and therefore cannot choose anything but evil;[4] and therefore they, and therefore their choice, and therefore their willing, is always evil and never good. They are thus the slaves of sin, which they obey; and while their free will avails for sinning, it does not avail for doing any good unless they be first freed by the grace of God. The superior depth of Augustine's view and its essential harmony with fact are apparent; if "the will" be conceived as simply the whole man in the attitude of willing, it would seem to be immediately evident that, however abstractly free the "will" is, it is conditioned in all its action by the character of the willing agent: a bad man does not cease to be bad in the act of willing, and a good man remains good even in his acts of choice.

In its *nature*, grace is assistance, help from God; and all divine aid may be included under the term—as well

[1] *On the Grace of Christ*, 4 sq.
[2] *On the Predestination of the Saints*, 10.
[3] *Against Two Letters of the Pelagians*, i. 5; *Epistle* 215, 4 and often.
[4] *Against Two Letters of the Pelagians*, i. 7; compare i. 5, 6.

what may be called natural as what may be called spiritual aid.[1] Spiritual grace includes, no doubt, all external help that God gives man for working out his salvation, such as the law, the preaching of the gospel, the example of Christ, by which we may learn the right way. It includes also forgiveness of sins, by which we are freed from the guilt already incurred. But above all it includes that help which God gives by His Holy Spirit, working within not without, by which man is enabled to choose and to do what he is enabled by the teachings of the law, or by the gospel, or by the natural conscience, to see to be right.[2] In this grace are included all those spiritual operations which we call regeneration, justification, perseverance to the end—in a word, all the divine assistance by which, in being made Christians, we are made to differ from other men. Augustine is fond of representing this grace as in essence the writing of God's law (or God's will) on our hearts, so that it appears hereafter as our own desire and wish. Even more prevalently he speaks of it as the shedding abroad of love in our hearts by the Holy Ghost given to us in Christ Jesus. It is, therefore, conceived by him as a change of disposition, by which we come to love and freely choose, in co-operation with God's aid, just the things which hitherto we have been unable to choose because of our bondage to sin. Grace, thus, does not make void free will.[3] It operates through free will, and acts upon it only by liberating it from its bondage to sin—*i.e.*, by liberating the agent that uses the free will, so that he is no longer enslaved by his fleshly lusts and is enabled to make use of his free will in choosing the good. Thus it is only by grace that free will is enabled to act in good part.

But just because grace changes the disposition, and so enables man, hitherto enslaved to sin, for the first time to desire and use his free will for good, it lies in

[1] *Sermon* 26.
[2] *On Nature and Grace*, 62 ; *On the Grace of Christ*, 13 ; *On Rebuke and Grace*, 2 sq.
[3] *On the Spirit and Letter*, 52 ; *On Grace and Free Will*, 1 sq.

the very nature of the case that it is *prevenient*.¹ Also, as the very name imports, it is necessarily *gratuitous* ;² since man is enslaved to sin until it is given, all the merits that he can have prior to it are bad merits and deserve punishment, not gifts of favour. When, then, it is asked, *on the ground of what* grace is given, it can only be answered, "on the ground of God's infinite mercy and undeserved favour."³ There is nothing in man to merit it, and it first gives merit of good to man. All men alike deserve death, and all that comes to them in the way of blessing is necessarily of God's free and unmerited favour. This is true equally of all grace. It is pre-eminently clear of that grace which gives faith, which is the root of all other graces and which is given of God, not to merits of good-will or incipient turning to Him, but of His sovereign good pleasure.⁴ But equally with faith, it is true of all other divine gifts. We may, indeed, speak of "merits of good" as succeeding faith ; but as all these merits find their root in faith, they are but "grace on grace," and men need God's mercy always, throughout this life, and even on the judgment day itself, when, if they are judged without mercy, they must be condemned.⁵ If we ask, then, why God gives grace, we can only answer that it is of His unspeakable mercy. And if we ask why He gives it to one rather than to another, what can we answer but that it is of His will? The *sovereignty* of grace results from its very gratuitousness :⁶ where none deserve it, it can be given only of the sovereign good pleasure of the great Giver—and this is necessarily inscrutable, but cannot be unjust. We can faintly perceive, indeed, some reason why God may be supposed not to have chosen to give His saving grace to all,⁷ or

---

¹ *On the Spirit and Letter*, 60, and often.
² *On Nature and Grace*, 4, and often.
³ *On the Grace of Christ*, 27, and often.
⁴ *Ibid.*, 34, and often.
⁵ *On Grace and Free Will*, 21.
⁶ *Ibid.*, 30, and often.
⁷ *On the Gift of Perseverance*, 16 ; *Against Two Letters of the Pelagians*, ii. 15.

even to the most.[1] But we cannot understand why He has chosen to give it to just the individuals to whom He has given it, and to withhold it from just those from whom He has withheld it. Here we are driven to the apostle's cry, "O the depth of the riches both of the mercy and the justice of God!"[2]

The *effects of grace* are according to its nature. Taken as a whole, it is the recreative principle sent forth from God for the recovery of man from his slavery to sin and for his reformation in the divine image. Considered as to the time of its giving, it is either *operating* or *co-operating*[3] grace, *i.e.*, either the grace that first enables the will to choose the good, or the grace that co-operates with the already enabled will to do the good. It is, therefore, also called either *prevenient* or *subsequent* grace.[4] It is not to be conceived as a series of disconnected divine gifts, but as one unbroken work of God. But we may look upon it in the various steps of its operation in men, as bringing forgiveness of sins, faith, which is the beginning of all good, love to God, progressive power of good working, and perseverance to the end.[5] In any case, and in all its operations alike, just because it is power from on high and the living spring of a new and re-created life, it is *irresistible* and *indefectible*.[6] Those on whom the Lord bestows the gift of faith, working from within, not from without, of course have faith and cannot help believing. Those to whom perseverance to the end is given will assuredly persevere to the end. It is not to be objected to this that many seem to begin well who do not persevere. This also is of God, who has in such cases given great blessings indeed, but not *this* blessing of perseverance to the end. Whatever of good men have, that God has given. And what they have not, why,

[1] *Epistle to Optatus*, 190.
[2] *On the Predestination of the Saints*, 17, 18.
[3] *On Grace and Free Will*, 33, and often.
[4] *On Grace and Free Will*, 17 ; *On the Proceedings of Pelagius*, 34, and often.
[5] Compare THOMASIUS' *Dogmengeschichte*, i. 510.
[6] *On Rebuke and Grace*, 40, 45 ; *On the Predestination of the Saints*, 13.

of course God has not given it. Nor can it be objected that this leaves all uncertain. It is only unknown to us ; but this does not argue uncertainty. We cannot know that we are to have any gift which God sovereignly gives, of course, until it is given ; and we therefore cannot know that we have perseverance unto the end until we actually persevere to the end.[1] But who would call uncertain what God does and knows He is to do, and what man is to do certain? Nor will it do to say that thus nothing is left for us to do. No doubt, all things are in God's hands and we should praise God that this is so, but we must respond to His touch ; and it is just because it is He that is working in us the willing and the doing, that it is worth our while to work out our salvation with fear and trembling. God has not determined the end without determining the appointed means.[2]

Now, Augustine argues, since grace certainly is gratuitous and given to no preceding merits, prevenient and antecedent to all good, and, therefore, sovereign and bestowed only on those whom God selects for its reception—we must, of course, believe that the eternal God has foreknown all this from the beginning. He would be something less than God, had He not foreknown that He intended to bestow this prevenient, gratuitous and sovereign grace on some men, and had He not foreknown equally the precise individuals on whom He intended to bestow it. To foreknow is to prepare beforehand. And this is *predestination*.[3] He argues that there can be no objection to predestination, in itself considered, in the mind of any man who believes in God. What men object to is gratuitous and sovereign grace : and to this no additional difficulty is added by the necessary assumption that it was foreknown and prepared for from eternity. That predestination does not proceed on the foreknowledge of good or of faith,[4] follows from its being noth-

---

[1] *On Rebuke and Grace*, 40.
[2] *On the Gift of Perseverance*, 56.
[3] *On the Predestination of the Saints*, 36 sq.
[4] *On the Gift of Perseverance*, 41 sq., 47.

ing more than the foresight and preparation of grace, which, in its very idea, is gratuitous and not according to any merits, sovereign and according only to God's purpose, prevenient and in order to faith and good works. It is the sovereignty of grace, not its foresight or the preparation for it, which places men in God's hands and suspends salvation absolutely on His unmerited mercy. But just because God is God, of course no one receives grace who has not been foreknown and afore-selected for the gift; and, as much of course, no one who has been foreknown and aforeselected for it, fails to receive it. Therefore the number of the predestinated is fixed, and fixed by God.[1] Is this fate? Men may call God's grace fate if they choose; but it is not fate, but undeserved love and tender mercy, without which none would be saved.[2] Does it paralyze effort? Only to those who will not strive to obey God because obedience is His gift. Is it unjust? Far from it: shall not God do what He will with His own undeserved favour? It is nothing but gratuitous mercy, sovereignly distributed, and foreseen and provided for from all eternity by Him who has selected us in His Son.

Augustine's doctrine of *the means of grace*, *i.e.*, of the channels and circumstances of the conference of grace upon men, is the meeting point of two very dissimilar streams of thought—his doctrine of grace and his doctrine of the Church. Profound thinker as he was, within whose active mind was born an incredible multitude of the richest conceptions, he was not primarily a systematiser, and these divergent streams of thought rather conditioned each the purity of the other's development at this point than were thoroughly harmonized.[3]

---

[1] *On Rebuke and Grace*, 39; compare 14.
[2] *On the Gift of Perseverance*, 29; *Against Two Letters of the Pelagians*, ii. 9 sq.
[3] Says HARNACK (*Dogmengeschichte*, iii. 90): "In conflict with Manicheanism and Donatism, Augustine acquired a doctrine of freedom, of the Church and of the means of grace which has little in common with his experience of sin and grace, and is in open strife with the theological development of this experience (doctrine of predestinational grace). It is possible even to draw out a double theology of

He does not, indeed, bind the conference of grace to the means in such a sense that the grace must be given at the exact time of the application of the means. He does not deny that "God is able, even when no man rebukes, to correct whom He will, and to lead him on to the wholesome mortification of repentance by the most hidden and most mighty power of His medicine."[1] Though the Gospel must be known in order that man may be saved[2] (for how shall they believe without a preacher?), yet the preacher is nothing and the preaching is nothing, but God only that gives the increase.[3] He even has something like a distant glimpse of what has since been called the distinction between the visible and invisible Church. He speaks of men not yet born as among those who are "called according to God's purpose" and therefore of the saved who constitute the Church,[4] and asserts that those who are so called, even before they believe, are "already children of God, enrolled in the memorial of their Father with unchangeable surety."[5] At the same time, he allows that there are many already in the visible Church who are not of it, and who can therefore depart from it. But he teaches that those who are thus lost out of the visible Church are lost because of some fatal flaw in their baptism, or on account of post-baptismal sins; and that those who are of the "called according to the purpose" are predestinated not only to salvation, but to salvation by baptism. Grace is not tied to the means in the sense that it is not conferred save in the means; but it is tied to the means in the sense that it is not conferred without the means. Baptism, for instance, is absolutely necessary for salvation: no exception is allowed except such as save the principle—baptism of blood (martyrdom),[6] and, somewhat grudgingly, bap-

Augustine, an Ecclesiastic and a Doctrine of Grace, and to present the whole in both."
[1] *On Rebuke and Grace*, 1.
[2] *On the Predestination of the Saints*, 17, 18 ; if the gospel is not preached at any given place, it is proof that God has no elect there.
[3] *On the Merits and Forgiveness of Sins*, etc., ii. 37.
[4] *On Rebuke and Grace*, 23.
[5] *Ibid.*, 20.
[6] *On the Soul and its Origin*, i. 11 ; ii. 17.

tism of intention. And baptism, when worthily received, is absolutely efficacious : " if a man were to die immediately after baptism, he would have nothing at all left to hold him liable to punishment." [1] In a word, while there are many baptized who will not be saved, there are none saved who have not been or are not to be baptized ; it is the grace of God that saves, but baptism is a channel of grace in the absence of which none actually receive it. [2]

One of the corollaries that flowed from this doctrine was that by which Augustine was led to assert that all those who died unbaptized, including infants, are finally lost and depart into eternal punishment. He did not shrink from the inference, although he assigned the place of lightest punishment in hell to those who were guilty of no sin but original sin, but who had departed this life without having washed this away in the "laver of regeneration." This is the dark side of his soteriology. But it should be remembered that it was not his theology of grace, but the universal and traditional belief in the necessity of baptism for remission of sins, which he inherited in common with all of his time, that forced it upon him. The theology of grace was destined in the hands of his successors, who have rejoiced to confess that they were taught by him, to remove this stumbling-block also from Christian teaching ; and if not to Augustine, it is to Augustine's theology that the Christian world owes its liberation from so terrible a tenet. Along with the doctrine of the damnation of all unbaptized infants, another stumbling-block also, not so much of Augustinian as of the Church theology inherited by Augustine, has gone. It was not because of his theology of grace or of his doctrine of predestination, that Augustine taught that comparatively few of the human race are saved. It was, again, because as a good churchman of his day he believed that baptism and incorporation into the visible Church were necessary for salvation. And it is

[1] *On the Merits and Forgiveness of Sins*, etc., ii. 46.
[2] On Augustine's teaching as to baptism, see Rev. JAMES FIELD SPALDING'S *The Teaching and Influence of Augustine*, pp. 39 sq.

only because of Augustine's theology of grace, which places man in the hands of an all-merciful Saviour and not in the grasp of a human institution, that men have come to see that, in the salvation of all who die in infancy, the invisible Church of God embraces the majority of the human race—saved not by the washing of water administered by the Church, but by the blood of Christ administered by God's own hand outside of the ordinary channels of His grace.[1] We are indeed born in sin, and those that die in infancy are, in Adam, children of wrath even as others; but God's hand is not shortened by the limits of His Church on earth that it cannot save.

Despite the strong churchly element within the theology of Augustine, the development of which has produced the ecclesiasticism of Romish thought, it must be admitted that, on the side that is presented in the controversy against Pelagianism, it is in its essence distinctly anti-ecclesiastical. Its central thought was the immediate dependence of the individual on the grace of God in Jesus Christ. It made everything that concerned salvation to be of God, and traced the source of all good to Him. "Without me ye can do nothing," is the inscription on one side of it; on the other stands written, "All things are yours." Augustine held that he who builds on a human foundation builds on sand, and founded all his hope on the Rock itself. And there also he founded his teaching; as he distrusted man in the matter of salvation, so he distrusted him in the form of theology. No other of the fathers so conscientiously wrought out his theology from the revealed Word; no other of them so sternly excluded human additions. The subjects of which theology treats, he declares, are such as "we could by no means find out unless we believed them on the testimony of Holy Scripture."[2] "Where Scripture gives no certain testimony," he says, "human presumption must

---

[1] This is shown in the accompanying essay on *The Development of the Doctrine of Infant Salvation*.
[2] *On the Soul and its Origin*, iv. 14.

beware how it decides in favor of either side."[1] " We must first bend our necks to the authority of Scripture," he insists, "in order that we may arrive at knowledge and understanding through faith."[2] And this was not merely his theory, but his practice.[3] No theology was ever, it may be more broadly asserted, more conscientiously wrought out from the Scriptures than that which he opposed to the Pelagians. It is not without its shortcomings. But its errors are on the surface and not of its essence. It came from God, and it leads to God ; and in the midst of the controversies of so many ages it has shown itself an edifice whose solid core is built out of material " which cannot be shaken."

[1] *On the Merits and Forgiveness of Sins*, etc., ii. 59.
[2] *Ibid.*, i. 29.
[3] Compare *On the Spirit and the Letter*, 63.

II.

THE DEVELOPMENT OF THE DOCTRINE OF INFANT SALVATION.

THE DEVELOPMENT OF THE DOCTRINE OF INFANT SALVATION.

THE task which we set before us in this brief paper is not to unravel the tangled skein of the history of opinion as to the salvation of those who die in infancy. We propose to ourselves only the much more circumscribed undertaking of tracing the development of doctrine on this subject. We hope to show that there has been a doctrine as to the salvation of infants, dying such, common to all ages of the Church. And we hope to show that there has taken place with reference to this, as with reference to other doctrines, a progressive correction of crudities in its conception, by which the true meaning and relations of the common teaching have been more and more freed from deforming accretions and its permanent core brought to ever purer expression. As the result of this process, as we hope to show, the Church has found its way to a tolerably complete understanding of the teaching of the Scriptures upon this important subject. Those portions of the Church which have chosen to sit still in the darkness of mediævalism will have advanced, to be sure, but a little way into this fuller and better apprehension. Those portions of the Church which have elected to light their path more or less by the rushlight of reason, rather than by the sun of revelation, have naturally wandered more or less aside from it. But wherever the Word of God has been the constant study of the Church, the darkness of this problem too has measurably given way before its light; and where the apprehension of scriptural truth in general has become most pure, there the depths of this doctrine too have been most thoroughly sounded and its relations most perfectly perceived.

The Patristic Doctrine.

It is fundamental to the very conception of Christianity that it is a remedial scheme. Christ Jesus came to save sinners. The first Christians had no difficulty in understanding and confessing that Christ had come into a world lost in sin to establish a kingdom of righteousness, citizenship in which is the condition of salvation. That infants were admitted into this citizenship they did not question. When the Apologist Aristides, for example, would make known to the heathen how Christians looked upon death, he did not confine himself to saying that "if any righteous person of their number passes away from the world, they rejoice and give thanks to God and follow his body as if he were moving from one place to another," but adds of the infant, for whose birth they (unlike many of the heathen) praised God, "if, again, it chance to die in its infancy, they praise God mightily, as for one who has passed through the world without sins."[1] Nor did those early Christians doubt that the sole gateway into this heavenly citizenship, for infants too, was not the natural birth of the flesh, but the new birth of the Spirit. Communion with God and the inheritance of life had been lost for all alike, and to infants too were restored only in Christ. To Irenæus, for example, it seems appropriate that Christ was born an infant and grew by natural stages into manhood, since, as he

---

[1] HELEN B. HARRIS, *The Newly Discovered Apology of Aristides*, London, 1891, p. 108.

says, "He came to save all by Himself—all, I say, who by Him are born again unto God, infants and children, and boys and young men, and old men," and accordingly passed through every age that He might sanctify all.[1]

Less pure elements, however, entered inevitably into their thought. The ingrained legalism of both Jewish and heathen conceptions of religion, when brought into the Church, quite obscured for a time the doctrines of grace. It seemed for a season almost as if Christ had died in vain, and as if Paul's whole proclamation of a free salvation had borne no fruit. Men persisted in looking for salvation by the works of the law, and found no ground of trust save in their own virtues. In this atmosphere the problem of the death of little children became an insoluble one. Dying before they had acquired merit, either good or bad, it seemed equally impossible to assign to them reward or punishment. Even a Gregory Nazianzen affirmed that they could be "neither glorified nor punished"[2]—that is, probably, that they went into a middle state similar to that taught by Pelagius. A heretical sect arose, called the Hieracitæ from their master Hierax, who, arguing that if one who strives cannot be crowned unless he strives lawfully it would be absurd to crown one who had not striven at all, consigned apparently all children dying before the use of reason to annihilation.[3] Gregory of Nyssa seems to have some such notion floating before his mind, when, at the opening of his treatise, *On Infants' Early*

---

[1] IRENÆUS, *Haer.*, ii., 22, 4, and iii., 18, 7.
[2] Cf. WALL, *Hist. of Infant Baptism.* Ed. 2,.1707, p. 365.
[3] See EPIPHANIUS, *Haer.*, 67 ; AUGUST., *Haer.*, 47 ; and compare SMITH and WACE, *Dictionary of Christian Biography*, iii., 24. It is possible that this heresy extended itself among the sectaries of the Middle Ages, and that it is some such notion as this that PETER THE VENERABLE intends when he accuses "the heretics" (*i.e.*, PETER DE BRUYS and his friends) of "denying that children who have not reached the age of intelligence can be saved by baptism, nor that another person's faith can profit those who cannot use their own, since our Lord says, 'Whosoever shall have believed and shall have been baptized shall be saved.'" Cf. A. H. NEWMAN, *A History of Anti-Pedobaptism*, p. 31.

Death, he speaks of such children as passing out of the world before they even become human.

This treatise, which is probably the most extended discussion of the question from this general point of view which has come down to us from the patristic age, is full of interest. It was written in Gregory's old age, at the request of Hierius, the governor of Cappadocia, and undertakes to solve, for the instruction of that official, the problem of justice which the early death of children raised under the legalistic viewpoint. Gregory begins by asserting the incongruity of imagining such an infant as standing before the judgment-seat of God, and the equal injustice of supposing him to pass at once into the lot of the blessed, without having acquired any merit. With apparently entire unconsciousness of the existence of anything like race-sin, he frankly proceeds in his argument on the assumption that future blessedness belongs of right to human beings who have not forfeited it by personally sinning, and that the infant, dying such, is therefore entitled to its natural happiness. The point of difficulty arises only from the consideration that then those are unjustly dealt with who are required to grow up in this earthly arena and to earn bliss only with difficulty or to lose it through their transgressions. This he attempts to meet by two suggestions. On the one hand, he suggests that though infants enter at once into happiness, they do not at once enter into all the happiness that rewards him who is victor here. "But the soul that has never felt the taste of virtue," he says, "while it may, indeed, remain perfectly free from the sufferings which flow from wickedness, having never caught the disease of evil at all, does nevertheless in the first instance partake only so far in that life beyond as this nurseling can receive ; until the time comes that it has thriven on the contemplation of the truly Existent as on a congenial diet, and, becoming capable of receiving more, takes at will more from that abundant supply of the truly Existent which is offered." By this only gradual participation in bliss he would avoid the injustice of placing one that had acquired no virtue on the

THE PATRISTIC DOCTRINE. 147

same level with him who had borne the heat and burden of the day. On the other hand, he suggests that the reason why God takes some away from the chance of failure here, removing them to certain bliss in their infancy, may be that He owes a debt to their parents' virtue, or that He foresees that the evil to which they would give themselves if left on earth would far exceed that wrought by any actually permitted to remain; or, at all events, he argues, it may be needful to leave some men on earth to sin, that their evil may serve as a foil for the virtue of the righteous, since it is beyond doubt an addition and intensification to the felicity of the good " to have its contrary set against it." We are in little danger of judging Gregory's theodicy successful;[1] but it is doubtless as successful a theodicy as could be wrought out on his premises. If the awards of the future life are to be conceived as distributed strictly according to personal merit, and infants, dying such, are to be esteemed free from sin, it would seem logically unavoidable that we should either suppose them to pass out of existence at death, or, like Pelagius, invent for them a middle place of natural felicity, neither heaven nor hell—or, at the best, like Gregory, less logically but more genially, fancy the Divine Father fitting them gradually for higher things " beyond the veil."

The same ingrained externalism in the conceptions of both Jewish and heathen converts to Christianity wrought, however, in the earliest ages of the Church, more powerfully and permanently another corruption of the Christian idea. The kingdom which Jesus came to found was not of this world, and was not, in its primary idea, an external organization. But it was inevitable that it should soon be identified with the visible Church, and the regeneration which was its door with the baptism by which entrance into the Church was accomplished. Already in Justin and Irenæus the word " regeneration" means "baptism;"

---

[1] The whole discussion can be conveniently read in vol. v. of *The Nicene and Post-Nicene Fathers.* Second series. New York, 1893, pp. 372–381.

and the language of John iii. 5, "Verily, verily, I say unto you, Except a man be born of water and the Spirit he cannot enter into the kingdom of God," was from a very early period uniformly understood to suspend salvation upon water-baptism. How early this doctrine of the necessity of baptism for salvation became the settled doctrine of the Church it is difficult to trace in the paucity of very early witnesses. Tertullian already defends it from objection.[1] The reply of Cyprian and his fellow-bishops to Fidus on the duty of early baptism, and especially his whole argument to Jubianus against the validity of heretical baptism, plainly presuppose it.[2] By this date clearly it was the accepted Church-doctrine; and although its stringency was mitigated in the case of adults by the admission not only of the baptism of blood, but also of that of intention,[3] the latter mitigation was not allowed in the case of infants. The watchword of the Church—first spoken in these exact words, perhaps, by Cyprian in his strenuous opposition to the validity of heretical baptism[4]—*Extra ecclesiam salus non est*, hardened in this sense into an undisputed maxim. The whole Patristic Church thus came to agree that, martyrs excepted, no infant dying unbaptized could enter the kingdom of heaven.

The fairest exponent of the thought of the age on this subject is Augustine, who was called upon to defend it against the Pelagian contention that infants dying unbaptized, while failing of entrance into the kingdom, yet obtain eternal life. His constancy in this controversy has won for him the unenviable title of *durus infantum pater*—a designation doubly unjust, in that not only did he not originate the obnoxious dogma or teach it in its harshest form, but he was even preparing its destruction by the doctrines of grace, of which he was more truly the father. Augustine ex-

[1] *De Bapt.*, c. 12.
[2] *Epistles* lviii. (lxiv.) and lxiii. (lxxii.).
[3] With what limitations may be conveniently read in WALL, *Hist. of Infant Baptism*, ed. 2, 1707, pp. 359 *sq*.
[4] *Epistle* lxiii. (lxxii.), § 21.

pressed the Church-doctrine moderately, teaching, of course, that infants dying unbaptized would be found on Christ's left hand and be condemned to eternal punishment, but also not forgetting to add that their punishment would be the mildest of all, and indeed that they were to be beaten with so few stripes that he could not say that it would have been better for them not to be born.[1] His zeal in the matter turned on his deepest convictions, and the essence of his argument may be exhibited by putting together two or three sentences from one of his polemic writings against the Pelagians. "We must by no means doubt," he says, "that all men are under sin, which came into the world by one man and has passed through unto all men, and from which nothing frees us but the grace of God through our Lord Jesus Christ." "For inasmuch as infants are only able to become His sheep by baptism, it must needs come to pass that they perish if they are not baptized, because they will not have that eternal life which He gives to His sheep." "Let then there be no eternal salvation promised to infants out of our own opinion, without Christ's baptism; for none is promised in that Holy Scripture which is to be preferred to all human authority and opinion."[2] The Pelagian, denying original sin, found it an easy matter to assign to infants, born innocent and taken out of life before their own activities could soil their consciences, a place outside of the kingdom of God, indeed, but also free from punishment. The semi-Pelagians, allowing original sin, were in deeper waters, and seem to have tentatively suggested that the fate of each infant was determined by what God knew it would have done had it lived to years of discretion. Augustine, with his profound conviction of the reality of innate sin and of its guilt before God,[3] could not

[1] Augustine's doctrine is most strongly expressed in *Sermo xiv*. In *De Peccat. Merit.*, c, 21 (xvi.), and *Contra Julian.*, v., 11, he speaks of the comparative mildness of the punishment.
[2] *De Peccat. Merit.*, c. 33 (xxii.), c. 40 (xxvii.).
[3] Mr. H. C. LEA, in his *History of Auricular Confession*, I., 97, adduces a curious instance of the perversity of Monkish thought from ST. ODO of Cluny. Augustine bases the condemnability of infants on their

but contend with all his force against these teachings; he was really striving for the essential doctrines of universal sinfulness and of eternal bliss only through the propitiating work of Christ. Because his doctrine was based on such broad grounds no one could surpass him in the strength of his conviction as to the doom of unbaptized children—*i.e.*, in his view, of children unsaved by Christ. But it is not to Augustine, but to Fulgentius († 533),[1] or to Alcimus Avitus († 523),[2] or to Gregory the Great († 604)[3] that we must go for the strongest expression of the woe of unbaptized infants.

Meanwhile, however, whether through the vigor of Augustine's advocacy or out of the natural and indeed inevitable revulsion of the Christian consciousness in the presence of Pelagian error, the Church had come at length to a fully reasoned reassertion of its primitive and essential faith, that infants, too, need salvation, and

---

original sin, and he sometimes accounts for the transmission of sin by the presence of concupiscence in the act of procreation. Odo, without more ado, traces the condemnability of infants to the sinfulness of conjugal intercourse! Since such infants are certainly not punished for guilt of their own, he argues, it is clear that they are punished for that sin by which they are conceived; "if, therefore," he continues, "the sin in conjugal intercourse is so great that an infant for that alone ought to be punished . . ."

[1] *E.g.*, *De Fide ad Petr.*, c. 27 : "It is to be most firmly held, and by no means doubted, that not only men already in the use of reason, but also children, whether they begin to live in their mother's womb and there die, or pass from this world after being born from their mothers without the sacrament of baptism, are to be punished with the everlasting penalty of eternal fire; because although they had no sin of their own committing, they nevertheless incurred by their carnal conception and nativity the damnation of original sin."

[2] *E.g.*, *Ad Fuscinam Sororem :*

"Omnibus id vero gravius, si forte lavacri
Divini expertem tenerum mors invidia natum
Præpitat, dura generatum sorte Gehennæ.
Qui mox, ut matris cessavit filius esse,
Perditionis erit ; tristes tunc edita nolunt
Quæ flammis tantum genuerunt pignora matres."

[3] *E.g.*, *Expos. in Job*, i. 16. Such phrases as these meet us in Gregory's writings : "Those who have done nothing here of themselves, but have not been freed by the sacraments of salvation, enter there into torments ;" "It is perpetual torment which those receive who have not sinned of their own proper will at all." (*Moralium*, ix., xii.).

none of any age enters life save through the saving work of Christ. This is the fundamental thought of the patristic age in the matter, to which only a form was given by its belief that saving grace came only through baptism. There were some outside Pelagian circles, like Gregory of Nazianzus, who sought for those who die in infancy unbaptized an intermediate place, neither salvation nor retribution. But probably, with the exception of Gregory of Nyssa, only such anonymous objectors as those whom Tertullian confutes,[1] or such obscure and erratic individuals as Vincentius Victor whom Augustine convicts, in the whole patristic age, doubted that the kingdom of heaven was closed to all infants departing this life without the sacrament of baptism. And now Augustine's scourge had driven out the folly of imaging an eternity of bliss for men outside the kingdom of heaven and apart from the salvation of Christ.

The Mediæval Mitigation.

If the general consent of a whole age as expressed by its chief writers, including the leading bishops of Rome, and by its synodical decrees, is able to determine a doctrine, certainly the Patristic Church transmitted to the Middle Ages as *de fide* that infants dying unbaptized (with the exception only of those who suffer martyrdom) are not only excluded from heaven but doomed to hell. Accordingly the mediæval synods so define. The second Council of Lyons and the Council of Florence declare that "the souls of those who pass away in mortal sin or in original sin alone descend immediately to hell, to be punished, however, with unequal penalties." On the maxim that *gradus non mutant speciem* we must adjudge Petavius'[2] unanswerable, when he argues that this deliverance determines the punishment of unbaptized infants to be the same in kind (in the same hell) with that of adults in mortal

[1] *De Bapt.*, c. 12.
[2] PETAVIUS, *Dog. Theol.*, ed. Paris, 1865, ii., 59 *sq.*

sin : "So infants are tormented with unequal tortures of fire, but are tormented nevertheless."

Nevertheless scholastic thought on the subject was characterized by a successful effort to mollify the harshness of the Church-doctrine, under the impulse of the prevalent semi-Pelagian conception of original sin. The whole troup of schoolmen unite in distinguishing between *pœna damni* and *pœna sensus*, and in assigning to infants dying unbaptized only the former —*i.e.*, the loss of heaven and of the beatific vision—and not the latter—*i.e.*, positive torment. They differ among themselves only as to whether this *pœna damni*, which alone is the lot of infants, is accompanied by a painful sense of the loss (as Lombard held), or is so negative as to involve no pain at all, either external or internal (as Aquinas argued). So complete a victory was won by this mollification that perhaps only a single theologian of eminence can be pointed to who ventured still to teach the doctrine of Augustine and Gregory— Gregory Ariminensis thence called *tortor infantum;* and Hurter reminds us that even he did not dare to teach it definitively, but only submitted it to the judgment of his readers.[1] Dante, whom Andrew Seth not unjustly calls "by far the greatest disciple of Aquinas," has enshrined in his immortal poem the leading conception of his day, when he pictures the "young children innocent, whom Death's sharp teeth have snatched ere yet they were freed from the sin with which our birth is blent," as imprisoned within the brink of hell, "where the first circle girds the abyss of dread," in a place where "there is no sharp agony" but "dark shadows only," and whence "no other plaint rises than that of sighs which from the sorrow without pain arise."[2] The novel doctrine attained papal authority by a decree of Innocent III. (c. 1200), who determined "the penalty of original sin to be the lack of the vision

---

[1] Hurter, *Theolog. Dogmat. Compend.*, 1878, iii., p. 516 : Tract. x., cap. iii., § 729. Wycliffe must be added ; but he stands out of the mass.

[2] *Hell*, iv., 23 *sq.*; *Purgatory*, vii., 25 *sq.*; *Heaven*, xxxii., 76 *sq.* (Plumptre's translation).

of God, but the penalty of actual sin to be the torments of eternal hell."

A more timid effort was also made in this period to modify the inherited doctrine by the application to it of a development of the baptism of intention. This tendency first appears in Hincmar of Rheims († 882), who, in a particularly hard case of interdict on a whole diocese, expresses the hope that "the faith and godly desire of the parents and godfathers" of the infants that had thus died unbaptized, "who in sincerity desired baptism for them but obtained it not, may profit them by the gift of Him whose Spirit (which gives regeneration) breathes where it pleases." It is doubtful, however, whether he would have extended this lofty doctrine to any less stringent case.[1] Certainly no similar teaching is met with in the Church, except with reference to the peculiarly hard case of still-born infants of Christian parents. The schoolmen (*e.g.*, Alexander Hales and Thomas Aquinas) admitted a doubt whether God may not have ways of saving such unknown to us. John Gerson, in a sermon before the Council of Constance, presses the inference more boldly.[2] God, he declared, has not so tied the mercy of His salvation to common laws and sacraments, but that without prejudice to His law He can sanctify children not yet born, by the baptism of His grace or the power of the Holy Ghost. Hence, he exhorts expectant parents to pray that if the infant is to die before attaining baptism, the Lord may sanctify it ; and who knows, he says, but that the Lord may hear them? He adds, however, that he only intends to suggest that all hope is not taken away ; for there is no certainty without a revelation. Gabriel Biel († 1495) followed in Gerson's footsteps,[3] holding it to be accordant with God's mercy to seek out some remedy for such infants. This teaching remained, however, without effect on the Church-dogma, although something similar to it was, among men who served God in the way

[1] Cf. WALL, *op. cit.*, p. 371.
[2] *Sermon, De Nat. Mar. Virg.*, consid. 2, col. 33.
[3] In iv., Sect. iv., p. 11.

154   THE DOCTRINE OF INFANT SALVATION.

then called heresy, foreshadowing an even better to come. John Wycliffe († 1384) had already with like caution expressed his unwillingness to pronounce damned such infants as were intended for baptism by their parents, if they failed to receive that sacrament in fact ; though he could not, on the other hand, assert that they were saved.[1] His followers were less cautious, whether in England or Bohemia ; and in this, too, they approved themselves heralds of a brighter day.

The Drift in the Church of Rome.

In the upheaval of the sixteenth century the Church of Rome found her task in harmonizing, under the influence of the scholastic formulas, the inheritance which the somewhat inconsistent past had bequeathed her. Four varieties of opinion sought a place in her teaching. At the one extreme the earlier doctrine of Augustine and Gregory, that infants dying unbaptized suffer eternally the pains of sense, found again advocates, and that especially among the greatest of her scholars, such as Noris, Petau, Diiedo, Conry, Berti. At the other extreme, a Pelagianizing doctrine that excluded unbaptized infants from the kingdom of heaven and the life promised to the blessed, and yet accorded to them eternal life and natural happiness in a place between heaven and hell, was advocated by such great leaders as Ambrosius Catharinus, Albertus Pighius, Molina, Sfondrati. The mass, however, followed the schoolmen in the middle path of *pœna damni*, and, like the schoolmen, differed only as to whether this punishment of loss involved sorrow (as Bellarmine held) or was purely negative.[2] The Council of Trent (1547) anathematized those who affirm that the " sacra-

---

[1] Cf. WALL, as above.
[2] For this classification see BELLARMINE, *De Amiss. Gratiæ*, etc , vi., 1 ; and compare GERHARD, *Loci* (Cotta's ed.), vol. ix., p. 279 ; CHAMIER, *Panstrat. Cath.* (1626), iii., 159 ; or SPANHEIM, *Chamierus Contractus* (1643), p. 797.

ments of the new law are not necessary to salvation, but superfluous ; and that, without them, or without the desire thereof, men obtain of God, through faith alone, the grace of justification ;" or, again, that " baptism is free, that is, not necessary to salvation."[1] This is explained by the Tridentine Catechism to mean that " baptism is necessary to every one without qualification," and that " the law of baptism is prescribed by our Lord to all, insomuch that they, unless they be regenerated to God through the grace of baptism, are born to eternal misery and perdition, whether their parents be Christian or infidel."[2] The Council of Trent thus made it renewedly *de fide* that infants dying unbaptized incur damnation, though it left the way open for discussion as to the kind and amount of their punishment.[3] The ordinary instruction in the Church of Rome has naturally been conformed to this point of view. Thus the *Catechism Prepared and Enjoined by Order of the Third Plenary Council of Baltimore* teaches that " baptism is necessary to salvation, because without it we cannot enter into the kingdom of heaven."[4] Müller's popular *Familiar Explanation of Catholic Doctrine* teaches that " baptism is the most necessary sacrament, because without it no one can be saved ;"[5] words which are repeated by Deharbe.[6] This is ex-

---

[1] SCHAFF'S *Creeds of Christendom*, ii., pp. 120, 123 (Seventh Session, March 3, 1547, Canon iv. on the Sacraments, and Canon v. on Baptism).
[2] *The Catechism of the Council of Trent, Translated into English ; with Notes by* THEODORE ALOIS BUCKLEY, B.A., pp. 150, 174, 175 (Part II., ch. i., *qq.* xvi., xxx., xxxiii.) ; cf. STREITWOLF and KLENER, *Libri Symbolici Eccles. Cath.*, tom. i., pp. 249, 274, 276. On the other hand, we are credibly informed that the council was near anathematizing as a Lutheran heresy the proposition that the penalty for original sin is the fire of hell (so Father PAUL, *Hist. of the Council of Trent*, c. 2).
[3] PERRONE, *Prælect. Theol. in Compend. Redact.*, i., p. 494.
[4] New York : The Catholic Publication Society—with the imprimatur of Cardinal McCloskey, and the approval of Archbishop (now Cardinal) Gibbons, dated April 6th, 1888 : No. 2, Lesson 14 (p. 27).
[5] No. IV., improved ed. New York : Benziger Bros. (1888), p. 309.
[6] *A Full Catechism of the Catholic Religion*, FANDER'S transla-

panded by Schouppe as follows : " This necessity is so absolute that children dying without baptism, though innocent of all actual sin, are excluded forever from heaven, on account of the original stain which they bear upon their souls. Therefore our Lord has permitted them to be baptized as soon as they are born, and has given the utmost facility to the administration of so indispensable a sacrament."[1] " Millions," says Wenham, " are saved with only this sacrament ; but no one is ordinarily saved without it."[2]

It is natural to catch at the word " ordinary" in such a deliverance. And the Tridentine declaration, of course, does not exclude the baptism of blood as a substitute for baptism of water, even for infants. Neither does it seem necessarily to exclude the application of a theory of baptism of intention to infants. Even after it, therefore, an alternative development seems to have been possible. The path already opened by Gerson and Biel might have been followed out, and a baptism of intention developed for infants as well as for adults. This might even have been logically pushed on so as to cover the case of all infants dying in infancy. The principle argued by Richard Hooker,[3] for example, appears reasonable, that the unavoidable failure of baptism in the case of the children of Christians cannot lose them salvation, because of the presumed desire and purpose of baptism for them in their Christian parents and in the Church of God. And it would be to proceed only a single step farther to have said that the desire and purpose of Mother Church to baptize all is intention of baptism enough for all dying in helpless infancy, or even that what has been called the implicit

tion, revised, etc., by Bishop LYNCH, of Charleston. New York : The Catholic Publication Society Co., 1891, p. 248.

[1] *Abridged Course of Religious Instruction*, etc. By the Rev. Father F. X. SCHOUPPE, S. J., new ed., etc. London : Burns & Oates, p. 188.

[2] *The Catechumen*, etc. By J. G. WENHAM, Provost of Southwark. 3d ed. London : St. Anselm's Society, 1892, p. 293.

[3] *Ecclesiastical Polity*, v., ch. 60, (ed. Dobson, I. 605.)

and interpretative faith[1] of their heathen parents may avail for them. Thus on principles agreeable to the general Roman line of thought a salvation for all dying in infancy might have been logically deduced, and infants, as more helpless and less guilty, have been given the preference over adults. On the other hand, it could be argued that as baptism either *in re* or *in voto* must mediate salvation, and as infants by reason of their age are incapable of the intention, they cannot be saved except they receive baptism in fact,[2] and thus infants be discriminated against in favor of adults. It

---

[1] What is meant by this language may be gathered from the following sentences from J. HENRY NEWMAN's *Letter Addressed to His Grace the Duke of Norfolk*, on the infallibility of the Pope: " I have employed myself, in illustration, in framing a sentence which would be plain enough to any priest, but I think would perplex any Protestant. I hope it is not too light to introduce here. We will suppose then a theologian to write as follows : ' Holding, as we do, that there is only *material* sin in those who, being *invincibly* ignorant, reject the truth, therefore in charity we hope that they have the future portion of *formal* believers, as considering that by *virtue* of their good faith, though not of the *body* of the faithful, they *implicitly* and *interpretatively* believe what they seem to deny.' What sense would this statement convey to the mind of a member of some Reformation Society or Protestant League ? He would read it as follows, and consider it all the more insidious and dangerous for its being so very unintelligible : ' Holding, as we do, that there is only a very considerable sin in those who reject the truth out of contumacious ignorance, therefore in charity we hope that they have the future portion of nominal Christians, as considering, that by the excellence of their living faith, though not in the number of believers, they believe without any hesitation, as interpreters [of Scripture ?], what they seem to deny.' " (P. 93.)

[2] Thus, *e.g.*, DOMINICUS DE SOTO expresses it (*De Natura et Gratia*, ii. 10) : " It is most firmly established in the Church that no infant apart from baptism *in re*—since he cannot have it *in voto*—enters the kingdom of heaven." In a more popular form it is put thus (*A Manual of Instruction in Christian Doctrine*, etc., 10th ed. London : St. Anselm's Society. Ed. 3 [1871], p. 282) : " Baptism is absolutely necessary to salvation for all infants, at least wherever the Gospel has been promulgated. . . . Children, therefore, who die unbaptized cannot enter into the beatific vision. . . . The case of adults is somewhat different. For them, when the actual reception of the sacrament is impossible, an act of perfect charity, which includes the desire of it, will suffice for salvation. . . . Again, martyrdom, which is the highest act of charity, has always been held to supply the place of baptism." The book bears the imprimaturs of Cardinals Wiseman and Manning.

was this second path which was actually followed by the theologians of the Church of Rome, with the ultimate result that not only are infants discriminated against in favor of adults, but the more recent theologians seem almost ready to discriminate against the infants of Christians as over against those of the heathen.

This certainly sufficiently remarkable result grows out of the development which has been given in later Romanism to the doctrine of ignorance, and especially of "invincible ignorance," the latter of which was at length authoritatively defined by Pope Pius IX. A very characteristic statement of the nature of this doctrine is to be found in the late Cardinal Newman's *A Letter Addressed to his Grace the Duke of Norfolk* on the infallibility of the Pope. He is illustrating the care with which doctrinal statements should be interpreted. "One of the most remarkable instances of what I am insisting on," he says, "is found in a dogma, which no Catholic can ever think of disputing, viz., that 'Out of the Church, and out of the faith, is no salvation.' Not to go to Scripture, it is the doctrine of St. Ignatius, St. Irenæus, St. Cyprian in the first three centuries, as of St. Augustine and his contemporaries in the fourth and fifth. It can never be other than an elementary truth of Christianity; and the present Pope has proclaimed it as all Popes, doctors, and bishops before him. But that truth has two aspects, according as the force of the negative falls upon the 'Church' or upon the 'salvation.' The main sense is, that there is no other communion or so-called Church but the Catholic, in which are stored the promises, the sacraments and other means of salvation; the other and derived sense is, that no one can be saved who is not in that one and only Church. But it does not follow, because there is no Church but one which has the Evangelical gifts and privileges to bestow, that therefore no one can be saved without the intervention of that one Church. Anglicans quite understand this distinction; for, on the one hand, their article says, 'They are to be had accursed (anathematizandi) that presume

THE DRIFT IN THE CHURCH OF ROME. 159

to say, that every man shall be saved *by* (in) the law or sect which he professeth, so that he be diligent to frame his life by that law and the light of nature;' while on the other hand they speak of and hold to the doctrine of the ' uncovenanted mercies of God.' The latter doctrine in its Catholic form is the doctrine of invincible ignorance—or, that it is possible to belong to the soul of the Church without belonging to its body; and at the end of 1800 years it has been formally and authoritatively put forth by the present Pope (the first Pope, I suppose, who has done so), on the very same occasion on which he has repeated the fundamental principle of exclusive salvation itself. It is to the purpose here to quote his words; they occur in the course of his Encyclical, addressed to the Bishops of Italy, under the date of August 10th, 1863 : ' *We and you know* that those who lie under invincible ignorance as regards our most Holy Religion, and who, diligently observing the natural law and its precepts, which are engraven by God on the hearts of all, and prepared to obey God, lead a good and upright life, are able, by the operation of the power of divine light and grace, to obtain eternal life.' "[1] Thus while an absolute necessity for baptism *in re* is posited for the infants of Christian parents, even though they die in the womb, on the other hand, as the law of baptism is in force only where it is known, and even an ignorance morally invincible (as among sectaries) is counted true ignorance, not even an intention of baptism is demanded of the heathen or of certain sectaries but may be held to be implicit—that is, they may be thought ready to do all that God requires if only they knew it. Among the heathen thus the old remedies for sin are held to be still probably valid, and their " primitive sacraments" are thought to retain their force;[2] and this rule may

[1] *Op. Cit.*, p. 122.
[2] From the theological point of view, GOUSSET, *Théolog. Dogmat.*, 10th ed., Paris, 1866, i., 548, 549, 351, ii.,382, may be profitably consulted on this whole subject. How it is popularly presented may be gathered from the following editorial remarks from *The Catholic Review*, 42, 25 (December 11-17, 1893) : " The truth is that God does not demand what is impossible ; the heathen who have not heard of the Gospel

with some prudence be extended to cover some sectaries. It may be extended also to cover the case of the infants of the heathen, dying such. St. Bernard, for example, is quoted approvingly by Gousset as saying, " Among the Gentiles as many as are found faithful, we believe that the adults are expiated by faith and the sacrifices; but the faith of the parents profits the children, nay, even suffices for them." If the fathers are saved, in other words, why not the children?

Sometimes a very sweeping application is given to this principle, as may be illustrated by a popular exposition of it made a few years ago in the pages of *The London Month*.[1] The writer is oppressed by the thought of the millions of unbaptized children who die annually. On the basis of John iii. 5 he declares that our Lord " excludes from the beatific vision all children who die unbaptized and who do not supply for the baptism of water by the baptism of desire, or the baptism of blood." It may be taken, therefore, as a first principle " that without baptism no little child, under the Christian dispensation, enters the kingdom of heaven." " But," he instructs his readers, " we must not omit to notice that we are speaking of the Christian dispensation and of it alone." God provided for the Jews a sort of anticipation of baptism; and we must suppose that something of the sort existed in the patriarchal age. " How long such traditional offering lasted on outside of the Jewish Covenant we do not know; it may be that during the whole period previous to the coming of our Lord, those who were believers in the true God had the opportunity of obtaining from Him the deliverance of their little children from original

---

will be judged by the light and grace given them. If we, with the Sacraments and the Sacrifice, are so apt to fall into sin, how hard it must be for the pagans to be faithful to natural virtue. Yet some of them, no doubt, have been true to the voice of conscience and are to-day in heaven. Having the disposition to do right, they had the implied desire for baptism, and St. Thomas says that if actual baptism had been essential for their salvation, the Almighty would have sent an angel from heaven to pour the cleansing water on them. They are few, probably, but few or many, they manifest the mercy of God and show that nowhere was salvation made impossible."

[1] *London Month*, February, 1893.

sin, when they offered them to be His, and dedicated them, according to the best of their ability and knowledge, to His service. Nay, we may even hope that in the present day the dwellers in lands where the name of Christ is still unknown may save their children, as they certainly can save themselves, from the eternal loss of God, if they offer their little ones to Him with a recognition of Him as their all-powerful King and Lord." As over against this " wider hope" for the children of the heathen, however, nothing so comforting can be said of the children of the faithful who die unbaptized. A few Catholic theologians may have indulged hope for them; but on insufficient grounds. " Here and there it may be that God, by an extraordinary intervention in behalf of some one of His faithful servants, may grant such a privilege to some favored little one, but only by a very special miracle of grace, and as a rare exception to the general law." And even this meagre comfort is disallowed by most writers, as, indeed, on the basis of the Tridentine decrees it must be. Why, however, the baptism of intention should receive so wide an extension to the heathen, so as to give even the infants of the heathen the benefit of it, and be so inflexibly denied to the infants of Christians, is a question which will not easily receive satisfactory answer.

The application of the baptism of intention to the infants of Christians was not abandoned without some protest from the more tender-hearted. Cardinal Cajetan defended in the Council of Trent itself Gerson's proposition that the desire of godly parents might be taken in lieu of the actual baptism of children dying in the womb.[1] Cassander (1570) encouraged parents to hope and pray for children so dying.[2] Bianchi (1768) holds that such children may be saved *per oblationem pueri quam Deo mater extrinsecus faciat*.[3] Eusebius Amort (1758) teaches that God may be moved by prayer to grant justification to such extra-sacramentally.[4] Even somewhat bizarre efforts have been made to es-

[1] In 3 Part. Thomæ, Q. 68, art. 2, et. 11.
[2] *De bapt. infant.* [3] *De Remedio . . . pro parentis.*
[4] *Theolog. Moral.*, ii., xi., 3.

cape the sad conclusion proclaimed by the Church. Thus Klee holds that a lucid interval is accorded to infants in the article of death, so that they may conceive the wish for baptism.¹ An obscure French writer supposes that they may, " shut up in their mother's womb, know God, love Him, and have the baptism of desire." ² A more obscure German conceives that infants remain eternally in the same state of rational development in which they die, and hence enjoy all they are capable of ; if they die in the womb they either fall back into the original force from which they were produced, or enjoy a happiness no greater than that of trees.³ These protests of the heart have awakened, however, no general response in the Church,⁴ which has preferred to hold fast to the dogma that the failure of baptism in infants, dying such, excludes *ipso facto* from heaven. What the Church of Rome, therefore, teaches as to the fate of infants of Christian parents dying such is, briefly, as follows : " Baptism is necessary as a means of salvation for both infants and adults. This necessity is not such as to exclude exceptions as regards the rite, though not as regards the substance and chief effects, in case actual baptism is impossible. . . . In the case of adults the effect can be obtained by contrition, perfect love of God, with a desire of baptism. . . . In the case of infants who are dead in sin through sharing in the guilt of Adam, and are incapable of making an act of attrition, the only way they can enter the kingdom of heaven is by baptism. . . . As infants are incapable of rational sentiments, their sanctification must be the work of a sacrament, that is, a divinely ordained rite that produces its effect while their souls are passive." ⁵

¹ *Dog*. iii., 2, § 1.
² DE LA MARNE, *Traité metaphysique des Dogmes de la Trinité*, etc., Paris, 1826.
³ HERMESSIUS, *Zeitschr. f. Phil. u. kath. Theol.*, Bonn, 1832.
⁴ Compare VASQUEZ, in 3 P. s. Th., disp. cli., cap. 1 ; HURTER, *op. cit*., 1878, iii., 516 *sq*. ; PERRONE, *Prælect. Theolog*. (1839), vi., 55.
⁵ The Very Rev. WILLIAM BYRNE, D.D., Vicar-General of the Archdiocese of Baltimore, *The Catholic Doctrine of Faith and Morals*, etc., Boston, 1892, pp. 224, 225.

The comfort which is refused from the application of the principle of baptism of intention to infants, is sought by the Church of Rome by mitigating still farther than the scholastics themselves the nature of that *pœna damni* which alone it allows as punishment of original sin. And if we may assume that such writers as Perrone, Hurter, Gousset and Kendrick are typical of modern Roman theology throughout the world, certainly that theology may be said to have come, in this pathway of mitigation, as near to positing salvation for all infants dying unbaptized as the rather intractable deliverances of early Popes and later councils permit to them. As the definitions of Florence and Trent require of them, they all teach, of course, (in the words of Perrone,[1]) " that children of this kind descend into hell, or incur damnation ;" but (as Hurter says [2]), " although all Catholics agree that infants dying without baptism are excluded from the beatific vision, and so suffer *loss*, are *lost* (*pati damnum, damnari*), they yet differ among themselves in their determination of the nature and condition of the state into which such infants pass." As the idea of " damnation" may thus be softened to a mere *failure to attain*, so the idea of " hell" may be elevated to that of a natural *paradise*.[3] Hurter himself is inclined to a somewhat severer doctrine. But Perrone (supported by

---

[1] *Compend.*, 1861, i., 494, No. 585.   [2] *Op. cit.*, No. 729.
[3] What is possible in the Church of Rome in the way of elevating the idea of hell to that of a paradise may be interestingly investigated by reading the notable discussion on *The Happiness in Hell* by Professor ST. GEORGE MIVART and others in *The Nineteenth Century* for December, 1892, and January, February, April, September, and December, 1893. Professor Mivart's language is such as this : " Hell in its widest sense—namely, as including all those blameless souls who do not enjoy the Beatific Vision—must be considered as, for them, an abode of happiness transcending all our most vivid anticipations, so that man's natural capacity for happiness is there gratified to the very utmost ; nor is it even possible for the Catholic theologian of the most severe and rigid school to deny that, thus considered, there is, and there will for all eternity be, a real and true *happiness in hell*" (Dec. 1892, p. 919). Professor Mivart's articles have been placed on the *Index*, and his language is extreme. But it is language which obviously expresses a widespread conviction among Roman teachers. And, indeed, a hell for " blameless souls" could scarcely be more severe.

such great lights as Balmes, Berlage, Oswald, Lessius, and followed not afar off by Gousset and Kendrick) reverts to the Pelagianizing view of Catharinus and Molina and Sfondrati—which Petau called a "fabrication" championed indeed by Catharinus but originated "by Pelagius the heretic," and which Bellarmine contended was *contra fidem*—and teaches that unbaptized infants enter into a state deprived of all supernatural benefits, to be sure, but endowed with all the happiness of which pure nature is capable. Their state is described as having the nature of penalty and of damnation when conceived of relatively to the supernatural happiness from which they are excluded by original sin ; but when conceived of in itself and absolutely, it is a state of pure nature, and accordingly the words of Thomas Aquinas are applied to it : " They are joined to God by participation in natural goods, and so also can rejoice in natural knowledge and love."[1]

Thus, after so many ages, the Pelagian conception of a middle state for infants dying unbaptized has obtained its revenge upon the condemnation inflicted upon it by the Church. To be sure, it is not admitted that this is a return to Pelagianism. Perrone, for example, argues that Pelagius held the doctrine of a natural beatitude for infants as one unrelated to sin, while " Catholic theologians hold it with the death of sin ; so that the exclusion from the beatific vision has the nature of penalty and of damnation proceeding from sin."[2] It may be doubted whether there is more than a verbal difference here. Both Pelagius and the Church of Rome consign infants dying unbaptized to a natural paradise. In deference to the language of fathers and councils and Popes, this natural paradise is formally assigned by Roman theologians to that portion of the other world designated " hell." But in its own nature it is precisely what the Pelagians taught should be the state of unbaptized infants after death. By what expedients such teaching is to be reconciled with the other doctrines of the Church of Rome, or with its former teaching on this same subject, or with its boast

[1] *Compend*, 1861, i., 494, cf. ii., 252.   [2] *Ibid.*, 1861, i., 494, No. 590.

of *semper eadem*, is more interesting to its advocates within that communion than to us.¹ Our interest as historians of opinion is exhausted in simply noting the fact that the Pelagianizing process, begun in the Middle Ages by ascribing to infants guilty only of original sin liability to *pœna damni* alone, culminates in our day in their assignment by the most representative theologians of modern Rome to a natural paradise, which has not been purchased for them by Christ but is their natural right. This is of the very essence of Pelagianism, and logically implies the whole Pelagian system.²

The Lutheran Teaching.

This Pelagianizing drift may no doubt be regarded as in part a reaction from the harshness of the Roman-

¹ See some of the difficulties very mildly stated in HURTER, *loc. cit.*
² It is not necessary to point out, *e.g.*, that such a determination implies a Pelagianizing doctrine of sin. When we make all the happiness of which nature is capable the desert of original sin, there is little to choose between this "doctrine of original sin" and its entire denial. Some Roman writers appear to stand, therefore, on the verge of sending all infants dying such to heaven, despite the explicit teaching of the Church to the contrary. For example, S. J. HUNTER, S.J. (*Outlines of Dogmatic Theology*. New York : Benziger Bros., 1896, vol. iii.) says at p. 229 : " We hold then that, after the promulgation of the Gospel, infants who die without baptism of water or of blood are not admitted to the supernatural vision of God, which constitutes the happiness of heaven ; that in consequence of the sin of Adam they will remain forever deprived of that happiness for which they were destined. But this privation is no injustice to them, for their nature gave them no claim in justice to a supernatural reward ; nor does it imply any unhappiness in them, for they need not be supposed to know what they have lost." And then he adds : " What little can be said concerning the difficult subject of their state will be found in the closing treatise of this volume." But when we turn to the closing treatise of the volume, what we find is this (pp. 441, 442) : "The Catholic doctrine is that hell is the portion of those who leave this life with the guilt of actual mortal sin. If a sin be such that the punishment of hell is more than is deserved by the malice involved, then that sin is not a mortal sin. . . . We have already said what was necessary concerning the lot of infants that die without baptism either of water or of blood, and therefore still under the guilt of original sin, but without actual sin." Thus we are sent back and forth on a fruitless errand—except so far as we gather this : that as hell is for those alone who are burdened with " the guilt of *actual* mortal sin," and as infants dying such are " without actual sin," hell is no place for them. As there is no permanent state of existence between heaven and hell, and infants are excluded from both, where do they go?

1st syllogism, "No man can attain salvation who is not a member of Christ; but no one becomes a member of Christ except by baptism, received either *in re* or *in voto*."[1] So considered, its fault is that it impinges by way of mitigation and modification on the *major* premise; which, however, is the fundamental proposition of Christianity. Its roots are planted, in the last analysis, in a conception of men, not as fallen creatures, children of wrath and deserving of a doom which can only be escaped by becoming members of Christ, but as creatures of God with claims on Him for natural happiness, but, of course, with no claims on Him for such additional supernatural benefits as He may yet lovingly confer on His creatures in Christ. On the other hand, that great religious movement which we call the Reformation, the constitutive principle of which was its revised doctrine of the Church, ranged itself properly against the fallacious *minor* premise, and easily broke its bonds with the sword of the Word. Men are not constituted members of Christ through the Church, but members of the Church through Christ: they are not made the members of Christ by baptism which the Church gives, but by faith, the gift of God; and baptism is the Church's recognition of this inner fact.

The full benefit of this better apprehension of the nature of that Church of God membership in which is the condition of salvation, was not reaped, however, by all Protestants in equal measure. It was the strength of the Lutheran movement that it worked out its positions not theoretically or all at once, but step by step, as it was forced on by the logic of events and experience. But it was an incidental evil that, being compelled to express its faith early, its first confession was framed before the full development of Protestant thought, and subsequently contracted the faith of Lutheranism into too narrow channels. The Augsburg Confession contains the true doctrine of the Church as the *congregatio sanctorum;* but it committed Lutheran-

---

[1] The words are AQUINAS's (p. 3, q. 68, art. 1); see them quoted and applied by PERRONE, *Compend.*, ii., 253.

ism to the doctrine that baptism is necessary to salvation. This it did by teaching that children are not saved without baptism (Art. IX.),[1] inasmuch as the condemnation and eternal death brought by original sin upon all are not removed except from those who are born again by baptism and the Holy Ghost (Art. II.).[2] Surely by this declaration the necessity of baptism is made the necessity of means. And the doctrine of the Augsburg Confession is repeated in the Formula Concordiæ. In this symbol the Anabaptists are condemned because they teach " that infants not baptized are not sinners before God, but just and innocent, and in this their innocence, when they have not as yet the use of reason, may, without baptism (of which, to wit, in the opinion of the Anabaptists they have no need) attain unto salvation. And in this way they reject the whole doctrine of original sin, and all the consequences that follow therefrom." From this it seems clear that to the framers of the Formula it is one of the consequences which follow from original sin that even infants, dying before the use of reason, cannot attain unto salvation without baptism; and this inference is strengthened by the subsequent article which condemns the Anabaptists for teaching " that the children of Christians, on the ground that they are sprung from Christian and believing parents, are in very deed holy, and are to be accounted as belonging to the children of God, even apart from and before the receiving of baptism." Whence it would seem to follow that they

---

[1] " Of baptism they teach that it is necessary to salvation. . . . They condemn the Anabaptists, who allow not the baptism of children, and affirm that children are saved without baptism," "and outside the Church of Christ," as is added in ed. 1540. (SCHAFF, *Creeds of Christendom*, iii., p. 13.)

[2] " Also they teach that, after Adam's fall, all men begotten after the common course of nature are born with sin ; . . . and that this disease of original fault is truly sin, condemning and bringing eternal death now also upon all that are not born again by baptism and the Holy Spirit. They condemn the Pelagians and others who deny this original fault to be sin indeed, and who, so as to lessen the glory of the merits and the benefits of Christ, argue that a man may, by the strength of his own reason, be justified before God" (SCHAFF, *loc. cit.*, p. 81.)

are made holy first and only by baptism.[1] These deliverances have naturally been felt to require some mollifying interpretation, and in this direction the theologians have urged : 1. That the necessity affirmed is not absolute but ordinary, and binds man and not God. 2. That as the assertion is directed against the Anabaptists, it is not the privation but the contempt of baptism that is affirmed to be damning. 3. That the necessity of baptism is not intended to be equalized with that of the Holy Ghost. 4. That the affirmation is not that for original sin alone any one is actually damned, but only that all are therefor damnable. There is force undoubtedly in these considerations. But they obviously do not avail wholly to relieve the Lutheran formularies of limiting salvation to those who enjoy the means of grace, and, as concerns infants, to those who receive the sacrament of baptism.

It is not to be contended, of course, that these formularies assert such an absolute necessity of baptism for infants, dying such, as can admit of no exceptions. From Luther and Melanchthon down, Lutheran theologians have always taught what Hunnius expressed in the Saxon Visitation Articles : " Unless a person be born again of water and the Spirit, he cannot enter into the kingdom of heaven. *Cases of necessity are not intended, however, by this."* [2] Lutheran theology, in other words, has taken its stand positively on the ground of baptism of intention as applied to infants, as over against its denial by the Church of Rome. " Luther," says Dorner,[3] " holds fast, in general, to the necessity of baptism in order to salvation, but in reference to the children of Christians who have died unbaptized, he says : ' The Holy and Merciful God will think kindly of them. What He will do with them He has revealed to no one, that baptism may not be despised, but has reserved to His own mercy ; God does wrong to no man.' "[4] From the fact that Jewish children dying be-

---

[1] Schaff's *Creeds of Christendom*, iii., pp. 174, 175.
[2] *Ibid.*, iii., 184.
[3] *Hist. of Protestant Theology* (E.T.), i., 171.
[4] *Opp.*, xxii., 872 (Dorner's quotation).

THE LUTHERAN TEACHING.

fore circumcision were not lost, Luther argues that neither are Christian children dying before baptism;[1] and he comforts Christian mothers of still-born babes by declaring that they should understand that such infants are saved.[2] So Bugenhagen, under Luther's direction, teaches that Christians' children intended for baptism are not left to the hidden judgment of God if they fail of baptism, but have the promise of being received by Christ into His kingdom.[3] It is not necessary to quote later authors on a point on which all are unanimous; let it suffice to add only the clear statement of the developed Lutheranism of John Gerhard (1610-22):[4] " We walk in the middle way, teaching that baptism is, indeed, the ordinary sacrament of initiation and means of regeneration necessary to all, even to the children of believers, for regeneration and salvation; but yet that in the event of privation or impossibility the children of Christians are saved by an extraordinary and peculiar divine dispensation. For the necessity of baptism is not absolute, but ordinary; we on our part are obliged to the necessity of baptism, but there must be no denial of the extraordinary action of God in infants offered to Christ by pious parents and the Church in prayers, and dying before the opportunity of baptism can be given them, since God does not so bind His grace and saving efficacy to baptism as that, in the event of privation, He may not both wish and be able to act extraordinarily. We distinguish, then, between necessity on *God's* part and on *our* part; between the case of *privation* and the *ordinary* way; and also between infants born *in* the Church and *out* of the Church. Concerning infants born out of the Church, we say with the apostle (1 Cor. v. 12, 13), 'For what have I to do with judging them that are without? Do not you judge them that are within? For them that are without God judgeth.' Wherefore, since there is no

---

[1] *Com. in Gen.*, c. 17.   [2] *Christliche Bedenken.*
[3] See for several such quotations brought together, LAURENCE, *Bampton Lectures*, 1804, ed. 1820, p. 272. Also GERHARD as in next note.
[4] Ed. Cotta, vol. ix., p. 284.

promise concerning them, we commit them to God's judgment; and yet we hold to no place intermediate between heaven and hell, concerning which there is utter silence in Scripture. But concerning infants born in the Church we have better hope. Pious parents properly bring their children as soon as possible to baptism as the ordinary means of regeneration, and offer them in baptism to Christ; and those who are negligent in this, so as through lack of care or wicked contempt for the sacrament to deprive their children of baptism, shall hereafter render a very heavy account to God, since they have 'despised the counsel of God' (Luke vii. 30). Yet neither can nor ought we rashly to condemn those infants which die in their mothers' wombs or by some sudden accident before they receive baptism, but may rather hold that the prayers of pious parents, or, if the parents are negligent of this, the prayers of the Church poured out for these infants are clemently heard, and they are received by God into grace and life."

From this passage we may learn not only the cordial acceptance given by Lutheran theologians to the extension of the baptism of intention to infants, but also the historical attitude of Lutheranism toward the entirely different question of the fate of infants dying outside the pale of the Church and the reach of its ordinances. These infants are a multitude so vast that it is wholly unreasonable to suppose them (like Christians' children deprived of baptism) simply exceptions to the rule laid down in the Augsburg Confession. And it is perfectly clear that the Lutheran Confessions extend no hope for them. It is doubtful whether it can even be said that they leave room for hope for them. Melanchthon in the *Apology* is no doubt arguing against the Anabaptists, and intends to prove only that children should be baptized; but his words in explanation of Art. IX. deserve consideration in this connection also—where he argues that " the promise of salvation" " does not pertain to those who are without the Church of Christ, where there is neither the Word nor the Sacraments, because the kingdom of Christ exists only with the Word and the Sacraments." Luther's personal opinion as to the fate of heathen children dying in infancy is in doubt : now he expresses the hope that the good and gracious God may have something good in view for them ;[1] and again, though leaving it to the future to decide, he only expects something milder for them than for the adults outside the Church :[2] and Bugenhagen, under his eye, contrasts the children of Turks and Jews with those of Christians, as not sharers in salvation because not in Christ.[3] From the very first the opinion of the theologians was divided on the subject. (1) Some held that all infants except those baptized in fact or intention are lost, and ascribed to them, of course—for this was the Protestant view of the desert of original sin—both privative and positive punishment. This party included such theologians as Quistorpius, Calovius, Fechter, Zeibichius, Buddeus. (2) Others judged that we may cherish the best of hope for their salvation. Here belong Dannhauer, Hulsemann, Scherzer, J. A. Osiander, Wagner, Musæus, Cotta, and Spener. (3) But the great body of Lutherans, including such names as Gerhard, Calixtus, Meisner, Baldwin, Bechmann, Hoffmann, Hunnius, held that nothing is clearly revealed as to the fate of such infants, and they must be left to the judgment of God. (*a*) Some of these, like Hunnius, were inclined to believe that they will be saved. (*b*) Others, with more (like Hoffmann) or less (like Gerhard) clearness, were rather inclined to believe they will be lost. But all of them alike held that the means for a certain decision are not in our hands.[4] Thus Hunnius says :[5] " That the infants of Gentiles, outside the Church, are saved, we cannot pronounce as certain, since there exists nothing definite in the Scriptures concerning the matter ; so neither do I dare simply to assert that these children are indiscriminately

---

[1] Cf. DORNER, *Hist. Prot. Theol.*, i., 171.
[2] Cf. LAURENCE, *Bampton Lectures*, p. 272.
[3] *Ibid.*
[4] This classification is taken from COTTA (Gerhard's *Loci*, ix., 282).
[5] *Quæst. in cap. vii. Gen.*

damned. . . . Let us commit them, therefore, to the judgment of God." And Hoffmann says :[1] "On the question, whether the infants of the heathen nations are lost, most of our theologians prefer to suspend their judgment. To affirm as a certain thing that they are lost could not be done without rashness."

This cautious agnostic position has the best right to be called the historical Lutheran attitude on the subject. It is even the highest position thoroughly consistent with the genius of the Lutheran system and the stress which it lays on the means of grace. The drift in more modern times has, however, been decidedly in the direction of affirming the salvation of all that die in infancy, on grounds identical with those pleaded by this party from the beginning—the infinite mercy of God, the universality of the atonement, the inability of infants to resist grace, their guiltlessness of despising the ordinance, and the like.[2] Even so, however, careful modern Lutherans moderate their assertions. They may affirm that "it is not the doctrine of our Confession that any human creature has ever been or ever will be lost purely for original sin ;"[3] but they speak of the matter as a "dark" or a "difficult question,"[4] and suspend the salvation of such infants on an "extraordinary" and "uncovenanted" exercise of God's mercy.[5] We cannot rise to a conviction or a "faith" in the matter, but may attain to a "well-grounded hope," based on our apprehension of God's all-embracing mercy.[6] In short, it is not contended that the Lutheran doctrine lays a foundation for a conviction of the salvation of all infants dying in infancy ; at the best it is held to leave open an uncontradicted hope. We are afraid we must say more : it seems to contradict this hope. For should this hope prove true, it would no longer be true that "baptism is necessary to salvation" even *ordinarily;* the exception would be the rule. Nor

[1] See KRAUTH, *Conservative Reformation*, p. 433.
[2] Compare the statements in COTTA and KRAUTH, *locc. citt.*
[3] KRAUTH, *l.c.*, p. 429.   [4] *Ib.*, pp. 561–563.
[5] *Ib.*, pp. 430, 437.
[6] *Ib., Infant Salvation in the Calvinistic System*, p. 22.

would the fundamental conception of the Lutheran theory of salvation—that grace is in the means of grace—be longer tenable. The logic of the Lutheran system leaves little room for the salvation of all infants, dying in infancy, and if their salvation should prove to be a fact, the integrity of the system is endangered.

That it is not merely the letter of the Lutheran formularies which needs to be transcended, if we are to cherish a hope for the salvation of all infants dying such, but the distinctive principle of the Lutheran system, is doubtless the cause of the great embarrassment exhibited by Lutheran writers in dealing with this problem, and of the extraordinary expedients which are sometimes resorted to for its solution. Thus, for example, Klieforth knows nothing better to suggest than that unbaptized children dying in their infancy, whether children of Christian parents or of infidel, stand in the same category with adult heathen, and are to have an opportunity to exercise saving faith when the Lord calls them before Him for judgment on His second coming. And the genial Norse missionary bishop Dahle, though he recognizes the scriptural distinction between the infants of Christian and those of heathen parents (1 Cor. vii. 14), seeks in vain to ground a hope on which he may rest his heart even for Christians' infants; and ends by falling back on the conjecture of the mediating theology of an opportunity for receiving Christ extended in the future life to those who have not enjoyed that opportunity here; thus, in other words, in his own way also assimilating the infant children of Christians with heathen. "The sum of the whole," he says, in concluding his discussion, "is that we may entertain a hope of salvation and bliss for our unbaptized children immediately after death, yet not more than a hope. But the question is still unanswered. Under any circumstances we have this consolation: that if the hope shall be unfounded such children will at least have the opportunity of the uncalled at some time to receive God's gracious call."[1] For

[1] LARS NIELSEN DAHLE, *Life After Death*, etc., translated from the Norse by the Rev. John Beveridge, M.A., B.D. (Edinburgh, 1896), p. 227.

the Lutheran the question is thus still unanswered, and must remain unanswered. The restrained paragraph with which Dahle opens his discussion appears, indeed, to put into words what every Lutheran must feel: "This is a very difficult—indeed, we might almost say a hitherto unanswered—question," he says. "All salvation is connected with Christ. But we come into connection with Him only through the means of grace; at all events, we do not know of any other way to Christ than this. Now, the means of grace are the Word and the sacraments. But the child is not susceptible to such means of grace as are afforded in the Word of God, which directs itself to the developed personal life; and so we have only the sacraments left. Of these, baptism is the one which incorporates into fellowship with Christ, and thereby with the Triune God, into whose name the candidate is baptized (Matt. xxvii. 19). Now, if a child is not susceptible to the means of grace of the Word, and does not receive the opportunity of baptism, is there any means whereby it can come into connection with Christ, apart from whom there is no salvation? This is the knot which no one yet has been able to undo."[1]

The Anglican Position.

A similar difficulty has been experienced by all types of Protestant thought in which the Roman idea of the Church, as primarily an external body, has been incompletely reformed. This may be illustrated, for example, from the history of opinion in the Church of England. The Thirty-nine Articles in their final form are thoroughly Protestant and Reformed. And many of the greatest English theologians, from the very earliest days of the Reformation, even among those not most closely affiliated with Geneva, have repudiated the "scrupulous superstition"[2] of the Church of Rome

---

[1] Lars Nielsen Dahle, *Life After Death*, translated from the Norse by the Rev. John Beveridge, M.A., B.D. (Edinburgh, 1896), pp. 219, 220.

[2] *Reform. Legum;* de Baptismo: "Illorum etiam videri debet scrupulosa superstitio, qui Dei gratiam et Spiritum Sanctum tanto-

as to the fate of infants dying unbaptized. But such repudiation neither was immediate, nor has it ever been universal. And it must needs be confessed that this "scrupulous superstition" was so deeply imbedded in the forms of the Book of Common Prayer, that it has survived all the changes which successive revisions have brought to its language, and remains to-day the natural implication of its Baptismal Offices.

The history of the formularies of the Church of England begins with the publication in 1536 of the somewhat more than semi-Romish *Articles devised by the Kinges Highnes Majestie, to stablyshe Christen quietnes and unitie amonge us, and to avoyde contentious opinions, which articles be also approved by the consent and determination of the hole clergie of this realme*,[1] commonly known as the "Ten Articles." These Articles explicitly teach the twin doctrines of baptismal regeneration and the necessity of baptism for salvation. Among the things which "ought and must of necessity" be believed regarding baptism, they tell us, is "that it is offered unto all men, as well infants as such as have the use of reason, that by baptism they shall have remission of sins, and the grace and favour of God;" that it is "by virtue of that holy sacrament" that men obtain "the grace and remission of all their sins;" and that it is "in and by this said sacrament" which they shall receive," that "God the Father giveth unto them, for His son Jesus Christ's sake, remission of all their sins, and the grace of the Holy Ghost, whereby they be newly regenerated and made the very children of God." Accord-

pere cum sacramentorum elementis colligant, ut plane affirment, nullum Christianorum infantem salutem esse consecuturum, qui prius morte fuerit occupatus, quam ad Baptismum adduci potuerit : quod longe secus habere judicamus." This code of laws seems to have been drawn up by a commission with CRANMER at the head of it. It was published by PARKER in 1571.

[1] "As seen by us, from the position we now occupy," says HARDWICK (*A History of the Articles of Religion*, etc. Third ed. revised by the Rev. FRANCIS PROCTER, M.A., etc. London : Bell, 1876, p. 42), "these articles belong to a transition-period. They embody the ideas of men who were emerging gradually into a different sphere of thought, who could not for the present contemplate the truth they were recovering, either in its harmonies or contrasts, and who conse-

ingly they "ought and must of necessity" also believe that "the sacrament of baptism was instituted and ordained in the New Testament by our Saviour Jesu Christ, as a thing necessary for the attaining of everlasting life;" that original sin cannot be remitted "but by the sacrament of baptism;" and that, therefore, since "the promise of grace and everlasting life (which promise is adjoined unto this sacrament of baptism) pertaineth not only unto such as have the use of reason, but also to infants, innocents, and children," they "ought therefore and must needs be baptized," and " by the sacrament of baptism, they do also obtain remission of their sins, the grace and favour of God, and be made thereby the very sons and children of God;" "insomuch as infants and children dying in their infancy shall undoubtedly be saved thereby, and else not."[1] The express assertion of the loss of all unbaptized infants included in these last words was taken over from the " Ten Articles" into *The Institution of the Christian Man*, commonly called " The Bishop's Book," which was published in 1537;[2] and thence, though with the omission of the final words in which the statement reaches its climax, into *The Necessary Doctrine and Erudition of Any Christian Man*, commonly called " The King's Book," which was published in 1543.[3] Here its career in the doctrinal formularies ceased.

quently did not shrink from acquiescing in accommodations and concessions, which to riper understandings might have seemed like the betrayal of a sacred trust." Dr. SCHAFF repels DIXON's description (*History of the Reformation*, i., p. 415) of these articles as bearing " the character of a compromise between the old and the new learning." " They are essentially Romish," he says (*Creeds of Christendom*, i., 611), " with the Pope left out in the cold;" and he endorses Foxe's characterization of them (which Hardwick deprecates) as intended for " weaklings, which were newly weyned from their mother's milke of Rome."

[1] The full text may be conveniently read in HARDWICK, as above, p. 242 *sq.*
[2] The text may be seen in Bishop LLOYD's *Formularies of Faith in the Reign of Henry VIII.*, p. 1.
[3] *Ibid.* Cf. FRANCIS PROCTER, *A History of the Book of Common Prayer*, etc. 15th ed. London and New York: Macmillan & Co., 1881, pp. 384, 385, *note* 1.

But it still had a part to play in the liturgical forms of the Church of England. The first *Book of Common Prayer* was published in 1549, and in it, among the rubrics which precede the Order of Confirmation, is found this parargaph : " And that no man shall think that any detriment shall come to children by deferring of their confirmation : he shall know for truth, that it is certain by God's word, that children being baptized (if they depart out of this life in their infancy) are undoubtedly saved."¹ In the Prayer Book for 1552 this was so far altered that its latter portion reads, " That children being baptized have all things necessary for their salvation, and be undoubtedly saved ;"² and so it stands in the Elizabethan Prayer Book of 1559, and substantially in later issues, until in the Prayer Book of 1661 it was transferred to the end of the order for the Public Baptism of Infants in the form : " It is certain by God's Word, that Children which are baptized, dying before they commit actual sin, are undoubtedly saved." Thus it still remains in the Book of Common Prayer according to the use of the Church of England, although it has dropped out of the Prayer Book according to the use of the Protestant Episcopal Church in the United States of America.

The successive alterations in this statement, no doubt, mark in a general way the growing Protestant sentiment in the Church of England, although it is noteworthy that the omission of the most obnoxious words, " and else not," in which the condemnation of unbaptized infants, dying in infancy, is made express, first occurs in the reactionary " King's Book," while the effect of the transposition of the rubric from the Confirmation Service to that for Baptism, which took place so late as 1661, was distinctly reactionary. Its primary effect, standing in the Confirmation Service,

¹ *The Two Liturgies, A.D. 1549 and A.D. 1552*, etc., *edited for the Parker Society, by the Rev.* JOSEPH KETLEY, M.A., etc. (Cambridge, 1844, p. 121).
² *Ibid.*, p. 295. The two may be found together in *The Two Books of Common Prayer set forth . . . in the Reign of King Edward the Sixth*, by EDWARD CARDWELL, D.D., etc. (Oxford, 1852, p. 544).

was to declare that confirmation is not necessary to salvation; and any implication which may be thought to reside in the words of the necessity of baptism to salvation was entirely incidental. While, standing at the end of the Baptismal Service, its primary effect seems to be to declare the certain efficacy of baptism when administered to infants, and the implication of the loss of the unbaptized infants dying in infancy is certainly more natural, even if not necessary. The explanation of this reactionary alteration is to be found, of course, in the general spirit which governed the revision of 1661, which not only was hostile to the more Protestant party in the Church, but was determined upon all possible insult and degradation to it.[1]

The more Protestant party had, of course, never been satisfied with this rubric; and it had, of late, necessarily received its share of criticism. The committee of divines appointed by the House of Lords in 1641 had proposed the omission from it of the words, "and be undoubtedly saved."[2] The Presbyterian divines at the Savoy Conference had commented on it: "Although we charitably suppose the meaning of these words was only to exclude the necessity of any other sacraments to baptized infants; yet these words are dangerous as to the misleading of the vulgar, and therefore we desire they may be expunged."[3] The

---

[1] Observe how even CARDWELL speaks of the general spirit of this revision (*A History of Conferences and other Proceedings connected with the Revision of the Book of Common Prayer*, etc. Third ed. Oxford, 1849, pp. 387 *sq.*) and the warning he draws from it (pp. 463 *sq.*): "Let it be remembered, also, on the part of nonconformists, that whenever objection is made against any expressions as ambiguous or indefinite, other parties, of different and even opposite opinions, will be as ready as they themselves are, to offer amendments. In such a case, the result will probably be that phrases, which had previously afforded a common shelter to both, will be made precise and contracted in accordance with the wishes of the more rigid interpreters. Let it be remembered that if one party complain of a strict adherence to forms and a tendency toward superstition, another party, more compact, more learned, and more resolute, may call for the restoration of prayers and usages which once found a place in the liturgy, and were removed by the fathers of the reformation as too nearly allied to Romanism."

[2] CARDWELL, as cited, p. 276.   [3] *Ibid.*, p. 327.

answer of the bishops was not conciliatory: "It is evident that the meaning of these words is, that children baptized, and dying before they commit actual sin, are undoubtedly saved, though they be not confirmed : wherein we see not what danger there can be of misleading the vulgar by teaching them truth. But there may be danger in this desire of having these words expunged, as if they were false ; for St. Austin says he is an infidel that denies them to be true. Ep. 23. ad Bonifac."[1] This defence of the rubric obviously is *ad rem* only in the form and place which it had in the Confirmation Service. When, as was immediately done, it was removed from its place in the Confirmation Service and, curtailed of all reference to confirmation, inserted into the Baptismal Order in the sharply assertive form : " It is certain by God's Word, that Children which are baptized, dying before they commit actual sin, are undoubtedly saved," it must be accounted one of the alterations designed to exclude a Protestant interpretation of the Book of Common Prayer ; and as, in the intention of the authors of the change at all events, no longer open to the interpretation that it does not imply the necessity of baptism for salvation but only asserts that confirmation is not necessary to salvation. It was obviously intended by those who gave it its present form and place to

---

[1] CARDWELL, as cited, p. 358. The reference to AUGUSTINE is to Ep. 98 in the Benedictine enumeration (§ 10). Augustine is discussing the propriety and effect of baptism prior to the exercise of active faith on the part of the recipient, and says : "During the time in which he is by reason of youth unable to do this, the sacrament will avail for his protection against adverse powers, and will avail so much on his behalf, that if before he arrives at the use of reason he depart from this life, he is delivered by Christian help, namely, by the love of the Church, commending him through the sacrament unto God, from that condemnation which by one man entered into the world. He who does not believe this, and thinks that it is impossible, is assuredly an unbeliever, although he may have received the sacrament of faith ; and far before him in merit is the infant which, though not yet possessing a faith helped by the understanding, is not obstructing faith by any antagonism of the understanding, and therefore receives with profit the sacrament of faith" (translation of the Rev. J. G. CUNNINGHAM, M.A., in *The Nicene and Post-Nicene Fathers*, first series, vol. i., p. 410).

assert baptismal regeneration, and to leave whatever implications the doctrine of baptismal regeneration may include as the natural teaching of the rubric.

Nor can it be denied that, as assertorial of baptismal regeneration, the rubric finds a very natural place in the Book of Common Prayer. It was inevitable that in the beginning of the Reformation movement remainders of the unreformed doctrine of baptismal regeneration should intrench themselves in the liturgical offices of the Church. As a matter of fact, the assumption of this doctrine underlay a good deal of the language relative to baptism in the first Prayer Book (1549).[1] This may be true even of the words of the opening address, which recite the fact of original sin and declare that "no man born in sin can enter into the kingdom of God (except he be regenerate and born anew of water and the Holy Ghost)." It is more clearly true of the language of the opening prayer, where the figure of baptism found in the flood and the passage through the Red Sea is developed rather on the negative than on the positive side ; and God is besought, therefore, to look mercifully upon these children, "that by this wholesome laver of regeneration, whatsoever sin is in them may be washed clean away ; that they, being delivered from His wrath, may be received into the ark of Christ's church, and so be saved from perishing." Similarly, after " the white vesture" had been given to the child " for a token of the innocence which by God's grace, in this holy sacrament of baptism, is given unto it," the priest was to bless the child in the name of the God "who hath regenerate it by water and the Holy Ghost, and hath given unto it remission of all its sins." When a child privately baptized was brought to the church for the priest to examine whether it had been lawfully baptized, if it were so decided, the minister was to certify the parents of their well-doing in having the child baptized, because it " is now, by the laver of regeneration

---

[1] The quotations that follow are taken from the text as given by CARDWELL, *The Two Books of Common Prayer . . . in the Reign of King Edward the Sixth*, etc., 3d ed. Oxford, 1852, pp. 320 *sq*.

THE ANGLICAN POSITION. 181

in baptism, made the child of God, and heir of everlasting life." The same implication naturally underlay also the whole form for the sanctification of the font, which appears only in this earliest of Anglican Prayer Books. In it God is said to have " ordained the element of water for the regeneration of His faithful people," and is asked to sanctify " this fountain of baptism . . . that by the power of His word all those that should be baptized therein might be spiritually regenerated and made the children of everlasting adoption." In the Catechism included in the Confirmation Service, the child is instructed to say that it was in its baptism that it " was made a member of Christ, the child of God, and the inheritor of the kingdom of heaven ;" while in the Invocation in the Confirmation Service itself God is addressed as He " who has vouchsafed to regenerate these His servants of water and the Holy Ghost, and also has given unto them forgiveness of all their sins."

The revising hand was, to be sure, as busy with this as with other portions of the Prayer Book. In particular, the opening prayer was already in the second Prayer Book (1552) brought into substantially the form which it still preserves : and this involved not only the omission of the words, " and so saved from perishing"—" expressions," as even Laurence is forced to admit, " too unequivocal to be misconceived," in their exclusion of all unbaptized infants from salvation[1]—but also a recasting of the whole tone of the prayer. But the revision was never complete enough to exscind the underlying doctrine of baptismal regeneration ; and, in the shifting opinion of the Church of England, after a while a reaction set in in its favor, which not only resisted all attempts to eliminate it,[2]

---

[1] LAURENCE, *Bampton Lectures for 1804*, rev. ed., Oxford, 1820, p. 71. Compare PROCTER, *A History of the Book of Common Prayer*, 15th ed, 1881, p. 374, *note* 1 ; SCHAFF, *Creeds of Christendom*, i., 642.

[2] It was naturally against this doctrine that the " Puritan party" directed their most persistent objection. See the form of their objections in the documents printed by CARDWELL, *A History of Confer-*

but added new expressions of it.[1] So it came about that when the Presbyterians at the Savoy Conference represented it as a hardship that ministers should " be forced to pronounce all baptized infants to be regenerate by the Holy Ghost, whether they be the children of Christians or not," and protested that they could not " in faith say," as required to say in the Thanksgiving, " that every child that is baptized is ' regenerated by God's Holy Spirit,' "[2] the bishops' reply simply asserts in terms the obnoxious doctrine : " Seeing that God's sacraments have their effects, where the receiver doth not ' ponere obicem,' put any bar against them (which children cannot do) ; we may say in faith of every child that is baptized, that it is regenerated by God's Holy Spirit."[3] There seems to be little room for doubting, therefore, that these expressions were retained by the revisers of 1661 not as " ambiguous and indefinite," but as distinct enunciations, and just because they were judged to be distinct enunciations, of the doctrine of baptismal regeneration. We must adjudge Laurence right, therefore, in finding this doctrine plainly taught in the Book of Common Prayer as now in use ; nor can we see how his summing up of the case can be set aside. " In the prayer after Baptism," he says, " every child is expressly declared to be regenerated : ' We yield thee hearty thanks, most merciful Father, that it hath pleased thee *to regenerate this infant with thy Holy Spirit*, to receive him for thine own child by adoption, and to incorporate him into thy holy Church.' And in the Office of private Baptism it is unreservedly stated, that he ' is now by the laver of regeneration in Baptism *received* into the number *of the children of God*, and *heirs of everlasting life*.' That all baptized children are not nominally,

---

ences, etc., 3d ed., Oxford, 1849, pp. 266, 276, 325, 326 ; and the answers of the bishops, pp. 357 and 358.

[1] For example, the thanksgiving address and prayer after baptism inserted in the Prayer Book of 1552, which declare the baptized child to be regenerate, and the questions, at the end of the Catechism, on the sacraments, added apparently in 1604, which declare that " we are made the children of grace" by baptism.

[2] CARDWELL, as cited, pp. 276, 325 ; cf. 326.   [3] *Ibid.*, p. 356.

but really, the elect of God, our Church Catechism likewise distinctly asserts. ' *Q*. Who gave you that name ? *A*. My Godfathers and Godmothers in my Baptism, wherein I was made *a member of Christ, the child of God,* and *an inheritor of the kingdom of heaven.*' . . . Nor is the position, that an actual regeneration always takes place confined to our Baptismal service, but also subsequently recognized in the Order of Confirmation, the first prayer of which thus commences : ' Almighty and everlasting God, who hast vouchsafed *to regenerate these thy servants* by water, and *the Holy Ghost,*' " etc. " Surely," he adds, with some justice, " it requires something more than a common share of ingenuity to pervert language like this from its plain grammatical sense, into one directly repugnant."[1]

On the basis of this doctrine of baptismal regeneration, thus clearly implied in her forms of worship and firmly retained in their latest revision, the Church of England is justified in asserting with the emphasis with which the rubric at the close of the Baptismal Service asserts it, that " it is certain" " that Children which are baptized, dying before they commit actual sin, are undoubtedly saved." Whether, however, this assertion carries with it, as Laurence contends, no implication of the loss of those who die unbaptized, is more questionable.[2] The mere change of language from the earlier form of " children being baptized" into the more distinguishing seventeenth-century form of " children which are baptized," bears a contrary suggestion. And the arguments which Laurence adduces from the known opinions of Cranmer and his coadjutors, and from the elimination from the earlier forms, under their hand, of phrases which assert the necessity of baptism to salvation, are vitiated by the fatal flaw

---

[1] *Op. cit* , pp. 440, 441.
[2] *Op. cit.*, pp. 70 and 176. Laurence contends that "the Reformers" intended by the language of the Prayer Book in no way " to establish any opinion inconsistent with the salvation of infants unbaptized :" " the very reverse of this is the fact," he thinks. And thus it has become customary to speak. So, *e.g.*, PROCTER, *Op. cit.*, p. 384, *note* 1 ; and even BLUNT, *The Annotated Book of Common Prayer* (London, 1866), ii., 230, although himself inclining to believe the loss

that he neglects to distinguish times and seasons.[1] That the leaders of the Reformation in England advanced rapidly from a semi-Romish, through a Lutheran, to a Reformed stage of opinion, and that their handiwork in the public formularies of the Church bears traces of this growth, is true enough. But it does not follow that every product of their labors must, therefore, have left their hands in a form which represents their highest attainments in doctrinal thought; or that every one has reached us in the precise form which they gave it. That much that was inconsistent with the better thought of the Protestant world was eliminated from the first Prayer Book of 1549 in its passage through the Book of 1552 to the Elizabethan Book of 1559 is thankfully to be recognized. But it must needs be recognized also that much was left in it which was scarcely consistent with the higher point of view which had been only gradually attained by the Reformers themselves; and that in the reactionary revision of the seventeenth century this unreformed element was even increased.[2]

of all infants dying unbaptized. These opinions would seem, however, to be too little determined by historical considerations. See further below.

[1] In some cases also his knowledge of historic facts was defective.

[2] It must be thankfully recognized also that a more complete reformation of doctrinal statement was accomplished in the doctrinal formularies of the Church of England than in her devotional forms. This is probably due to the singular discontinuity in the growth of the doctrinal formularies, by which the later Articles were saved from corruption through inheritance from the earlier and more tentative attempts to state the reformed faith. The first Prayer Book (1549) stands at the basis of and contributes its substance to the whole series of Prayer Books. But the first doctrinal formularies, the "Ten Articles" and the "Bishop's" and "King's Books," though they contributed to the Prayer Book the very rubric in which the assertion of baptismal regeneration reaches its climax, had little effect on the development of the "Articles of Religion." For them, an entirely new beginning was made in the "Thirteen Articles" of 1538, which were formed under Lutheran influence and rather on the basis of Lutheran than earlier Anglican formularies. In these Articles the Lutheran doctrine of the sacraments, of course, finds expression, and is sometimes even strengthened. In Article 2, for example, it is asserted that original sin condemns and brings eternal death "to those who are not born again by baptism and the Holy Spirit." In Article 4 it is declared that "by the word and sacraments, as by in-

Whatever may be thought, however, of the implications of the doctrine taught in the Prayer Book, this much is at least certain—that the formularies of the Church of England hold out absolutely no hope for the salvation of infants who die unbaptized. They assert with great strength of language the certainty of the salvation of all baptized children dying in infancy. As to those who die unbaptized, they at the least preserve a profound silence. "This assertion," says Mr. Francis Procter, the learned historian of the Book of Common Prayer, "carefully avoids all mention of children unbaptized. . . . Our Reformers are intending to speak only of that which is revealed—the covenanted mercy of Almighty God."[1] Whence we may learn that, in the judgment of Mr. Procter at least, the Prayer Book knows of no covenanted mercy of God for children dying before baptism, and can find nothing in God's revealed word which will justify an

---

struments, the Holy Spirit is given, who effects faith when and where it seems good to God, in those who hear the Gospel." These statements came from the Augsburg Confession. Article 6, "on Baptism," teaches, in the words of the Augsburg Confession, that "baptism is necessary to salvation, and by baptism remission of sins and the grace of Christ are offered to infants and adults." Then it is added that "by baptism infants receive remission of sins and grace and are the children of God," and "that the Holy Spirit is efficacious even in infants and cleanses them"—a statement which is repeated in Article 9. These Articles were never published, and have influenced the development of the Articles of the Church of England only through their use by the framers of the Forty-two Articles of 1553. The first draught of these was from the hand of Cranmer himself, and reflects his more advanced Reformed opinions, deriving practically nothing from former Articles except where the "Thirteen Articles" have been drawn upon. In the portions at least which have been retained in the Thirty-nine Articles the influence of even the "Thirteen Articles" has affected rather language than doctrine, in which latter particular the new Articles follow Reformed rather than Lutheran modes of statement. If the language of the "Thirteen Articles," by which the sacraments are said, "as by instruments," to convey the Holy Spirit who effects faith, seems to be repeated here in the Article on Baptism (Art. 28 of 1553, 27 of 1563-71), it is along with an important caveat by which the effect is confined "to those that receive baptism rightly." By this the stress is thrown rather on the subjective attitude of the recipient than on the mere reception of the rite.

[1] *A History of the Book of Common Prayer*, etc., 15th ed. (London and New York, 1881), p. 384, *note* 1.

assured hope for them. In the same spirit is conceived the comment in Mr. Blunt's *Annotated Book of Common Prayer*, which runs as follows : " Neither in this Rubric, nor in any other formulary of the Church of England, is any decision given as to the state of infants dying without Baptism. Bishop Bethell says [*Regeneration in Baptism*, p. xiv.] that the common opinion of the ancient Christians was, that they are not saved : and as our Lord has given us such plain words in John iii. 5, this seems a reasonable opinion. But this opinion does not involve any cruel idea of pain or suffering for little ones so deprived of the Sacrament of new birth by no fault of their own. It rather supposes them to be as if they had never been, when they might, through the care and love of their parents, have been reckoned among the number of those ' in whom is no guile,' and ' who follow the Lamb whithersoever He goeth.' " [1] This position has indeed the best right to be called the historical understanding of the Church of England as to the teaching of her Prayer Book, as we may be advised by the statement of it by the great historian of infant baptism, William Wall, writing indeed two hundred years ago, but putting into his carefully chosen and sober language just what, as we have seen, the best accredited expounders of the Prayer Book in our own day repeat. " The Church of England," says Wall,[2] " have declared their sense of its [*i.e* baptism's] necessity by reciting the saying of our Saviour, John iii. 5, both in the Office of Baptism of Infants and also in that for those of riper years. . . . Concerning the everlasting state of an infant that by misfortune dies unbaptized, the Church of England has determined nothing (it were fit that all churches would leave such things to God) save that they forbid the ordinary *Office for Burial* to be used for such an one ; for that were to determine the point and acknowledge him for a Christian brother. And though the most noted men

[1] *The Annotated Book of Common Prayer*, etc., edited by the Rev. JOHN HENRY BLUNT, M.A., F.S.A., etc. (London, 1866), ii., 230.
[2] *Hist. of Infant Baptism*, ed. 2, 1707, p. 377.

in the said Church from time to time since the Reformation of it to this time have expressed their hopes that God will accept the purpose of the parent for the deed ; yet they have done it modestly and much as Wycliffe did, rather not determining the negative than absolutely determining the positive, that such a child shall enter into the kingdom of heaven."

The Church of England holds thus the unenviable place among Protestant churches of alone of them having no word of cheer to say as to the destiny of the children of Christian parents who depart from this world without baptism. There is no covenant with reference to them ; it may be that they may be saved —but if so, she is sure she cannot tell how ; or if they be not saved, it may be that they shall be " as if they had never been :" there is no word of God with reference to them. Surely this is all cold comfort enough. And if this is all that can be said of the children of the faithful, lacking baptism, where will those of the infidel appear ?

The hope which the formularies of the Church of England can find no basis for in the Word of God, and which those whose views of Divine truth are moulded by these formularies must deny or at least withhold, has nevertheless, as Wall tells us, been " from time to time since the Reformation" freely expressed by individual teachers in that Church, and that especially, as he adds, by " the most noted men" in it. Those to whose labors and sufferings the Church of England owed her very existence were in no respect behind their successors in this. We have seen that the *Reformation of the Ecclesiastical Laws,* drawn up by a commission with Cranmer at its head, affirmed, of the opinion that no infant dying without baptism could be saved —which Cranmer and his coadjutors had themselves incorporated into the earliest formularies—that it was a " scrupulous superstition" and far different from the opinion of the Church of England.[1] Obviously " in the

---

[1] See above, foot-note on p. 174.

meantime," as Dr. Schaff suggests, Cranmer "had changed his opinion."[1] What was the current conviction on this subject among the leading reformers we may learn, as well as from another, from one of Cranmer's chaplains, Thomas Becon, who chances to have written repeatedly and at length upon it.

In the second part of his treatise on *The Demands of Holy Scripture*, the preface to which is dated on the first of September, 1563, Becon raises the question, "What if the infants die before they receive the sacrament of baptism?" and answers it succinctly as follows: "God's promise of salvation unto them is not for default of the sacrament minished, or made vain and of no effect. For the Spirit is not so bound to the water that it cannot work his office when the water wanteth, or that it of necessity must always be there where the water is sprinkled. Simon Magus had the sacramental water, but he had not the Holy Ghost, being indeed an hypocrite and filthy dissembler. In the chronicle of the apostles' Acts we read that, while Peter preached, the Holy Ghost came upon them that heard him, yea, and that before they were baptized; by the reason whereof Peter brast out into these words, and said: 'Can any man forbid water, that these should not be baptized, which have received the Holy Ghost as well as we?' True Christians, whether they be old or young, are not saved because outwardly they be washed with the sacramental water, but because they be God's children by election through Christ, yea, and that before the foundations of the world were laid, and are sealed up by the Spirit of God unto everlasting life."[2]

In the voluminous *Catechism*, which he wrote somewhat earlier (1560) for the instruction of his children and presents to them in a touching and beautiful preface, he develops his views on this matter at great length. "The infants of the heathen and unbelieving," "for-

---

[1] *Creeds of Christendom*, i., p. 642.
[2] *Prayers and Other Pieces by Thomas Becon, S.T.P.*, edited for the Parker Society by the Rev. JOHN AYRE, M.A. (Cambridge, 1844), p. 617.

asmuch as they belong not unto the household of faith, neither are contained in this covenant, ' I will be thy God, and the God of thy seed ; ' again, ' I will pour out my Spirit upon thy seed, and my blessing upon thy buds,' " he leaves " to the judgment of God, to whom they either stand or fall." But "with the children of the faithful God hath made a sure and an everlasting covenant, that he will be their God and Saviour, yea, their most loving Father, and take them for his sons and heirs, as St. Peter saith, ' The promise was made to you and to your children.' " He knows well " how hard and rigorous divers fathers of Christ's church are to such infants as die without baptism," but he judges this opinion of theirs to be injurious to the grace of God and dissenting from the verity of God's Word. Injurious to the grace of God, because " the Holy scripture in every place attributeth our salvation to the free grace of God, and not either to our own works, or to any outward sign or sacrament." " Hath God so bound himself and made himself thrall to a sacrament, that without it his power of saving is lame, and of no force to defend from damnation ?" Baptism is to Christians what circumcision was to the Jews, not a thing that makes righteous, but " ' a seal of righteousness,' and a sign of God's favor toward us," and so " the outward baptism, which is done by water, neither giveth the Holy Ghost, nor the grace of God, but only is a sign and token thereof," and therefore, " if any of the Christian infants, prevented by death, depart without baptism (necessity so compelling), they are not damned, but be saved by the free grace of God ; forasmuch, as we tofore heard, they be contained in the covenant of grace, they be members of God's church, God promiseth to be their God, they have faith, and be endued with the Spirit of God, and so finally ' sons and heirs of God, and heirs annexed with Christ Jesu.' " His firm conviction from Scripture is " that the grace and Spirit of God cometh where and when it pleaseth God, yea, and that they be not bound to any external ceremony, as to be present and to be given when the sacraments are ministered, and otherwise not, so that the Spirit and grace of God must wait and attend upon these outward signs, as servants do attend and wait upon their lords and masters"— "which is nothing else," he declares, "than to bring God into bondage to his creatures, and to make him not master of his own." " They, therefore," he concludes, " that teach and hold this doctrine are not only enemies to the salvation of the infants, but they also utterly obscure, yea, and quench the grace and election of God and the secret operation of the Holy Ghost in the tender breasts of the most tender infants, and attribute to an external sign more than right is."[1] In a word, Thomas Becon plants himself squarely on that "covenanted mercy of Almighty God," which Mr. Procter tells us the framers of the Prayer Book failed to discover for those who die unbaptized ; and finds no difficulty in showing from Scripture that it underlies baptism which is its seal, and does not rather wait on baptism as its cause.

Such an instance as that of John Hooper is, of course, even more striking. He had come under distinctly Zwinglian influences, and, like Zwingli and possibly first after Zwingli, taught the salvation not only of the infants of Christians dying unbaptized, but also of all infants dying such, whether the children of Christians or of infidels. As to baptismal regeneration, he speaks of " the ungodly opinion, that attributeth the salvation of man unto the receiving of an external sacrament," " as though God's holy Spirit could not be carried by faith into the penitent and sorrowful conscience except it rid always in a chariot and external sacrament." With reference to the salvation of unbaptized infants, therefore, he says : " It is ill done to condemn the infants of the Christians that die without baptism, of whose salvation by the Scripture we be assured : *Ero Deus tuus, et seminis tuis post te.* I would likewise judge well," he adds, " of the infants of the infidels who hath

[1] *The Catechism of Thomas Becon, S T.P.,* etc., edited for the Parker Society by the Rev. JOHN AYRE, M.A. (Cambridge, 1844), pp. 214–225.

none other sin in them but original, the sin of Adam's transgression. And as by Adam sin and death entered into the world, so by Christ justice and life. *Ut quemadmodum regnaverat peccatum in morte, sic et gratia regnaret per justiciam ad vitam æternam per Jesum Christum.* Rom. v. Whereas the infants doth not follow the iniquity of the father, but only culpable for the transgression of Adam, it shall not be against the faith of a Christian man to say, that Christ's death and passion extendeth as far for the salvation of innocents, as Adam's fall made all his posterity culpable of damnation. *Quia quemadmodum per inobedientiam unius hominis peccatores constituti fecimus multi, ita per obedientiam unius justi constituentur multi.* The Scripture also preferreth the grace of God's promise to be more abundant than sin. *Ubi exuberavit peccatum, ubi magis exuberavit gratia.* Rom. v. It is not the part of a Christian to say, this man is damned, or this is saved, except he see the cause of damnation manifest. As touching the promises of God's election, *sunt sine pœnitentia dona et vocatio Dei.*"[1]

Naturally many other opinions have found expression in the bosom of this most inclusive communion. In the vexed time of the seventeenth century, for example, men like William Perkins[2] and James Usher[3] approached the question from the side of the Reformed

---

[1] *An Answer unto My Lord of Winchester's Booke*, etc., 1547, in the Parker Society's *Early Writings of Bishop Hooper*, pp. 129, 131.

[2] "Reprobates are either infants or men of riper age. In reprobate infants the execution of God's decree is this: As soon as they are born, for the guilt of original and natural sin, being left in God's secret judgment unto themselves, they dying are rejected of God forever" (*The Golden Chain*, ch. 53, in *Works*, ed. 1608, i., p. 107). "We are to judge that Infants of believing parents in their infancy dying, are justified" (*How to Live Well*, i., 486).

[3] "Some Reprobates dying Infants . . . Being once conceived they are in a state of Death (Rom. 5. 14), by reason of the sin of *Adam* imputed, and of original corruption cleaving to their Nature, wherein also, dying they perish: As (for instance) the Children of Heathen Parents. For touching the Children of Christians, we are taught and account them holy. 1 Cor. 7. 14" (*Body of Divinity*, 4to ed., 1702, p. 165).

theology; others, like Jeremy Taylor,[1] from a fundamentally Pelagianizing standpoint; others, like Matthew Scrivener,[2] from a "churchly" one. From a somewhat earlier period, the argument of Richard Hooker may be taken as fairly representing the more considerate churchmanship of the time. Holding to the necessity of baptism, not indeed as "a cause of grace," but as "an instrument or means whereby we receive grace," ordained as such by Christ, he argues that "if Christ himself which giveth salvation do require Baptism; it is not for us that look for salvation to sound and examine him, whether unbaptized men may be saved; but seriously to do that which is required, and religiously to fear the danger that may grow by the want thereof." Nevertheless he remarks that the "Law of Christ, which in these considerations maketh Baptism necessary, must be construed and understood according to rules of natural equity;" "and (because equity so teacheth) it is on our part gladly confessed, that there may be in divers cases life by virtue of inward Baptism, even when outward is not found." Whether this principle may be extended to infants dying unbaptized, he makes the subject of special consideration. Inasmuch as "grace is not absolutely tied unto Sacraments;" and God accepts the will for the deed in cases where the deed is impossible; and there is a presumed desire and even purpose in Christian parents and the Church to give these children baptism; and their birth of Christian parents marks them, according to Scripture, as holy, and gives them "a present interest and right to those means wherewith the ordinance of Christ is that his Church shall be sanctified:" "it is not to be thought that he

[1] *The Whole Works of*, etc. (London, 1828), vol. ii., p. 258 *sq.*, 289 *sq.*; vol. viii., 150 *sq.*; vol. ix., p. 12 *sq.*, 90 *sq.*, 369 *sq.*
[2] "Either all children must be damned, dying unbaptized, or they must have baptism. . . . The principle in Christian religion is, That children come into the world infected with original sin; and therefore, if there be no remedy against that, provided by God, all children of Christian parents, which St. Paul says are holy, are liable to eternal death without remedy. Now, there is no remedy but Christ; and his death and passion are not communicated to any but by outward signs and sacraments. And no other do we read of but that of water in baptism" (*Course of Divinity*, London, 1674, p. 196).

which, as it were, from Heaven, hath nominated and designed them unto holiness by special privilege of their very birth, will himself deprive them of regeneration and inward grace, only because necessity depriveth them of outward sacraments."[1]

It would seem that on grounds such as these, even the highest churchmanship might find it possible to assert the certain salvation of all the children of Christians, at least, which die unbaptized ; and, as has been pointed out on an earlier page,[2] the considerations thus so judiciously set forth would even appear to open a way for the development, on churchly grounds, of a baptism of intention as applied to infants, which could be extended, without danger to any important interest, to embrace all infants that die in infancy. Nevertheless it has not been on the part of high-churchmen that, in the Church of England, the salvation of infants dying such has been affirmed. This has rather been the part of low-churchmen, like John Newton[3] and Thomas Scott[4] and Augustus Toplady,[5] while high-

[1] *Ecclesiastical Polity*, Book V., § 60. (Dobson's ed , i., 600-607 ; Keble's ed. ii., 341-347.)
[2] See above, p. 156.
[3] *Works*, IV., 182 : "I cannot be sorry for the death of infants. How many storms do they escape ! Nor can I doubt, in my private judgment, that they are included in the election of grace. Perhaps those who die in infancy are the exceeding great multitude of all people, nations, and languages mentioned (Rev. 7 : 9) in distinction from the visible body of professing believers, who were marked on their foreheads and openly known to be the Lord's."
[4] *The Articles of the Synod of Dort*, etc. (Philadelphia, 1818, p. 189) : "The salvation of the offspring of believers dying in infancy is here scripturally stated, and not limited to such as are baptized. Nothing is said of the children of unbelievers dying in infancy, and the Scripture says nothing. But why might not these Calvinists have as favorable a hope of all infants dying before actual sin as anti-Calvinists can have ?"
[5] *The Works of*, etc. (new ed., London, 1837, pp. 645, 646) : "But you observe . . . that ' With regard to infants, the rubrick declares it is certain by God's word that children which are baptized, dying before they commit actual sin, are undoubtedly saved.' I firmly believe the same ; nay, I believe more. I am convinced that the souls of all departed infants whatever, whether baptized or unbaptized, are with God in glory. . . . I believe that in the decree of predestination to life, God hath included all whom he hath decreed to take away in infancy ; and that the decree of reprobation has nothing to do with them." So, again, p. 142, *note m :* " No objection

churchmen have ever shown a tendency to doubt or deny the salvation of those who die without having been "admitted into covenant with God" by baptism. This is the language of *Tract No. 35*[1] (written by A. C. Percival) of the Oxford *Tracts for the Times*, within which were included also Dr. Pusey's voluminous treatises on baptismal regeneration. These treatises have not failed of their effect, and possibly at no time before the present in the whole history of the Church of England since the first years of its reformation, has there ever been a more widespread tendency to stand simply upon the wording of the rubric at the end of the Baptismal Service, as if it included all ascertainable truth, and to affirm only the certainty of the salvation of those infants dying in infancy which have been baptized. All others, though they be the children of God's recognized children, are, sometimes with a certainly not very easily understood complacency, at the best committed to the "uncovenanted mercies of God,"[2] at the worst consigned to a place among those

can hence arise against the salvation of such as die in infancy (all of whom are undoubtedly saved) ; nor yet against the salvation of God's elect among the Heathens, Mohametans, and others. The Holy Spirit is able to inspire the grace of actual faith into those hearts (especially at the moment of dissolution) which are incapable of exerting the explicit act of faith."

[1] "The Sacrament of Baptism, by which souls are admitted into covenant with God, and without which none can enter into the kingdom of heaven (John 3 : 5)" (*Tract No. 35*, p. 1). Cf. the words of *Tract No. 67* which affirms that the relationship of sonship to God is imparted through baptism, and is not imparted without it.

[2] Efforts to assign salvation to them on the "uncovenanted mercies of God," proceed ordinarily either upon a Romish conception of "ignorance," or upon the conjecture of a proclamation of the Gospel to them in the intermediate state. Thus a recent writer declares that "those souls who have, until this season, been ignorant of their God, or seen Him, at the best, but dimly, through their heathen faiths, and yet, despite of this, have followed and obeyed, as best they could, His guidings and 'enlightenings' of their minds—those souls, I say, will doubtless, in that 'Vision' at last receive the Full Light, hear His Gospel, and know Him as their Lord." Then he adds in a note : "In this category, also, evidently belong unbaptized infants" (ALAN S. HAWKESWORTH, *De Incarnatione Verbi Dei*, p. 64). Why "unbaptized infants," even of believers, "evidently" belong in the category of the heathen, we are not told ; nor why, if they are so classed by God, they should belong in the category of those heathen who "have followed and obeyed, as best they could ;" nor what reason we have to

who know not God and obey not the Gospel of our Lord Jesus.

The Reformed Doctrine.

It was among the Reformed alone that the newly recovered scriptural apprehension of the Church to which the promises were given, as essentially not an external organization but the true Body of Christ, membership in which is mediated not by the external act of baptism but by the internal regeneration of the Holy Spirit, bore its full fruit in rectifying the doctrine of the application of redemption. This great truth was taught alike, to be sure, by both branches of Protestantism, Lutheran as well as Reformed. But it was limited in its application in the one line of teaching by a very high doctrine of the means of grace; while in the other, wherever the purity of the Reformed doctrine was not corrupted by a large infusion of Romish inheritance, it became itself constitutive of the doctrine of the means of grace. There were some Reformed theologians, even outside the Church of England, no doubt, who held a high doctrine of the means. Of these Peter Jurieu (1637–1713) may be taken as a type.[1] This famous writer, to whom Witsius somewhat rashly promised the grateful veneration of posterity, taught that even elect infants, children of covenanted parents, are children of wrath until they are baptized, and up to that time have not received their complete reconciliation, nor have been washed from the stains with which they are born, nor are the objects of God's love of complacency; that baptism is as necessary to salvation as eating is to living or taking the remedy is to recovery from disease; that therefore infants properly baptized and dying in infancy are certainly saved, and their baptism is an indubitable proof of their election, while of the salvation of those who die before baptism we can have no certainty, but only a

think that all of either these or those will receive the Gospel when it is offered them.

[1] See his views quoted and discussed by WITSIUS, *De Efficace et Utilitate Bapt.* in *Miscel. Sacra* (1736), ii., 513.

judgment of charity; that God no doubt does save some infants without baptism, but this is done in an extraordinary, and, so to speak, miraculous way, and so that the death of the infant may be supposed to supply the defect of baptism, as martyrdom does for adults in the Romish teaching. Such opinions, however, were not characteristic of the Reformed churches, the distinguishing doctrine of which, rather, by suspending salvation on membership in the invisible instead of in the visible Church, transformed baptism from a necessity into a duty, and left men dependent for salvation on nothing but the infinite love and free grace of God.

From this point of view the absolutely free and loving election of God alone is determinative of the saved. How many are saved, and who they are, can therefore be known absolutely to God alone; to us, only so far forth as may be inferred from the presence of the marks and signs of election revealed to us in the Word. Faith and its fruits are the chief signs in the case of adults; and accordingly he that believes may know that he is of the elect and be certain of his salvation. In the case of infants dying in infancy, birth within the bounds of the covenant is a sure sign, since the promise is "unto us and our children." But present unbelief is not a sure sign of reprobation in the case of adults; for who knows but that unbelief may yet give place to faith? Nor in the case of infants, dying such, is birth outside the covenant a trustworthy sign of reprobation; for the election of God is free. Accordingly there are many—adults and infants—of whose salvation we may be sure: but of reprobation we can never be sure; a judgment to that effect is necessarily unsafe even as to such adults as are apparently living in sin, while as to infants who " die and give no sign," it is presumptuous and rash in the extreme. The above is practically an outline of the teaching of Zwingli.[1] He himself, after

---

[1] Zwingli's teaching may be conveniently worked out by the aid of AUGUST BAUR's valuable *Zwingli's Theologie*, especially vol. ii. (Halle, 1889). Zwingli's peculiar doctrine of original sin had practically very little influence on his resolution of the question of the sal-

some preliminary hesitation,[1] worked it out in its logical completeness, and taught that: 1. All believers are elect and hence are saved; though we cannot know infallibly who are true believers, except each man in his own case.[2] 2. All children of believers dying in infancy are elect, and hence are saved; their inclusion in the covenant of salvation rests on God's immutable promise, and their death in infancy must be taken as a sign of election.[3] 3. It is probable, from the super-

vation of infants, which rather turned on his doctrine of the extent of the atonement.

[1] *Works*, i., 423 (1523).

[2] The word "church," says Zwingli, "is used variously in the Scriptures. First of all, it is used for those elect who are destinated by the will of God to eternal life. . . . This is known to God alone, for He, according to the word of Solomon, alone knows the hearts of the sons of men. But none the less, those who are members of this church know that they themselves, since they have faith, are elect and are members of this first church; but they are ignorant of other members than themselves. . . . Those then who believe are ordained to eternal life. But who truly believe no one knows except the believer himself. . . . From these, therefore, it follows that that first church is known to God alone, and only those who have certain and unshaken faith know that they are members of this church." (*Works*, iv., p. 8.) "It follows, therefore, that those who believe know they are elect; for those who believe are elect. Election is, therefore, the antecedent of faith. . . . It is proper to pronounce concerning those only who persist in disbelief until death. However much any give open signs, whether by cruelty or lust, that they are repudiated by God, nevertheless we ought not before the end or 'departure' (as the poet says) to condemn any one." (*Works*, iv., 723 *sq.*, 1530.)

[3] "We are more certain of the election of none than of infants who are taken away in youth, while as yet they are without law; for human life is sometimes not truly, but only apparently innocent, while there cannot be any stain (*labes*) in infants who spring from believers. For original sin is expiated by Christ; for as in Adam all died, so in Christ we are all restored to life—we, that is, who either believe or are of the church by promise. But no stain of misdeeds (*labes facinorum*) can contaminate them, for they are not yet under law. But since no cause disjoins them from God except sin, and they are alien from all sin, it follows that none can so irrefragably be known to be among the elect as those infants who are taken away by fate in youth; for in their case to die is the sign of election, just as faith is in adults. And those who are reprobated or repudiated by God do not die in this state of innocence, but are preserved by Divine providence, that their repudiation may be manifested by a wicked life." (*Works*, iv., 127, 1530.) "Therefore the infants of Christians, since they are not less than adults of the visible Church of Christ, are not less to be (so it follows) in the number of those whom

abundance of the gift of grace over the offence, that all infants dying such are elect and saved ; there is, indeed, no sure promise of their salvation, which must, therefore, be left with God, but it is certainly rash and even impious to affirm their damnation.[1] 4. All who are saved, whether adult or infant, are saved only by the free grace of God's election and through the redemption of Christ.[2]

we judge to be elect than their parents. Hence it happens that those judges act impiously and presumptuously who devote the infants of Christians to dreadful things, since so many clear testimonies of Scripture contradict this . . ." (*Works*, iv., 8.)

[1] " Since those alone who have heard and then either believed or remained in unbelief are subject to our judgment, it follows that we vehemently err in judging infant children, whether of Gentiles or of Christians. Of Gentiles, because no law condemns them, for they do not fall under that of ' Who shall not believe,' etc. Hence, since the election of God is free, it is impious to exclude from it those of whom by these signs, faith and unbelief, we are not able to determine whether they are in it or not. With reference to those of Christians, however, we are not only intruding rashly into the election of God, but we are not even believing His word by which He manifests this election to us. For since He admits us into the covenant of Abraham, this word now renders us no less certain of their election than formerly of the Hebrews. For that word, that they are within the covenant, testament, people of God, makes us certain of their election until God shall announce something else concerning any one." (*Works*, iii., 427, cf. 429, 1527.) " Hence it follows that if in Christ, the second Adam, we are restored to life, just as we were handed over to death in the first Adam, we rashly condemn the children born of Christian parents ; nay, even the children of Gentiles. But as to the infants of Gentiles, whatever opinion may be held, we confidently assert that on account of the virtue of the pre-eminent salvation of Christ, they go beyond the mark who adjudge them to eternal malediction, both because of the reparation spoken of and because of the free election of God, which does not follow, but is followed by, faith. . . . They ought not, therefore, to be rashly condemned by us who, by reason of age, have not faith ; for although they do not as yet have it, the election of God is nevertheless hidden from us, with respect to which, if they are elect, we judge rashly concerning things of which we know nothing." (*Works*, iv., 7.)

[2] " But I have spoken in this manner, That the children of Christians cannot be damned by original sin for this reason, because though sin should condemn according to the law, yet on account of the remedy exhibited in Christ it cannot condemn, especially not those included in the covenant made with Abraham ; for concerning these we have other clear and solid testimonies : concerning the rest, who are born out of the church, we have nothing except the present testimony" (*i.e.*, " As in Adam, so in Christ, but more"), " so far as I know, and similar ones in this fifth chapter of Romans, by which to prove that

It is probable that Zwingli stood alone among the Reformers in his extension of salvation to all infants dying in infancy. That all children of believers, dying in infancy, are included in the covenant of God and enter at once into glory was the characteristic feature of the Reformed doctrine; the boldness of which and the relief which it brought to the oppressed heart are alike scarcely estimable by us after centuries of emancipation from the dreadful burden of what had up to the rise of the Reformed theology been for ages the undoubting belief of the Church—viz., that all unbaptized infants are excluded from bliss. With this great advance the minds and hearts of most men were satisfied, and, happy in teaching from positive Scriptures the certain salvation of all the children of Christian parents departing from their arms to the arms of Jesus, they were content to leave the children of unbelievers, dying such, to the just but hidden judgment of God. It has been thought by many, indeed, that both John Calvin and Zwingli's successor in the leadership of the Church at Zurich, Henry Bullinger, shared to the full extent the hope of Zwingli, and were ready, with him, to extend their assurance of infant salvation to all who die in infancy of whatever parentage. It is true that it is not easy to adduce from the writings of these great teachers passages which clearly affirm the opposite; what have been brought forward as such are usually rather assertions of the presence and desert of "original sin" in infants than declarations of the punishment which they actually undergo. But, on the other hand, there is a more entire lack of positive evidence for the affirmation; and there are not altogether

those who are born outside the Church are cleansed from original contamination. But if any one should say that it is more probable that the children of the Gentiles are saved by Christ than that they are damned, certainly he is less making Christ void than those who damn those born in the Church, if they die without baptism; and he will have more foundation and authority from the Scriptures than those who deny this, for he would assert nothing more than that the children of the Gentiles, too, while of tender age, are not damned on account of original vice, but this, of course, through the benefit of Christ." (*Works*, 637, 1526.)

wanting passages from either writer which appear, in their natural sense, to imply belief that some infants dying such pass into doom.. It would seem difficult to read, for example, Calvin's rejoinders to Pighius, Servetus and Castellio without becoming convinced that he did not think of all infants, dying such, as escaping the just recompense of their sinfulness. Even such a comment as that which he makes on Rom. v. 7 seems, indeed, to carry this implication on its face : " Hence, in order to partake of the miserable inheritance of sin, it is enough for thee to be a man, for it dwells in flesh and blood ; but in order to enjoy the righteousness of Christ, it is necessary for thee to be a believer, for a participation of Him is obtained by faith alone. He is communicated to infants in a peculiar manner ; for they have in the covenant the right of adoption, by which they pass over into participation of Christ. It is of the children of the pious that I am speaking, to whom the promise of grace is directed. For the rest are by no means released from the common lot."[1] Similarly Bullinger's language, as he argues for the inclusion of believers' infants within the covenant and their consequent right to baptism, now and again appears inconsistent with the supposition that he supposed all infants dying such to be alike included in the election of God. Thus a fundamental distinction between the children of the faithful and those of unbelievers, not only in privileges but also in ultimate destiny, seems to color the whole language of a passage like the following : " Wherefore, I, trusting to God's mercy and his truth and undoubted promise, believe that infants, departing out of this world by a too timely death, before they can be baptized, are saved by the mere mercy of God in the power of his truth and promise through Christ, who saith in the Gospel, ' Suffer little ones to come unto me ; for of such is the kingdom of God :' Again, ' It is not the will of my Father which is in heaven that one of these little ones should

---

[1] Amsterdam ed. of CALVIN's *Opera*, vii., 36a : " De piorum liberis loquar, ad quos promissio gratiæ dirigitur. Nam alii à communi forte nequaquam eximuntur."

perish.' For verily God who cannot lie hath said, 'I am thy God, and the God of thy seed after thee.' Whereupon St. Paul also affirmeth that they are born holy which are begotten of holy parents; not that of flesh and blood any holy thing is born, for 'that which is born of flesh is flesh:' but because that holiness and separation from the common seed of men is of promise, and by right of the covenant. For we are all by natural birth born the sons of wrath, death, and damnation: but Paul attributeth a special privilege to the children of the faithful, wherewith by the grace of God they which by nature are unclean are purified. So the same apostle, in another place, doth gather holy branches of a holy root; and again elsewhere saith: 'If by the sin of one many be dead, much more the grace of God and the gift of grace which is by one man, Jesus Christ, hath abounded unto many.'"[1] As over against the natural implications of such passages there is nothing positive to set, and it is certainly within the mark to say that as yet no decisive evidence has been adduced to show that either Calvin[2] or Bullinger[3] agreed with Zwingli in cherishing the hope

[1] *Decades*, Parker Soc. ed., iv., 373; cf. 382, 313, 344.
[2] Dr. CHARLES W. SHIELDS, in a very thorough and learned paper in *The Presbyterian and Reformed Review* for October, 1890 (vol. i., pp. 634-651), has said everything possible to be said in favor of including Calvin in the class of those who teach the salvation of all infants dying such. Dr. Shields's ingenious and powerful argument is vitiated, however, by two faults of interpretation. He does not always catch the drift of Calvin's argument, as directed rather to showing against the Anabaptists that infants, too, as subjects of salvation, are also subjects of baptism; and he refers Calvin's repeated assertions of the presence of personal guilt as distinguished from imputed guilt in all those who are lost, to guilt arising from actual sinning, whereas Calvin means it of guilt arising from inherent corruption or "original sin." Calvin says that every soul that is lost deserves it not merely because it is implicated in the guilt of Adam's first sin, but also because it is inwardly corrupt and wrath-deserving; he does not say it is not condemned unless it has committed overt acts of sinning. When these two errors of interpretation are eliminated, no passages remain in which would seem to imply the salvation of all who die in infancy.
[3] That Bullinger agreed with Zwingli in holding that all who die in infancy are saved is repeatedly asserted by Dr. SCHAFF, but without the adduction of evidence, unless we are to read the note in *Creeds of Christendom*, i., 642, note 3, as directing us to the passages

that all infants dying in infancy are saved; the probability is distinctly to the contrary.

The constitutive principles of Zwingli's teaching, however, are not only the common conviction of all the Reformed, but are even the essential postulates of the whole Reformed system. That the salvation of men depends ultimately upon nothing except the free election of God must be the hinge of all Reformed thinking in the sphere of soteriology; and differences relative to the salvation of infants can arise within the limits of Reformed thought only on the two points of what the signs of election and reprobation are, and how surely these signs may be identified in men. On these points the Reformed were early divided into five distinguishable classes.

cited in Laurence's *Bampton Lectures*, pp. 266, 267, as such. But these passages do not support the contention; they only prove that Bullinger taught that infants, too, are salvable (arguing for their baptism as against the Anabaptists), not that all that die in infancy are saved. In the seventh volume of his *History of the Christian Church*, published in 1892, Dr. Schaff somewhat qualifies the sharpness of his previous statement by adding a justifying clause. Bullinger, he here says, "agreed with Zwingli's extension of salvation to all infants and to elect heathen; *at all events, he nowhere dissents from these advanced views, and published with approbation Zwingli's last work, where they are most strongly expressed*" (p. 211). That the young Bullinger—he was then thirty-two—did put forth his beloved master's last work, the *Expositio Fidei*, addressed to King Francis, with a preface of hearty appreciation and praise, is certainly true. But this can scarcely be said to commit him to every statement in the work. We know that he did not share his master's doctrine of original sin, but labors to explain away its peculiarities and reduce it to only a verbal deviation from the common doctrine of the Reformers (*Decades* as above, ii., 394, 388). Why should the case be different with reference to matters lying on the periphery of the doctrinal system? Surely the argument from silence here is most precarious. Nor is it clear that he nowhere betrays dissent from these views of his master. We have adduced passages which appear to imply that he did not contemplate heathen infants dying in infancy as saved. And in a little book on the Judgment Day, published in 1572 (*Von höchster Freud und gröstem Leyd des künftigen jüngsten Tags, u.s.w.*), he certainly does not speak in Zwingli's manner of the heathen. The learned Zwingli scholar, Dr. J. W. Wÿss, of Zurich, suggests that Bullinger may have changed his mind in the interval between the ages of thirty-two and sixty-eight, a suggestion which seems unnecessary in the entire absence of proof that he ever had a different mind from that suggested in the *Decades* of 1551 as well as in his *Judgment Day* of 1572.

1. There were a few, from the very beginning, who held with Zwingli that death in infancy is one of the signs of election, and hence that all who die in infancy are the children of God and enter at once into glory. After Zwingli it is probable that Bishop Hooper was the first to embrace this view.[1] It is presented in a characteristically restrained and winning way by Francis Junius in his work on *Nature and Grace*, which was published in 1592. "Some one will say, perhaps," he says, "'But infants surely who are called from this life before they commit actual sin are not to be assigned to destruction nor held by us to be lost on account of that natural vitiosity which they have contracted as an inheritance from their parents?' I respond that there is a double question raised here under the appearance of one : one is, What end do they deserve according to God's justice by their vitiosity? the other is, What end will they actually have? The first we answer, briefly, thus : they cannot but deserve for their vitiosity, according to God's justice, separation from God—that is, destruction and eternal death. . . . Let us look, then, at the second question. None of us is so wild, or has ever been known to be so wild, as to condemn infants *simpliciter*. Let those who teach otherwise look to it by what right they do it, and relying on what authority. For, although they are in themselves and in our common nature condemnable, it does not follow that we ought to pass the sentence of condemnation upon them. What then? Will they be saved? We hold that all those will be saved who belong to the covenant and who belong to the election. But those infants belong to the covenant who spring from covenanted parents, whether immediately—*i.e.*, from covenanted father and mother, or either ; or mediately—*i.e.*, from covenanted ancestors, even though the continuity has been broken, as God says He 'will show mercy unto thousands of generations' (Ex. xx.). And this is the way in which Paul speaks of the Jews as being included in his time (Rom. xi.) ; nor do we doubt that by

---

[1] See reference, *ante*, p. 191.

the same force of the covenant God sanctifies by the covenant as His own some from the number of unbelievers—for the sake of the covenant, we mean, that their ancestors received. Some also, however, belong to the election, for God has not cut off from Himself the right and authority to communicate more widely the grace of His own election to those of whom it cannot be said that either their parents or ancestors belonged to the covenant; for just as of old He called into the covenant afresh, according to His election, those who were not in the covenant, in order that they might be in it, so also in every age the same benefit may be conferred by His most free action. And why may not this happen to infants as well as to others, since of them may be justly said what the author of the Book of Wisdom wrote of Enoch, that 'he was taken away lest evil should change his mind or guile ensnare his soul'? All infants, therefore, are in themselves condemnable by the justice of God; and if God have condemned any (a matter to be left to Him) they are justly condemned; but we nevertheless affirm that those who are of the covenant and those who are of the election are saved—whomsoever He has ordained to eternal life; and out of charity we presume that those whom He calls to Himself as infants and snatches seasonably out of this miserable vale of sins are rather saved according to His election and fatherly providence than expelled from the kingdom of heaven. We rest utterly in His counsel."[1] More lately this genial judgment has become the ruling view, especially among English-speaking Calvinists, and we may select Augustus M. Toplady[2] and Robert S. Candlish as its types. The latter, for example, writes:[3] "In many ways I apprehend it may be inferred from Scripture

[1] Francis Junius, *De Natura et Gratia*, 1592, pp. 83, 84: the closing words are: "Ex charitate antem eos quos ad se infantes vocat, et tempestive ex hac misera valle peccatorum eripit, potius servari præsumimus, secundum electionem et providentiam ipsius paternam, quam à regno cœlorum abdicari. Omnino conquiescimus in consilio ejus."
[2] See reference, *ante*, p. 193.
[3] *The Atonement*, etc., 1861, pp. 183, 184.

that all dying in infancy are elect, and are, therefore, saved. . . . The whole analogy of the plan of saving mercy seems to favor the same view, and now it may be seen, if I am not greatly mistaken, to be put beyond question by the bare fact that little children die. . . . The death of little children must be held to be one of the fruits of redemption. . . ."

2. At the opposite extreme a very few Reformed theologians taught that the only sure sign of election is faith with its fruits, and, therefore, that we can have no real ground of conviction concerning the fate of any infant. As, however, God certainly has His elect among infants too, each man can cherish the hope that his own children are of the elect. This sadly agnostic position, which was afterward condemned by the whole body of the Reformed assembled in the Synod of Dort, is at least approached by Peter Martyr, who writes: " Neither am I to be thought to promise salvation to all the children of the faithful which depart without the sacrament, for if I should do so I might be counted rash ; I leave them to be judged by the mercy of God, seeing I have no certainty concerning the secret election and predestination ; but I only assert that those are truly saved to whom the divine election extends, although baptism does not intervene. Just so, I hope well concerning infants of this kind, because I see them born from faithful parents ; and this thing has promises that are uncommon ; and although they may not be general, *quoad omnes*, yet when I see nothing to the contrary it is right to hope well concerning the salvation of such infants."[1] Even after the declaration of the Synod of Dort there remained some to whom it did not seem possible to speak with the Synod's confidence of the salvation of all the children of believers dying in infancy. Thus, Thomas Gataker writes to Richard Baxter on November 1st, 1653,[2] that he dares not " herein speak so peremptorilie as the Synod of

---

[1] *Loci Communes*, i., class. 4, cap. 5, § 16 (compare iv., 100).
[2] This letter is preserved in the Williams Library, London, and was printed by Dr. BRIGGS in *The Presbyterian Review*, v., 705 *sq*. See pp. 708 and 706.

Dort doth;" "nor," he adds, "do Zanchie, Ursine, or divers other of our Divines, of whom see Malderi Antisynodica,' pp. 63, 64. Tho I confess that some of them in their Discourses and Disputes overthrow sometime with one hand, what they seem to build up with the other." That the infants of believing parents are included in the covenant he did not doubt; but he conceived of this covenant as rather conditional than absolute, and therefore felt it to be "more than can certainlie be avowed or from Scr. can be averred," "that the Child is therein considered as a member of the Parents, and is by its parents' faith discharged of the guilt of its sin, and put in an actual state of Salvation." "Concerning the state of infants, even of true believers," therefore, he thinks that the Scripture is "verie sparing; and in averring ought therein peremptorilie we have great cause therefore to be verie warie." Something of the same hesitancy characterizes also Baxter's own statements on the subject. In his *Plain Scripture Proof of Infant Church-Membership and Baptism*, the third edition of which was issued shortly before the date of the letter to which Gataker's was a reply, he speaks in a very similar manner. "We have," he says, "a stronger probability than he [Tombes] mentioneth of the salvation of all the Infants of the Faithfull so dying, and a certainty of the salvation of some.... If any will go farther and say that God's assuring mercy to them, and calling them blessed, and covenanting to be their God, with the rest of the Arguments, will prove more than a probability, even a full certainty of the salvation of all Believers' Infants so dying; though I dare not say so my selfe, yet I profess to think this opinion far better grounded than Mr.

---

[1] Dr. Briggs prints "Antisquodica," which is a mere blunder, of course, for Gataker's "Antisynodica." Malderus was bishop of Antwerp and a prolific writer, author of a number of commentaries and theological and ethical treatises. The book cited by Gataker was published at Antwerp by Balthasar Moretus, in 1620, and is a volume of over 300 8vo pages. Its full title is: *Antisynodica*, sive Animadversiones in decreta conventus Dordraceni, quam vocant synodum nationalem, de quinque doctrinæ capitibus inter Remonstrantes et Contra-Remonstrantes controversis.

T[ombs]'s, that would shut them all out of the Church."[1] Twenty years later he returns to the question, and treats it at great length. He thinks that "there can no promise or proof be produced that all unbaptized Infants are saved, either from the *pœna damni* or *sensus*, or both;" but, on the other hand, he can now " say, as the Synod of *Dort*, Art. I., that *Believing Parents have no cause to doubt of the salvation of their children that dye in infancy*, before they commit *actual sin;* that is, not to trouble themselves with fears about it :" and he thinks " it very probable that this ascertaining promise belongeth not only to the *natural* seed of believers, but to all whom they have the true *power* and *right* to dedicate in covenant to God." Still, however, he " dares not say" that he is " *undoubtedly certain of it ;*" he is giving opinions, not convictions.[2] A hint of the same unwillingness to make the affirmation of the salvation of the children of believers absolute is found even in the statement of the *Compendium* of John Marck. " Nor is it to be doubted," he says, " that to those reprobated, there are likewise most justly to be referred as well the Gentiles who are strangers to the proclamation of the Gospel as the infants of unbelievers, while we have good hope for those of believers because of God's promise (Gen. xvii. 7, etc.), although they are in themselves not less damnable, and possibly some of them are even to be damned (*cæteroquin in se non minus damnabilibus, et forte quibusdam etiam damnandis*). For although concerning individual persons of Gentiles and of infants born of unbelievers we neither can nor wish to determine anything particularly, because of God's freedom and the frequently hidden paths of the Spirit, yet all these are by nature children of wrath, impure, alien, and remote from God, without hope, left to themselves (cf. Eph. ii. 3 ; 1 Cor. vii. 14 ; Eph. ii. 12, 17 ; Acts xiv. 16, etc.) ; God has revealed nothing concerning a salvation decreed or to be wrought

[1] *Op. cit.*, ed. 3, 1653, pp. 76 and 78.
[2] *A Christian Directory*, etc., London, 1673, p. 807 *sq.* See p. 809. ("Christian Ecclesiastics: Ecclesiastical Cases of Conscience," Quest. 35.)

for them ; and they are destitute of the ordinary means of grace."[1]

To the great body of Calvinists, however, both of these views seemed insufficiently in accord with " what is written." The one appeared to err by going beyond, and the other by falling short of, the warrant of Scripture. All their thought on this subject took its start from the cardinal scriptural fact of the covenant, and they were jealous of everything which seemed to dull the sharpness of the distinction between the covenanted children of believers and the uncovenanted children of unbelievers. Triglandius speaks not for himself alone but for practically the whole body of the Reformed when, in answer to the suggestion of Episcopius that " it makes no difference whether the infants are children of believers or unbelievers, since the same innocence is found in all infants as such," he replies : " But to us the two do not stand on the same footing ; since the one are included in the covenant of God and the others are strangers to that covenant (Gen. xvii. 7 ; Eph. ii. 11, 12). For this reason children of unbelieving Gentiles are said to be *impure*, but those of believers *holy* (1 Cor. vii. 14) ; wherefore also Peter says, when exhorting the Jews to repentance and faith (Acts ii. 39), ' To you is the promise (*i.e.*, of remission of sins and the gift of the Holy Ghost), and to your children, and to all who are afar off whom our Lord God shall call.' "[2] And John Gerhard might have quoted many more names than those of Calvin, Beza, Sadeel, Ursinus, Gentilis, and Musculus, as affirming that " the infants of believers, all alike, whether baptized or unbaptized, are rightly holy from their mothers' womb by the inheritance of the promise, and enjoy eternal salvation in the covenant and company of God."[3] With this central point of agreement, the great

---

[1] JOANNIS MARCKII *Compendium*, etc. (1752), p. 147 (cap. vii., § xxxiii.). In defending Marck's suggestion, DE MOOR quotes a similar passage from the *Censura Confess. Remonstr.*, and another from TRIGLANDIUS very much to the same effect as GATAKER'S.
[2] *Antapolog.*, caput. 13, p. 207a.
[3] *Loci.*, ix., p. 281, edition of 1769.

body of Calvinists differed among themselves only in their belief concerning the destiny of infants dying outside the covenant, and on this point parted into three varieties of opinion.

3. Many held that faith and the promise are sure signs of election, and accordingly that all believers and their children are certainly saved ; but that the lack of faith and the promise is an equally sure sign of reprobation, so that all the children of unbelievers dying such are equally certainly lost. The younger Spanheim, for example, writes : " Confessedly, therefore, original sin is a most just cause of positive reprobation. Hence no one fails to see what we should think concerning the children of pagans dying in their childhood ; for unless we acknowledge salvation outside of God's covenant and Church (like the Pelagians of old, and with them Tertullian, Epiphanius, Clement of Alexandria, of the ancients, and of the moderns, Andradius, Ludovicus Vives, Erasmus, and not a few others, against the whole Bible), and suppose that all the children of the heathen, dying in infancy, are saved, and that it would be a great blessing to them if they should be smothered by the midwives or strangled in the cradle, we should humbly believe that they are justly reprobated by God on account of the corruption (*labes*) and guilt (*reatus*) derived to them by natural propagation. Hence, too, Paul testifies (Rom. v. 14) that death has passed upon them which have not sinned after the similitude of Adam's transgression, and distinguishes and separates (1 Cor. vii. 14) the children of the covenanted as holy from the impure children of unbelievers."[1] Somewhat similarly Stapfer, after affirming the salvation of the infants of believers, dying such, continues : " As to the children of unbelievers, we believe, indeed, that they will be separated from communion with God ; and hence, because as children of wrath and cursing they are excluded from the beatific communion with God, they will be damned"—though he eases the apparent harshness of his language by recalling

[1] *Opera*, iii., cols. 1173-74, § 22.

the fact of various degrees of punishment in hell.¹ On an earlier page² we have quoted a passage from Usher's *Body of Divinity* to the same effect. That work was a compilation, and we find the same words in an earlier *Catechism* published by Samuel Crooke,³ which may stand as an example from English ground of this very widespread opinion.

4. More held that faith and the promise are certain signs of election, so that the salvation of believers' children is certain, while the lack of the promise only leaves us in ignorance of God's purpose; nevertheless that there is good ground for asserting that both election and reprobation have place in this unknown sphere. Accordingly they held that all the infants of believers, dying such, are saved, but that some of the infants of unbelievers, dying such, are lost. Probably as much as this is intended to be asserted by Thomas Goodwin when to the question, " Doth God inflict eternal death merely for the corruption of nature upon any infants?" he answers: " My brethren, it must be said, Yes: we are children of wrath by nature; and unless there come in election amongst them, for it is election saveth and is the root of salvation, it must needs be so. . . . But you will say, Do these perish? or Doth God let those perish? Doth His wrath seize upon them? Not only what the text [Eph. ii. 3] saith, but that in Rom. v. is clear for it. . . . It is true election knows its own amongst infants, but it must be free grace, it must be by grace that ye are saved, for clearly by nature ye are all children of wrath. Therefore the Lord, as He will have instances of all sorts that are in heaven, so He will have some that are in hell for their sin brought into the world."⁴ But probably no higher expression of this general view can be found than John Owen's. He argues that there are two ways in which God saves infants. "(1) By interesting them in the covenant, if their immediate or remote parents have

---

¹ *Institut. Theolog. Polemic.*, 1716, iv., 518.
² See above, p. 191.
³ *Guide unto True Blessedness*, etc., ed. 2, 1614.
⁴ *Works*, ii., 135–36.

been believers. He is a God of them and of their seed, extending his mercy to a thousand generations of them that fear him.[1] (2) By his grace of election which is most free and not tied to any conditions, by which I make no doubt but God taketh many unto him in Christ whose parents never knew or had been despisers of the Gospel."[2]

5. Most Calvinists of the past, however, have held that faith and the promise are marks by which we may know assuredly that all those who believe and their children, dying such, are elect and saved; while the absence of sure marks of either election or reprobation in infants, dying such outside the covenant, leaves us without ground for inference concerning them, and they must therefore be left to the judgment of God, which, however hidden from us, is assuredly just and holy and good. This agnostic view of the fate of uncovenanted infants has been held, of course, in conjunction with every degree of hope or the lack of hope concerning them, and thus in the hands of the several theologians it approaches each of the other views. Petrus de Witte may stand as one example of it. He says: " We must adore God's judgments and not curiously inquire into them. Of the children of believers it is not to be doubted but that they shall be saved, inasmuch as they belong unto the covenant. But because we have no promise for the children of unbelievers we leave them to the judgment of God."[3] Our own Jonathan Dickinson[4] may stand as another. " It may be further urged against this proposition," he says, "*That it drives multitudes of poor* infants to Hell *who never committed any actual Sin; and is therefore a Doctrine so cruel and unmerciful as to be unworthy of God.* To this I answer that greatest Modesty becomes us in drawing any Conclusions on this Subject. We have indeed the highest

---

[1] It is, perhaps, worth noting that this is the general Calvinistic view of what " children of believers" means. Compare CALVIN, *Tracts*, vol. iii., p. 351; and also JUNIUS as quoted above, p. 203.
[2] *Works*, x., 81; compare v., 137.
[3] *Catechism*, q. 37.
[4] *The True Scripture Doctrine concerning some Important Points of Christian Faith*, etc. Boston, 1741, pp. 123, 124.

Encouragement to dedicate our children to Christ, since he has told us, *Of such is the Kingdom of Heaven;* and the strongest Reason to Hope as to the Happiness of those deceased Infants, who have been thus dedicated to him. But God has not been pleased to reveal to us how far he will extend His *uncovenanted* Mercy to others that die in Infancy.—As, on the one Hand, I don't know that the Scripture anywhere assures us that they shall *all* be *saved:* So, on the other Hand, we have not (that I know of) any Evidence, from Scripture or the Nature of Things, that *any* of them will eternally *perish.*— All those that die in Infancy may (for aught we know) belong to the *Election of Grace;* and be *predestinated to the Adoption of Children.* They may, in Methods to us unknown, have the benefits of Christ's Redemption applied to them; and thereby be made Heirs of Eternal Glory. They are (it is true) naturally under the Guilt and Pollution of Original Sin; but they may, notwithstanding this, for any thing that appears to the contrary, be renewed by the gracious Influences of the Spirit of God, and thereby be made mete for Eternal Life. It therefore concerns us, without any bold and presumptuous conclusions, to leave them in the Hands of that God whose *tender Mercies are over all His Works.''* It is this cautious, agnostic view which has the best historical right to be called the general Calvinistic one, and it has persisted as such until the present day in all but English-speaking lands. One of the ablest living Calvinistic thinkers, for example, Dr. A. Kuyper, of Amsterdam, writes as follows: " Constantly and unwaveringly the Reformed Confession stations itself on the standpoint of the *covenant* and withholds baptism from all who stand outside the covenant, because it belongs to those within the covenant. To be sure, the Reformed Confession does not pass judgment on the children of heathen who die before coming to years of discretion. They depend on God's mercy, widened as broadly as possible. But where the Scriptures are silent, the Confession, too, preserves silence. Men know nothing here and can say nothing. Mere conjecture and imagination have no right to enter so serious a matter. The lot of these numerous children belongs to the hidden things that are for the Lord God, and is not included among the things which He has revealed to the children of men. Revealed, however, is the matter of the covenant, and this covenant makes known to us the remarkable rule that God has been pleased to set His holy election in connection with the bond of generation."[1] Van Mastricht correctly says that while the Reformed hold that infants are liable to reprobation, yet "concerning *believers'* infants . . . they judge better things. But *unbelievers'* infants, because the Scriptures determine nothing *clearly* on the subject, they judge should be left to the Divine discretion."[2]

The Reformed Confessions with characteristic caution refrain from all definition upon the negative side of this great question, and thus confine themselves to emphasizing the gracious doctrine common to the whole body of Reformed thought. The fundamental Reformed doctrine of the Church is nowhere more beautifully stated than in the sixteenth article of the Old Scotch Confession, while its polemical appendix of 1580, in its protest against the errors of "antichrist," specifically mentions "his cruell judgement againis infants departing without the sacrament: his absolute necessitie of baptisme." No synod probably ever met which labored under greater temptation to declare that some infants, dying in infancy, are reprobate, than the Synod of Dort. Possibly nearly every member of it held as his private opinion that there are such infants. And the certainly very shrewd but scarcely sincere methods of the Remonstrants in shifting the form in which this question came before the Synod were very irritating. But the fathers of Dort, with truly Reformed loyalty to the positive declarations of Scripture, confined themselves to a clear testimony to the positive doctrine of infant salvation and a repudiation of the calumnies of the Remonstrants, without a word of negative inference. "Since we are to judge of the

[1] *De Heraut*, for September 7th, 1890.
[2] *Theoretico-Pract. Theol.* (1724), p. 308.

will of God from His Word," they say, "which testifies that the children of believers are holy, not by nature, but in virtue of the covenant of grace, in which they together with their parents are comprehended, godly parents have no reason to doubt of the election and salvation of their children whom it pleaseth God to call out of this life in their infancy" (cap. i., art. xvii.). Accordingly they repel in the Conclusion the calumny that the Reformed teach "that many children of the faithful are torn guiltless from their mothers' breasts and tyrannically plunged into hell."[1] It is easy to say that nothing is here said of the children of any but the "godly" and of the "faithful." This is true. And therefore it is not implied (as is often thoughtlessly asserted) that the contrary of what is here asserted is true of the children of the ungodly; but nothing is taught of them at all. It is more to the purpose to observe that it is asserted here that all the children of believers, dying such, are saved; and that this assertion is an inestimable advance on that of the Council of Trent and that of the Augsburg Confession that baptism is necessary to salvation, as well as upon the ominous silence of the Anglican Prayer Book as to all who die unbaptized. It is, in a word, the confessional doctrine of the Reformed churches and of the Reformed churches alone, that all believers' children, dying in infancy, are saved.

What has been said of the Synod of Dort may be repeated of the Westminster Assembly. The West-

---

[1] The language here used has a not uninteresting history. It is CALVIN's challenge to Castellio : " Put forth now thy virulence against God, who hurls innocent babes torn from their mothers' breasts into eternal death" (*De Occulta Dei Providentia*, in *Opp.* ed., Amst., viii., pp. 644-45). The underlying conception that God condemns infants to eternal death may, no doubt, be Calvin's ; but the mode of expression is Calvin's *reductio ad absurdum* (or rather *ad blasphemiam*) of Castellio's opinions. Nevertheless the Remonstrants allowed themselves in their polemic zeal to apply the whole sentiment to the orthodox, and that, even in a still more sharpened form—viz., with reference to *believers'* children. This very gross calumny the Synod repels. Its deliverance is subjected to a very sharp and not very candid criticism by EPISCOPIUS (*Opera* I., i., p. 176, and specially II., p. 28).

minster divines were generally at one in the matter of infant salvation with the doctors of Dort, but, like them, they refrained from any deliverance as to its negative side. That death in infancy does not prejudice the salvation of God's elect they asserted in the chapter of their Confession which treats of the application of Christ's redemption to His people: "All those whom God hath predestined unto life, and those only, He is pleased, in His appointed and accepted time, effectually to call, by His word and Spirit, . . . so as they come most freely, being made willing by His grace. . . . Elect infants dying in infancy are regenerated and saved by Christ, through the Spirit who worketh when, and where, and how He pleaseth."[1] With this declaration of their faith that such

[1] *Westminster Confession of Faith*, X., i. and iii. The opinion that a body of non-elect infants dying in infancy and not saved is implied in this passage, although often controversially asserted, is not only a wholly unreasonable opinion exegetically, but is absolutely negatived by the history of the formation of this clause in the Assembly as recorded in the *Minutes*, and has never found favor among the expositors of the Confession. DAVID DICKSON'S (1684) treatment of the section shows that he understands it to be directed against the Anabaptists; and all careful students of the Confession understand it as above, including SHAW, A. A. HODGE, MACPHERSON, MITCHELL, and BEATTIE. This is true of all schools of adherents to the Confession. See, *e.g.*, LYMAN BEECHER (*Spirit of the Pilgrims*, 1828, i., pp. 49, 81): "The phrase 'elect infants,' which, in his usual way, the reviewer takes for granted implies that there are infants who are not elect, implies no such thing." "But this Confession, which represented the Calvinism of Old England and New, and which expresses also the doctrinal opinions of the Church of Scotland and of the Presbyterian Church in the United States, teaches neither directly nor by implication that infants are damned." Compare also PHILIP SCHAFF, *Creeds of Christendom*, i., 380, 795. Compare also *The Presbyterian Pastor's Catechism*, by the Rev. JOHN H. BOCKOK, D.D. (Presbyterian Board, 1857): "Q. 13. *Why do we not baptize the infant children of unbelievers?* A. 1. Not because we think such children would be lost if they died in infancy. We do not think children will be saved on account of their baptism, but through the merits of Christ. Baptism does not confer salvation, but only acknowledges and recognizes it. 2. Non-elect infants are such as do not die in infancy, but grow up to be wicked and impenitent men, as Cain, Herod, Judas, Voltaire, Paine." The impression that the phrase "elect infants dying in infancy," implies as its contrast "non-elect infants dying in infancy," rather than "elect infants living to grow up," is probably due in some measure to lack of acquaintance with the literature of the subject. A glance into CORNELIUS BURGES'S

216 THE DOCTRINE OF INFANT SALVATION.

of God's elect as die in infancy are saved by His own mysterious working in their hearts, although incapable of the response of faith, they were content. Whether these elect comprehend all infants, dying such, or some only—whether there is such a class as non-elect infants dying in infancy, their words neither say nor suggest. No Reformed confession enters into this question; no word is said by any one of them which either asserts or implies either that some infants are reprobated or that all are saved. What has been held in common by the whole body of Reformed theologians on this subject is asserted in these confessions; of what has been disputed among them the confessions are silent. And silence is as favorable to one type of belief as to another.

treatise entitled *Baptismal Regeneration of Elect Infants*, which was published in 1629, will supply a number of instances of the use of the phrase in the latter contrast. For example: "Elect infants that live to years . . . yet such as dye in infancy" (p. 166). Some think Calvin in his *Institutes*, iv., 16, 21, speaks only of the "case of elect infants dying in infancy," "but he is not so to be taken, as if he held that only elect infants who dye in infancy doe receive the Spirit in baptism: but that all the elect, whether they live or dye, doe ordinarily partake of the Spirit in that ordinance" (p. 164). "That all elect infants doe ordinarily, in Baptism, receive the Spirit of Christ, to seaze upon them for Christ, and to be in them as the roote and first principle of regeneration and future newnesse of life. . . . This I speake . . . with reference only unto such Infants as dye not in infancy, but live to years of discretion, and then come to be effectually called, and actually converted by the ordinary means of the word applied by the same Spirit unto them, when and how he pleaseth. As for the rest of the elect who dye infants, I will not deny a further worke, sometimes in, sometimes before baptisme, to fit them for heaven" (p. 3). The relation of this sentence to the statement in the *Westminster Confession* is obvious. Among the testimonies which Burges cites from leading Reformed theologians in support of his contentions, we may adduce two, the language of which is closely similar to that of the *Confession*. One is from the Continental divine JUNIUS (*De Pædobapt.* 7), and asserts that "elect infants are regenerated when they are ingrafted unto Christ (regenerantur infantes electi cum Christo inseruntur), and this is sealed to them when they are baptized" (quoted p. 26). The other is from the English divine WHITAKER (*De Sacram. in Genere, quæst.* i., cap. 3, p. 15), and affirms that "God renews elect infants dying in infancy by the power of His Spirit (infantes electos, morientes antequam adoleverint, Deus virtute Spiritus sui renovat): but if it falls to them to live to greater age, they are the more incited to seek renewal, because they know they received its badge while infants" (quoted p. 211).

Although, thus, the cautious agnostic position as to the fate of uncovenanted infants dying in infancy may fairly claim to be historically the Calvinistic view, it is perfectly obvious that it is not *per se* more Calvinistic than the others. The adherents of all the types enumerated above are clearly within the limits of the Reformed system, and hold with the same firmness to the fundamental Reformed position that salvation is absolutely suspended on no earthly condition, but ultimately rests on God's electing grace alone, while our knowledge of who are saved depends on our view of what are the signs of election and of the clearness with which they may be interpreted. As these several types differ only in the replies they offer to the subordinate question, there is no "revolution" involved in passing from one to the other; and as in the lapse of time the balance between them swings this way or that, it can only be truly said that there is advance or retrogression, not in fundamental conception, but in the clearness with which details are read and with which the outline of the doctrine is filled up. In the course of the latter half of the eighteenth century the agnostic view of the fate of uncovenanted infants, dying such, gradually gave place, among English-speaking Calvinists at least, to an ever-growing universality of conviction that these infants too are included in the election of grace; so that in the first half of the nineteenth century it was almost forgotten among American theologians that anything else had ever been believed among them. Men like Henry Kollock and James P. Wilson, of course, retained consciousness of the past and spoke with caution. "It is in perfect consistence," says the one, "with both these doctrines [of original sin and the necessity of atonement], that we maintain that God has ordained to confer eternal life on all whom He has ordained to remove from this world before they arrive at the years of discretion."[1] And the other, having spoken of the desert of original sin, adds similarly: "Nevertheless it does not follow that any dying

[1] *Sermons* (Savannah, Ga., 1822), iii., pp. 20 *sq.* (esp. p. 23); cf. iv., p. 273 *sq.*

218   THE DOCTRINE OF INFANT SALVATION.

in infancy are lost, since their salvation by Christ is more than possible."[1] But Dr. Lyman Beecher, in a sermon which this declaration made famous, was almost ready to assert that there never had been a Calvinist who believed that any of those dying in infancy were lost. "I am aware," he said in his inimitable way, "that Calvinists are represented as believing and teaching the monstrous doctrine that infants are damned, and that hell is doubtless paved with their bones. But having passed the age of fifty, and been conversant for thirty years with the most approved Calvinistic writers, and personally acquainted with many of the most distinguished Calvinistic divines in New England, and in the Middle and Southern and Western States, I must say that I have never seen nor heard of any book which contained such a sentiment, nor a man, minister or layman, who believed or taught it. And I feel authorized to say that Calvinists as a body are as far from teaching the doctrine of infant damnation as any of those who falsely accuse them. And I would earnestly and affectionately recommend to all persons who have been accustomed to propagate this slander that they commit to memory without delay the ninth commandment, which is, 'Thou shalt not bear false witness against thy neighbor.' "[2] A challenge delivered in such a tone as this could not fail of a reply,[3] and Dr.

---

[1] *An Essay on the Probation of Fallen Man*, etc., 1827, pp. 15, 16. Dr. H. M. DEXTER, in *The Congregationalist*, December 10th, 1874, says that Dr. Wilson, editing Ridgeley's *Body of Divinity*, "dissents from his author, and argues effectively and at great length in proof that all infants dying before actual transgression are 'saved by sovereign mercy, by free favor, to the praise of the glory of God's grace.'" The reference given is vol. i., p. 422, but it is wrong; and we have, consequently, not been able to verify the statement.

[2] *The Government of God Desirable.* A sermon delivered at Newark, N. J., October, 1808, during the session of the Synod of New York and New Jersey. By LYMAN BEECHER, A.M., Pastor of the Church of Christ in East Hampton, L. I. Seventh edition. Boston: T. R. Marvin, 1827, 8vo, pp. 27. P. 15, note. This footnote was added in this (seventh) edition. The sermon is also reprinted in Dr. Beecher's *Works*.

[3] In three articles in *The Christian Examiner* for 1827 and 1828 (vols. iv. and v.), said to be by F. Jenks. In *The Spirit of the Pilgrims*, i. (1828), pp. 42 *sq.*, 78 *sq.*, and 149 *sq.* Dr. Beecher explained

Beecher's history was soon set right ; but his testimony to the state of opinion in his own day on the subject is, of course, unaffected by his historical error. The same state of affairs is witnessed also by Dr. Charles Hodge, who, as the end of his long life of service as a teacher of theology was drawing to a close, could remark of the opinion, "'that only a certain part, or some of those who die in infancy, are saved :'' '' We can only say that we never saw a Calvinistic theologian who held that doctrine." [1] Dr. Hodge's predecessor as teacher of theology at Princeton spoke of the salvation of all infants dying such in something of the tone prevalent early in the century : " As infants, according to the creed of all Reformed churches, are infected with original sin, they cannot without regeneration be qualified for the happiness of heaven. Children dying in infancy must, therefore, be regenerated without the instrumentality of the Word ; and as the Holy Scriptures have not informed us that any of the human family departing in infancy will be lost, we are permitted to hope that all such will be saved." [2] Dr. Hodge himself speaks with more decision ; [3] and to-day few English-

that in writing the note attacked his mind was more upon contemporary than past teachers. He says further : " I have only to add that I have nowhere asserted that Calvinists as a body teach that all infants are *certainly* saved. I am aware that many, with Dickinson and the Reformers" (doubtless a blunder, from Van Mastricht's *Reformati*) " and 'moderate Calvinists' have hoped that they are saved, and referred the event to the unerring discretion of heaven" (p. 51).

[1] *Systematic Theology*, iii., 605, note 4, published in 1872. In the succeeding words Dr. Hodge approaches, but fortunately does not attain, the unhistorical assertion of Dr. Beecher. He adds : " We are not learned enough to venture the assertion that no Calvinist ever held it ; but if all Calvinists are responsible for what every Calvinist has ever said, and all Lutherans are responsible for everything Luther or Lutherans have ever said, then Dr. Krauth as well as ourselves will have a heavy burden to carry." Dr. Krauth, of course, found no more difficulty than the writer in *The Christian Examiner* had found in reply to Dr. Beecher, in bringing together, in reply to Dr. Hodge, a great list of Calvinists who had held this doctrine. The result is found in his *Infant Baptism and Infant Salvation in the Calvinistic System*, etc. (Phila., 1874, p. 83.)

[2] *The Life of Archibald Alexander*, *D.D.*, etc., by JAMES W. ALEXANDER, D.D., p. 585.

[3] *Systematic Theology*, i., 26 ; iii., 605.

speaking Calvinists can be found who do not hold with Toplady, and Thomas Scott, and John Newton, and J. H. A. Bomberger,[1] and Nathan L. Rice, and Robert J. Breckinridge, and Robert S. Candlish, and Thomas Hamilton,[2] and Charles Hodge, and William G. T. Shedd,[3] and the whole body of those of recent years whom the Calvinistic churches delight to honor, that all who die in infancy are the children of God and enter at once into His glory—not because original sin alone is not deserving of eternal punishment (for all are born children of wrath), nor because those that die in infancy are less guilty than others (for relative innocence would merit only relatively light punishment, not freedom from all punishment), nor because they die in infancy (for that they die in infancy is not the cause but the effect of God's mercy toward them), but simply because God in His infinite love has chosen them in Christ, before the foundation of the world, by a loving foreordination of them unto adoption as sons in Jesus Christ. Thus, as they hold, the Reformed theology has followed the light of the Word until its brightness has illuminated all its corners, and the darkness has fled away.

"*Ethical*" *Tendencies*.

The most serious peril which the orderly development of the Christian doctrine of the salvation of infants has had to encounter, as men strove age after age more purely and thoroughly to apprehend it, has arisen from the intrusion into Christian thought of what we may without lack of charity call the unchristian conception of man's natural innocence. For the task which was set to Christian thinking was to obtain a clear understanding of God's revealed purpose of mercy to the infants of a guilty and wrath-deserving race. And the Pelagianizing conception of the inno-

[1] *Infant Salvation in its Relation to Infant Depravity, Infant Regeneration and Infant Baptism.* Philadelphia, 1859, pp. 64, 109, 196.
[2] *Beyond the Stars*, ch. vii. (pp. 184, etc.).
[3] *Dogmatic Theology*, ii., 714.

cence of human infancy, in however subtle a form it may be presented, puts the solution of the problem in jeopardy by suggesting that no such problem exists and no solution is needed. We have seen how some Greek Fathers cut the knot with the facile formula that infantile innocence, while not deserving of supernatural reward, was yet in no danger of being adjudged to punishment. We have seen how, in the more active hands of Pelagius and his companions, as part of a great unchristian scheme, the assertion that there has been no such thing as a "fall" and that every human being comes into the world in the same condition as Adam when he came from his Maker's hands, menaced Christianity itself and was repelled only by the vigor and greatness of an Augustine. We have seen how the same conception, creeping gradually into the Latin Church in the modified form of semi-Pelagianism, lulled her heart to sleep with suggestions of less and less ill-desert for original sin, until she neglected the problem of infant salvation altogether and comforted herself with a constantly attenuating doctrine of infant punishment. If infants are so well off without Christ, there is little impulse to consider whether they may not be in Christ.

The Reformed churches could not hope to work out the problem free from menace from the perennial enemy. From the very beginning of their history, of course, they were continually called upon to meet the assaults of individuals who found that the most telling form they could give their Pelagian attack was to charge the Reformed with dishonoring God by attributing to Him cruel treatment of "innocent infants."[1] The

[1] Outstanding instances may be found in CASTELLIO and SERVETUS. The latter taught that infants are born with hereditary disease (morbus) of sin, indeed, but without guilt, which comes only with responsibility, *i e.*, with the knowledge of good and evil, the age for which he sets at about twenty. Those who die before that age go, like all men, to the purifying pains of Hades—a sort of purgatory : whence they are released by Christ at the resurrection. They are soiled by the serpent of original sin ; but they are guilty of no impiety, and hence the merciful and pitiful Master who gave His blessing to unbaptized babes in this life will not condemn them, but will raise them up at the last day and convey them to heavenly bliss. These tenets may be veri-

crisis came, however, with the Remonstrant controversy, which marked the first considerable Pelagianizing defection from the Reformed ranks. Like all their predecessors, the Remonstrants put themselves forward as the defenders of "innocent infancy" against the "barbarity" of the Reformed doctrine, which represented them as born, on account of original sin, under the condemnation of God ; and they accordingly passionately asserted the "salvation" of all that die in infancy. "Neither does it matter," said Episcopius,[1] "whether these infants are the children of believers or of heathen, for the innocence is just the same in infants as infants." The anthropology of the Remonstrants, however, was distinctly semi-Pelagian, and on that basis no solid advance was possible toward a sound doctrine of infant salvation. Nor was the matter helped by their postulation of a universal atonement, which lost in intention as much as it gained in extension. Infants may have very little to be saved from, but their salvation from even that cannot be wrought by an atonement which only purchases for them the opportunity for salvation. Of this opportunity they cannot avail themselves, however uninjured by the fall the natural power of free choice may be, for the simple reason that they die infants. Nor can God be held to make them, without their free choice, partakers in the atonement without an admission of that sovereign discrimination among men which it was the very object of the whole Remonstrant theory to exclude. It is not strange that the Remonstrants looked with some favor on the Romish theory of *pœna damni*,

fied from the extracts given from the *Christianismi Restitutio* by Dr. SCHAFF, *History of the Christian Church*, vii., pp. 748 *sq*. Dr. Schaff is wrong, however, in paralleling Servetus's doctrine of original sin with Zwingli's. Zwingli taught the universality of the guilt of Adam's first sin, only denying that hereditary corruption is the source of guilt ; while Servetus makes no more of *ad*herent than he does of *in*herent guilt, denying guilt altogether to infants. On the other hand, Servetus's doctrine is curiously similar to that of our modern Pelagianizing Arminians, as represented, say, by Drs. Whedon, Miner Raymond and John Miley.

[1] *Opera Theologica*, ed. Curcellæus, altera pars. Goudæ, 1665, p. 153*a*.

which would have been more conformable to their Pelagianizing standpoint. Though the doctrine of the salvation of all infants dying in infancy became one of their characteristic tenets, therefore, it had no logical basis in their scheme of faith, and their proclamation of it could have no direct effect in working out the problem. Indirectly it had, however, a twofold effect. On the one hand, it retarded the true course of the development of doctrine, by leading those who held fast to biblical teaching on original sin and particular election to oppose the doctrine of the salvation of all dying in infancy, as if it were necessarily inconsistent with those teachings. Probably Calvinists were never so united in affirming that some infants, dying such, are reprobates, as in the height of the Remonstrant controversy. On the other hand, so far as the doctrine of the salvation of all infants, dying such, was accepted by the anti-Remonstrants, it tended to bring in with it, in more or less measure, the other tenets with which it was associated in the teaching of the Remonstrants, and thus to lead men away from the direct path along which alone the solution was to be found.

Wesleyan Arminianism brought only an amelioration, not a thoroughgoing correction, of the faults of Remonstrantism. The theoretical postulation of original sin and natural inability, corrected by universal justification and the gift to all men of a gracious ability on the basis of universal atonement in Christ, was a great advance. But it left the salvation of infants dying in infancy logically as unaccounted for as had been done by original Remonstrantism. A universal atonement could scarcely bring to these infants more than it brought to such infants as did not die in infancy but grew up to exhibit the corruption of their hearts in appropriate action; and surely this was something short of salvation—at the most an ability to improve the grace given alike to all. But infants, dying such, cannot improve grace; and, therefore, it would seem, cannot be saved, unless we suppose a special gift to them over and above what is given to other men—a supposition subversive at once of the whole Arminian contention. The assertion of the salvation of all infants dying in infancy, although a specially dear tenet of Wesleyan Arminianism, remains, therefore, as with the earlier Remonstrants, unconformable to the system. The Arminian difficulty, indeed, lies one step further back; it does not make clear how *any* infant dying in infancy is to be saved. This is thrown into startling relief by such sentences as these from a sermon by Dr. Phillips Brooks : " What do we mean by original sin ? Not surely that each being comes into the world guilty, already bearing the burden of responsible sin. If that were so, every infant dying before the age of conscious action must go to everlasting punishment, which horrible doctrine, I think, nobody holds to-day."[1] This "horrible doctrine" probably no one in any age ever avowed ;[2] but the noteworthy point is that Dr. Brooks found it inconceivable that anything deserving the name of salvation could take place " before the age of conscious action." If " salvation" were needed before that, there would be no hope for those needing it. And this is logically involved in the Arminian principle.

The difficulty which faces Arminian thought at this point is fairly illustrated by the evident embarrassment of Arminian theologians in dealing with the whole question of infant salvation. There are doubtless few who will be willing to follow Dr. James Strong in his admission that the Arminian doctrine of salvation is inapplicable to infants, and his consequent suggestion that those who die in infancy are incapable of salvation ; that, like " idiots, lunatics, and other irresponsible human beings" (all of whom present the same difficulty to a type of thought which suspends salvation absolutely on a personal act of rational choice), it may be doubted whether they have souls, since " the existence of an absolutely undeveloped soul is to us inconceivable."[3] But it cannot be said that the attempts

---

[1] *Sermons*, vol. vi., Sermon 1, on *The Mystery of Iniquity*.
[2] Something similar to it has occasionally been held ; see above, p. 145.
[3] *The Doctrine of a Future Life* (New York, 1891), p. 94, *note*. The text is speaking of probation and of the fact of reprobation found-

that have been made to explain, conformably to Arminian principles, the salvation of those who die before reaching the age of responsible action have met with much success. The original Wesleyan position, in its effort to evangelicalize the Arminian scheme, began with allowing the evangelical doctrine of original sin and the consequent guilt of the whole human race, and laid, therefore, the whole weight of infant salvation upon the cancelling grace supposed to come equally to all men on the basis of the atonement in Christ. Though all men are by nature guilty and condemned, yet no one comes into being under mere nature but under grace; and "the condemnation resting upon the race as such is removed by the virtue of the one oblation beginning with the beginning of sin."[1] Every man comes into the world, therefore, in a saved state; and if he departs from the world again before reaching the age of responsible action, he enters at once into the fruition of this salvation. This is essentially the doctrine not only of Wesley, and indeed of Arminius before him,[2] but hitherto of the leading Wesleyan thinkers—of Fletcher[3] and Richard Watson,[4] and, in our own day, of W. B. Pope[5]

ed on it; and the note adds: "All this is, of course, inapplicable to infants, idiots, lunatics and other irresponsible human beings who can hardly be called *persons* in the strict sense. Their case has its peculiar difficulties. . . . We may be permitted, however, to venture the suggestion that where the moral disability is congenital and total there is grave reason to doubt the existence of an immortal spirit; and perhaps we may be forced to believe that immortality itself is *developed* rather than innate. Certain it is that the soul, as a thinking, moral substance, is itself at least developed at some point of embryonic life, and why may not its immortality be likewise a stage in its progress? The perpetuity or even the existence of an absolutely undeveloped soul is to us inconceivable."
[1] W. B. POPE, *Christian Theology*, ii., 59.
[2] He is defending his friend BORRIUS, and denies that Borrius would have infants saved without the intervention of Christ; and affirms that Borrius's doctrine of infant salvation rested on the conception that "God has taken the whole human race into the grace of reconciliation, and has entered into a covenant of grace with Adam and with the whole of his posterity in him." (*Works*, Nichols's translation, ii., 10, 11.)
[3] *Works*, i., 283, 284.
[4] *Theological Institutes*, ii., 57 *sq.*
[5] As above.

and T. O. Summers[1] and all who follow the original type of Wesleyan theology.² It may, indeed, be looked upon as the official teaching of the great Methodist Episcopal Church, which says in its *Discipline:* " We hold that all children, by virtue of the unconditional benefits of the atonement, are members of the kingdom of God, and therefore graciously entitled to baptism."³

Therefore it is customary among Methodist theologians, in treating of the benefits of the atonement, to separate between the "immediate" or "unconditional" and the "conditional" benefits, and to speak of the salvation of infants under the former and of the salvation of adults under the latter caption. There have naturally arisen minor differences among them as to exactly what is included in these " unconditional benefits" conferred prenatally on all who come into being. The ordinary custom is to identify them with "justifica-

---

[1] *Systematic Theology*, ii. 39.
[2] This includes very explicitly the late Dr. HENRY J. VAN DYKE, who wrote : " We believe that the satisfaction which He [Christ] as the seed of the woman and Saviour of the world, rendered to God's broken law, takes away the guilt and condemnation of Adam's sin from the whole human race. We do not say the inherited corruption and depravity of our nature, which is commonly called original sin ; but we say the guilt and condemnation of original sin ; so that the multitude of the redeemed which no man can number will include not only all believers, but ' all who have not sinned after the similitude of Adam's transgression,' that is to say, who die in infancy" (*The Presbyterian Review* for January, 1885, vol. vi., p. 58 ; cf. *The Church: Her Ministry and Sacraments*, p. 106, where the middle clause of the above is omitted, but without change of sense). So also Dr. HENRY VAN DYKE (*God and Little Children*, N. Y., 1890, p. 62 *sq.*) : " The obedience of Christ countervails the disobedience of Adam and blots it out completely. . . . Original sin is all atoned for ; the guilt of it is taken away from the race by the Lamb of God." Perhaps a shade less clearly assertory of the fundamental Arminian soteriologic principle is Dr. HENRY E. ROBINS (*The Harmony of Ethics with Theology*, 1891, p. 63 *sq.*): "The sentence of acquittal is the first indispensable step in the process of redemption which will go on to its consummation unless thwarted by personal moral resistance. Now, since infants dying in infancy, idiots, the congenitally insane, and all who in the infallible judgment of God have not reached the stature of moral personality, are incapable of such intelligent moral resistance, incapable of resisting the new terms of salvation proposed under the grace system, they become, we believe, on that account, subjects of regeneration by the Holy Spirit."
[3] *Methodist Discipline*, § 43 (1892).

tion," and to speak, as standing over against the "decree of condemnation" which has been "issued against original sin, irresponsibly derived from the first Adam," of another "decree of justification" which has "issued from the same court, whose benefits are unconditionally bestowed through the second Adam."[1] Others have seen that such a justification must necessarily drag in its train a "regeneration" also, by which the sinful depravity, which otherwise infants would bring with them into the world, is removed. While Richard Watson draws off to himself in his cautious hesitancy to affirm even actual "justification" of all who come into the world, preferring to say that they are "all born under the 'free gift,' the effects of the 'righteousness' which extended to 'all men;' and this free gift is bestowed on them *in order to* justification of life;" which "justification" follows unconditionally, by a process of which we are not informed, in the case of all who die in infancy.[2] These minor variations of statement, however, while they illustrate the difficulties of its construction, do not affect the common doctrine; which is, briefly, that all men are born into the world, in principle, saved, and it is therefore that they who die in infancy enter into life. Nor do they affect the portentous consequences which flow from this doctrine—fatal, it would seem, to the whole system. For that all men enter the world in a saved state is assuredly not verifiable from experience; those that do not die in infancy certainly do not exhibit the traits of salvation: and, in order to believe that all are born in a saved state, we would seem to be forced to postulate a universal individual apostasy to account for universal sin—a thing which the Wesleyan theologians are naturally somewhat loath to do.[3] Further, if all men enter the world in a saved state, but with the certainty of apostatizing if they live to

---

[1] The words quoted here are Dr. JOHN J. TIGERT's in SUMMERS's *Systematic Theology*, ii., 39.
[2] *Theological Institutes*, ii., 59.
[3] Dr. POPE, for example, says: "We do not assume a second personal fall in the case of each individual reaching the crisis of responsibility" (*Comp. Christ. Theology*, ii., 59.)

years of discretion, the difficulty of justifying the ways of God with man is surely vastly increased ; for we have now the permission of two universal apostasies to account for instead of one. Moreover, it would look as if, in that case, grace were openly exhibited as hopelessly weaker than nature ; and one would seem justified in doubting whether the grace which protects none from sin who live beyond infancy can be depended on to introduce all who die in infancy into certain glory.

It cannot be held strange, therefore, that a strong tendency has recently developed itself among Arminian theologians to discard entirely the assuredly very artificial scheme which postulates a purely theoretical race sin, corrected by an equally theoretical race salvation that cannot be traced in any portion of the race subject to our scrutiny, and to revert to the Pelagianizing anthropology of the Dutch Arminians. From this point of view, which denies the guilt of original sin, infants are thought to enter into the world unfortunates indeed, and soiled by an inherited depravity which will inevitably cause them to sin when responsible action begins, but in the meantime under no condemnation ; so that if they die in infancy they are liable to no punishment and must perforce enter into life, for which they are then unconditionally fitted by grace. This is, in general, the doctrine of Drs. Whedon,[1] Raymond,[2]

[1] *The Methodist Quarterly Review*, 1883, p. 757. *Commentary* on Eph. ii. 3 *et al.*
[2] *Systematic Theology*, ii., 311 *sq.* Dr. RAYMOND is not without some little hesitation in his rejection of the older Wesleyan view. " The doctrine of inherited depravity," he says, " involves the idea of inherited disqualification for eternal life. The salvation of infants, then, has primary regard to a preparation for the blessedness of heaven—it may have a regard to a title thereto ; not all newly created beings, nor those sustaining similar relations, are by any natural right entitled to a place among holy angels and glorified saints. The salvation of infants cannot be regarded as a salvation from the peril of eternal death. They have not committed sin, the only thing that incurs such a peril. The idea that they are in danger of eternal death because of Adam's transgression, is at most nothing more than the idea of a theoretic peril. But if it be insisted that ' by the offence of one, judgment came upon all men to [a literal and actual] condemnation,' we insist that, from that condemnation, be it what it may, theoretic or literal, all men are saved ; for ' by the righteousness of one,

John Miley,[1] C. W. Miller,[2] G. W. King,[3] and a great host of others who are in our day illustrating the inevitable tendency of consistent Arminian thought to find its level in a Pelagian anthropology. The gain to Arminian thought, however, of substituting for the formula, " All infants are born saved," the simpler one of " All infants are born innocent and need no salvation," is certainly not apparent enough to justify the price at which it is purchased—which is no less than the denial that Jesus is, in any proper sense, the Saviour of those that die in infancy. For, this account of the "salvation" of infants, no less than that which it would supplant, is fundamentally destructive to the very principle of Arminianism. For, whether the grace of Christ is called in for the pardon of the sin of those who die in infancy or merely for the removal of their uncondemnable depravity, in either case their destiny is determined irrespective of their choice, by an

---

the free gift came upon all men unto justification of life,' so that the conditions and relations of the race in infancy differ from those of newly created beings solely in that, by the natural law of propagation, a corrupted nature is inherited. As no unclean thing or unholy person can be admitted to the presence of God . . . it follows that if infants are taken to heaven, some power, justifying, sanctifying their souls, must be vouchsafed unto them ; the saving influence of the Holy Spirit must be, for Christ's sake, unconditionally bestowed. Not only their preparation for, but also their title to, and enjoyment of, the blessedness of heaven comes, as came their existence, through the shed blood of our Lord Jesus Christ. . . . Our Lord's assurance of infant salvation is sufficient ; that, if saved, they are saved by His blood, admits of no doubt ; hence we catalogue among the unconditional benefits of atonement the secured salvation of those dying in infancy."

[1] *Systematic Theology*, i., 518, 532 ; ii., 247, 408, 505 *sq*. Dr. MILEY is very decided in his Pelagianizing construction and controverts at length the earlier Wesleyan view. We are indebted to him for a number of references.

[2] *The Conflict of Centuries* (Nashville, Tenn., Southern Meth. Pub. House, 1884,) pp. 115 *sq*., 166, 208. " The fundamental truth is here affirmed ' that there is no corruption in children which is truly and properly sin,' " etc.

[3] *Future Retribution* (New York, 1891) : " This is not the place to discuss the question of the relation of children to the atonement, and we need only say that, not being sinners in any true definition of sin, their relation to Christ must be wholly peculiar, as is their relation to probation and the new birth" (p. 159 *note*).

unconditional decree of God, suspended for its execution on no act of their own; and their salvation is wrought by an unconditional application of the grace of Christ to their souls, through the immediate and irresistible operation of the Holy Spirit prior to and apart from any action of their own proper wills. We can scarcely speak of their death in infancy as their own voluntary act, and we are therefore forbidden to say that their salvation is conditioned on their death in infancy—that is no proper condition which depends on God's providence and not their act. And if death in infancy does depend on God's providence, it is assuredly God in His providence who selects this vast multitude to be made participants of His unconditional salvation. It would be hard to contend that He did not foreknow those who would die in infancy, when He gave Christ to die for the sin of the world; and it would be inevitable that He should have had them in mind as certainly and unconditionally recipients of the benefits of His atonement, whatever other benefits it might bring conditionally to others. And this is but to say that they were unconditionally predestinated to salvation from the foundation of the world. If only a single infant dying in irresponsible infancy be saved, the whole Arminian principle is traversed. If all infants dying such are saved, not only the majority of the saved, but doubtless the majority of the human race hitherto, have entered into life by a non-Arminian pathway.

The truth, indeed, seems to be that there is but one logical outlet for any system of doctrine which suspends the determination of who are to be saved upon any action of man's own will, whether in the use of gracious or natural ability. That lies in the extension of " the day of grace" for such as die before the age of responsible action, into the other world. Otherwise, there will inevitably be brought in covertly, in the salvation of infants, that very sovereignty of God, " irresistible" grace and passive receptivity, to deny which is the whole *raison d'être* of these schemes. There are indications that this is being felt increasingly and in ever wider circles among those who are most concerned; we have noted it recently among the Cumberland Presbyterians,[1] who, perhaps alone of Christian denominations, have embodied in their confession their conviction that all infants, dying such, are saved.[2] The theory of a probation in the other world for such as have had in this no such probation as to secure from them a decisive choice, has come to us from Germany, and bears accordingly a later Lutheran coloring. Its roots are, however, planted in the earliest Lutheran thinking,[3] and are equally visible in the writings of the early Remonstrants; its seeds are present, in fact, wherever man's salvation is causally suspended on any act of his own, and they are already germinated wherever the Scriptural declaration that none can be saved except through Christ is transmuted into its pseudo-disjunctive that none can be lost except through rejection of Christ—as if from the proposition that none can live without food it followed that none can die who do not reject food. But the outcome offered by this theory certainly affords no good reason for affirming that all infants, dying such, are saved. It is not uncommon, indeed, for its advocates to suppose the present life to be a more favorable opportunity for moral

---

[1] *Cumberland Presbyterian Review*, July, 1890, p. 369; cf. January, 1890, p. 113.

[2] "All infants dying in infancy are regenerated and saved by Christ through the Spirit, who worketh when, and where, and how He pleaseth; so also are others who have never had the exercise of reason, and who are incapable of being outwardly called by the ministry of the Word."—*The Confession of Faith of the Cumberland Presbyterian Church*, revised and adopted by the General Assembly at Princeton, Ky., May, 1829 (Nashville, Tenn., Board of Publication C. P. Church, 1880, ch. x., § 3). In the revision of 1883, this runs: "All infants dying in infancy, and all persons who have never had the faculty of reason, are regenerated and saved."—*Confession of Faith and Government of the Cumberland Presbyterian Church*. (Nashville, etc., 1893, § 54, p. 34.)

[3] Cf. e.g., ANDREÆ (*Actis Colloq. Montisbelligart*, p. 447, 448), who argues that those who are adjudicated to eternal punishment are not condemned for the reason that they have sinned, but because they have refused to embrace Christ in true faith. BEZA very appropriately replied: "This that you say, 'these are not therefore damned because they have sinned,' is something wholly new to me and hitherto unheard of, since sin is the sole cause of eternal damnation, why the wicked are left in their wickedness and condemned."

renewal in Christ than the next.[1] Some, no doubt, think otherwise. But in either event what can assure us that *all* whose opportunity comes to them only on the other side of the grave will be so renewed? Surely we must bear constantly in mind that, however the circumstances in that world may differ from those of life here, there will nevertheless always " remain the mystery of that freedom which makes it possible to reject Christ,"[2] and therefore a probability less or greater, according to our estimate of the relative favorableness of the opportunity for moral renewal in Christ, offered then and now, that fewer or more of those that die in infancy will use their freedom in rejecting Christ, and so pass to doom.

Efforts enough, no doubt, have been made to show that, even on the so-called " ethical" postulates, it is reasonable to believe that all infants, dying such, will attain blessedness, and that, without the assumption of any proper probation beyond the grave. We are ready to accept the subtle argument in Dr. Kedney's valuable work, *Christian Doctrine Harmonized*,[3] as the best that can be said in the premises. Dr. Kedney denies the theory of "future probation," but shares the general " ethical" view on which it is founded, and projects the salvation of infants dying in infancy into the next world on the express ground that they are incapable of choice here. He assures us that they will surely welcome the knowledge of God's love in Christ there. But we miss the grounds of assurance, on the fundamental postulates of the scheme. He reasons that we may fairly believe " that even in such cases the moral trend is in this life determined, and through mystical influence, as in all cases whatever, such determination sure to issue in self-determination, foreseen by God and the environment adapted accordingly." "This simply locates the will," he adds, " back of the point of clear self-consciousness, and uses the word to

---

[1] Cf. *Progressive Orthodoxy*, p. 76 : " There is much reason also, in the nature of the case, to believe that the present life is the most favorable opportunity for moral renewal in Christ."
[2] *Progressive Orthodoxy*, p. 93.   [3] Vol. ii., pp. 91 *sq*.

represent the rudimentary consciousness, which last has spiritual elements." " Hence the inference," he concludes, " that infants dying are on the way to perfection, since the knowledge of God's love in Christ is sure to reach them under the coming environment, and that, not to be possibly rejected, but sure to be welcomed, and to carry them to the blessed end. This supply of the highest possible motive-spring, in every case needful for perfection, is not probation, but elevation." We certainly rejoice in this conclusion. But as certainly we do not find it possible to view it as a logical corollary from Dr. Kedney's general principle that every man's eternal state is determined by a true probation, personally undergone by him under influences and providential provisions for making a holy choice easy. Rather it appears to us to rest on assumptions which stand in flagrant contradiction with this principle; and it is hard for us to see why, if the great majority of those who are saved are saved by a mystical influence of the Holy Spirit's, acting beneath consciousness, such as makes their choice of Christ certain, we need be so strenuous in denying with reference to the minority the morality of so blessed and sure a salvation.[1]

Dr. Kedney's inconsistency [2] appears to us happy in-

[1] It is a view not essentially differing from Dr. Kedney's that the Rev. D. FISK HARRIS, himself a Congregational minister (*Calvinism Contrary to God's Word and Man's Moral Nature*, p. 107), tells us " seems to be the prevailing view of Congregationalists." This he states thus : " All infants become moral agents after death. Exercising a holy choice, they ' are saved on the ground of the atonement and by regeneration.'" Suppose they do not exercise a "holy choice"? What is to assure us that they will *all* " exercise a holy choice"? If the choice of these infants while it remains free can be made certain *there*, why not the same for adults here? And if their choice is made certain, by what is it that their destiny is *determined* —by their choice, or by the Divine act which makes it certain? Assuredly, no thoroughfare is open along this path for a consistent doctrine of the salvation of all that die in infancy, unless the whole principle of the theory is given up and the Reformed doctrine of the sovereign and irresistible grace of God sub-introduced.

[2] This inconsistency naturally appears in all writers of similar tendencies, and the popular religious literature of the day is accordingly full of it. An example may be found in Bishop HUGH MILLER THOMPSON's Baldwin Lectures on *The World and the Man* (New York,

deed when we consider what the more consistent solution of the problem would be, as it is offered, say, by 1890). His conception of Christianity is the so-called "ethical" one (pp. 59, 150), and his central idea is that the world is "the wilderness" or trial-ground necessary for fitting men for heaven. In the middle of a chapter the very object of which is to show that the sons of God must needs be trained by tests and trials, attempts and temptations, and that the law that "resistance is the measure of advance" is *universal*, he needs to stop suddenly and say : " And it does not change the law that myriads of the children of our race are spared this trial. The majority of those born into the wilderness are taken out of it before temptation begins." "There is no sense in this," he adds justly, " if we look at our ' science ' only. The death of infants is absolutely irrational in the face of the law of survival, if we confine that law only to time and the world. I dare say there is nothing more preposterously senseless than the death, at a year old, of a child who in head and hand, in health and intellect, was the perfect flower of his race ! But the great Father has other schools besides this. He is not confined to one curriculum for the training of His sons, and those He takes away need other discipline than this wilderness affords. He trains some here. He need not train all" (p. 96). It certainly is interesting to learn that a "universal" law is not affected by its inapplicability to " the majority" of those over whom it was to rule. It is equally worthy of note that Dr. Thompson's "ethical" theory of the necessity of " probation" forces him to assume that children departing this life must enter, not a place of bliss, but a new trial-place in the same sense in which this life is a trial-place, and equally including likewise the risk and certainty of many failures. There is, in other words, no pathway open along this road for belief in the salvation of all who die in infancy, nor even for the immediate salvation of *any* who die in infancy. All who are saved must be saved through trial, here or hereafter. Whether Dr. Thompson would assent to this or not, we do not know ; his theory involves it. Compare the following words of Dr. E. H. PLUMPTRE (*The Wider Hope*, edited by James Hogg, London, 1890, p. 132) : " I dwelt . . . on the fact that for a large number of human souls, whom the great mass of Christians recognize as heirs of immortality, there has been absolutely no possibility of any action that could test or develop character. ' As yet I am compelled to believe that where there has been no adequate probation or none at all, there must be some extension of the possibility of development or change beyond the limits of this present life. Take the case of unbaptized children. Shall we close the gates of Paradise against them and satisfy ourselves with the *levissima damnatio* which gained for Augustine the repute of the *durus pater infantum?* And if we are forced in such a case to admit the law of progress, is it not legitimate to infer that it extends beyond them to those whose state is more or less analogous ? ' " Dr. Plumptre does not once think of the possibility of infants passing at once to bliss,—" *unbaptized* children," he says out of his Anglican consciousness ; the best he can hope for is that they " may have a chance" under probation : and that is certainly the best that can be hoped under his " ethical" view.

Dr. Emory Miller.[1] Because his theory forces him to consider that the racial and social life existent in this world affords the lowest and easiest conditions which "all-conditioning love" can prepare for the rise, progress and perfection of finite personalities, Dr. Miller can find nothing better to say of "infants of days," dying such, than that, along with idiots, as they have "never exercised self-determination, they have not attained to individual self-consciousness," and are persons "only in the sense of a bundle of personal conditions;" and hence " physical death, which is merely racial retribution, the dissolution of race conditions, must, so far as we can determine without a revelation on the subject, end their being." Even for children of a somewhat larger growth, " who have passed from human conditions without human temptation or probation into the conditions and associations of the blessed," though he is forced to allow that their new conditions are those of " overwhelming motives to love and entire absence of temptation," he yet, because he is required to contend that any conceivable conditions are less easy for attaining perfection than those provided in this world, can only promise relatively low attainments and doubtful advance toward perfection. These new conditions, after all, are not such as will afford opportunity of " self-determined conquest of natural susceptibilities to selfishness," or of the attainment " of the consciousness of moral security as against supposable temptation to sin." By them alone, therefore, perfect personality or the highest order of moral character cannot be reached ; though it must be admitted that through association with the "faithful" who have determined their own security (and whom Dr. Miller strangely speaks of as constituting the "main body" of the perfect universe, as if the number of these conquering " faithful" could possibly exceed the combined numbers of " angels, infants, and innocent heathen") they too may eventually acquire a like tran-

[1] *The Evolution of Love.* By EMORY MILLER, D.D., LL.D. (Chicago, 1892), p. 330 ; cf. pp. 254 and 336, which speak of *children* and not merely *infants.*

scendent security. From such speculations one turns with the sense of a great relief to the simplicity of the Word, which does not suspend salvation upon man's action, but solely upon the loving act of God, for whom nothing is " too hard ;" and with a deepened conviction that it is better to fall into the hands of God than in those of men, however well-intentioned.

The drifts of doctrine which have come before us in this rapid sketch may be reduced to three generic views. 1. There is what may be called the *ecclesiastical doctrine*. According to this the Church, in the sense of an outwardly organized body, is set as the sole fountain of salvation in the midst of a lost world ; the Spirit of God and eternal life are its peculiar endowments, of which none can partake save through communion with it. Accordingly to all those departing this life in infancy, baptism, the gateway to the Church, is the condition of salvation. 2. There is what may be called the *gracious doctrine*. According to this the visible Church is not set in the world to determine by the gift of its ordinances who are to be saved, but, as the harbor of refuge for the saints, to gather into its bosom those whom God Himself in His infinite love has selected in Christ Jesus before the foundation of the world in whom to show the wonders of His grace. Men accordingly are not saved because they are baptized, but they are baptized because they are saved ; and the failure of the ordinance does not argue the failure of the grace. Accordingly to all those departing this life in infancy, inclusion in God's saving purpose alone is the condition of salvation : we may be able to infer this purpose from manifest signs, or we may not be able to infer it, but in any case it cannot fail. 3. There is what may be called the *humanitarian doctrine*. According to this the determining cause of man's salvation is his own free choice, under whatever variety of theories as to the source of his power to exercise this choice, or the manner in which it is exercised. Accordingly whether one is saved or not is dependent not on inclusion by baptism in the Church, the God-endowed institution of salvation, nor on inclusion by grace in God's hidden purpose of mercy, but on the decisive activity of the individual soul itself.

The first of these doctrines is characteristic of the early, the mediæval, and the Roman churches, and is not without echoes in those sections of Protestantism which love to think of themselves as " more historical" or less radically reformed than the rest. The second is the doctrine of the Reformed churches. These two are not opposed to one another in their most fundamental conception, but are related rather as an earlier misapprehension and a later correction of the same basal doctrine. The phrase *extra ecclesiam nulla salus* is the common property of both ; they differ only in their understanding of what is meant by the " ecclesia" outside of which is no salvation, whether the visible or the invisible church, whether the externally organized institution or the true " body of Christ" bound to Him by the indwelling Spirit. The third doctrine, on the other hand, has cropped out ever and again in every age of the Church, has dominated the thought of whole sections of it and of whole ages, but has never, in its purity, found expression in any great historic confession or exclusively characterized any age. It is, in fact, not a development of Christian doctrine at all, but an intrusion into Christian thought from without. In its purity it has always and in all communions been recognized as deadly heresy ; and only as it has been more or less modified and concealed among distinctively Christian adjuncts has it ever made a position for itself in the Church. Its fundamental conception is the antipodes of that of the other doctrines, inasmuch as it looks to man and not to God as the decisive actor in the saving of the soul.

The first sure step in the development of the doctrine of infant salvation was taken when the Church drew from the Scriptures that foundation which from the beginning has stood firm, *Infants too are lost members of a lost race, and only those savingly united to Christ are saved.*

It was only in its definition of what infants are thus savingly united to Christ that the early Church missed the path. All that are brought to Him in baptism, was its answer. And long ages needed to pass before a second step in the development of the doctrine was taken in a corrected definition. The way for a truer apprehension was prepared indeed by Augustine's doctrine of grace, by which salvation was made dependent on the dealings of God with the individual heart, and thus in principle all ecclesiastical bonds were broken. But his own eyes were holden that he should not see it. It was thus reserved to Zwingli to proclaim the true answer clearly, *All the elect children of God, who are regenerated by the Spirit, who works when, and where, and how He pleases.* The sole question that remains is, Who of those that die in infancy are the elect children of God? Tentative answers have been given. The children of God's people, some have said. Others have said, The children of God's people, with such others as His love has set upon to call. *All those that die in infancy*, others still have said. And it is to this reply that Reformed thinking and not Reformed thinking only, but in one way or another, logically or illogically, the thinking of the Christian world has been converging. Is it the Scriptural answer? If it be really conformable to the Word of God it will stand ; and the third step in the development of the doctrine of infant salvation is already taken.

But if this answer stand, it must be clearly understood that it can stand on no other theological basis than that of the Reformed theology. If all infants dying in infancy are saved, it is certain that they are not saved by or through the ordinances of the visible Church ; for they have not received them. It is equally certain that they are not saved through their own improvement of a grace common to all men ; for, just because they die in infancy, they are incapable of personal activity. It is equally certain that they are not saved through the granting to them of a bare opportunity of salvation in the next world ; for a bare opportunity indubitably falls short of salvation. If all that die in infancy are saved, it can only be through the almighty operation of the Holy Spirit, who works when, and where, and how He pleases, through whose ineffable grace the Father gathers these little ones to the home He has prepared for them. If, then, the salvation of all that die in infancy be held to be a certain or probable fact, this fact will powerfully react on the whole complex of our theological conceptions, and no system of theological thought can live in which it cannot find a natural and logical place. It can find such a place in the Reformed theology. It can find such a place in no other system of theological thought.